SIERRA TROUT GUIDE

SIERRA TROUT GUIDE

Ralph Cutter

Illustrations by Lisa Cutter
Trout Drawings by Joe Tomelleri
Photos by Ralph Cutter

Frank Amato Publications
Portland, Oregon

10 9 8 7 6 5

© 1991, Ralph Cutter • Printed in Hong Kong

Book Design: Joyce Herbst • Typesetting: Charlie Clifford

Hardbound ISBN: 1-878175-03-3   Softbound ISBN: 1-878175-02-5

DEDICATION

This book is dedicated to Teal, Haley and others who contribute to the preservation of the earth.

Kennedy Meadows about 1910. From left to right: Ed Cutter and sons Bob, Fred, and Ted. As an organizer of "milk can" transplants in the barren waters of the high Sierra, Ed greatly influenced the Sierra fisheries as we know them today.

Bob and Fred organized and led Sierra Club "expeditions" into the Sierra for over four decades.

While fly fishing on the Kern River, Bob was nearly bitten by rattlesnakes three times in a single day. A short time later he invented a revolutionary snake bite kit for hikers.

On another occasion, After being driven out of the Sierra by hordes of mosquitos, the brothers collectively went to work and developed an "incredibly effective" mosquito repellent. Both the snake bite kit and bug repellent are still being marketed today by Cutter Laboratories.

ABOUT THE AUTHOR AND ARTISTS

Cutter's love of the Sierra and its trout was cast as a small boy when his grandfather taught him to drift a fly on the Truckee River.

His first fishery research project goes back to the seventh grade where he won first place in a regional science fair with his experiment of rearing salmon eggs and fry in various polluted media.

For their honeymoon in 1976, Ralph and Lisa backpacked from Mexico to the northern Sierra border. During the nine month walk they swept back and across the Sierra, hiking nearly every pass and fishing much of the waters.

Ralph's job as a paramedic/firefighter at North Lake Tahoe provides 220 days a year off to work on environmental issues, dive in Sierra waters, fish, and enjoy his family.

The black and white illustrations were sketched by Lisa Cutter. Lisa builds architectural models for a living and has won awards for her graphics design. She is an avid skier, hiker and fly fisher.

The color illustrations were drawn by Joe Tomelleri. While working on his master's thesis on the fish of Big Creek, Kansas, Joe decided to sketch the fish rather than photograph them. With no art training, Joe went into a hobby shop and the salesman sold him a box of colored pencils. That was in 1983. Seven years later, he is widely recognized as the finest fish illustrator alive.

Ralph operates Cutter's California School of Flyfishing, P.O. Box 8212, Truckee, CA 96162, (916) 587-7005.

A "secret" spring creek loaded with picky trout bubbles out of this Sierra meadow, flows for a mile, then melts back into the ground. Photo by author.

ABOUT THE TROUT
DRAWINGS

Joseph R. Tomelleri
© '88

Joe Tomelleri drew the trout in this book from specimens fresh from their native waters. In the summer of 1990 I drug Joe and his fishing partner Guy Ernsting throughout the Sierra in search of genetically pure trout. It was a tremendously fun time, but more importantly, it was a chance to freeze for posterity a few trout living uncomfortably close to the edge of extinction.

We would catch a number of pure fish and Joe would choose the one that best represented the species. While the trout was kept alive, we would shoot numerous photos as Joe sketched notes.

In his studio, using six-ply, 100-percent cotton rag museum board, Joe outlines a life sized fish, then, using water color, paints a background wash. With Berol Prismacolor and Verithin pencils Joe draws the fish, scale by scale, sometimes layering up to five different colors. Once the fish is completed, he takes an off white pencil and burnishes the drawing to give it depth and highlight. The last step is to take an Exacto knife and carve away the colored pencil around each and every scale; this allows the water color wash to bleed around the scales and glow like a living trout. The average trout in this book took about forty hours to draw.

The finished trout is scientifically accurate. If the living specimen has 124 scales on the lateral line and 10 rays on the dorsal fin...so does the drawing.

Gary Soucie, the executive editor of *Audubon* magazine says, "Joseph Tomelleri is the best fish illustrator I've ever seen. Period. His handling of natural detail, scientific accuracy, and aesthetic elegance is nothing short of incredible."

SIGNED TROUT PRINTS ARE AVAILABLE

CONTACT: Ralph Cutter, P.O. Box 8212. Truckee, CA 96162. Cost is $60.00 each, or four for $200.00.

ACKNOWLEDGEMENTS

Without help from many dozens of people this book would never have been written. Over the course of this book I established many new friendships and renewed a number of old ones.

The personnel at the California Department of Fish and Game went out of their way to help me find information. I spent days on end tearing apart filing cabinets and tying up phone lines. They went so far as to give me a desk to set up my computer. Thanks go to Phil Bartholomew, Almo Cordone, Leonard Fisk, John Hiscox, Fred Kopperdahl, Dennis Lee, Laird Marshall, Dave Rodgers, Bill Snyder, Stan Stephens, and John Turner.

Special appreciation needs to be directed to fishery biologists Dan Christenson, John Dienstadt, Eric Gerstung, Chuck von Geldern, Russ Wickwire, and Darrell Wong.

Contributors from the Nevada Department of Fish and Wildlife include: Marvin Burgoyne, Jim Curran, Ted Frantz, Kay Johnson, Ralph Phenix, and Dave Rice.

Personnel from both the U.S. Forest Service and the National Park Service were enthusiastic and supportive. Vast stores of information and often irreplaceable documents were placed at my disposal. Many thanks to Steve Botti, Dick Riegelhuth, Donna Ward, and Harold Werner. A special thanks goes to the librarian in the Yosemite Research library...I lost her name.

Dr. Bill Berg (University of California, Davis) provided fascinating information on Sierra trout morphology, evolution, and genetics. Bill unselfishly allowed me to USE much of his unpublished work regarding the golden trout.

Dr. Bob Behnke (Colorado State University) and Eric Gerstung (California Fish and Game) greatly enhanced my knowledge of the cutthroat trout.

Dr. Peter Moyle (University of California, Davis) contributed information regarding the rainbow trout and gave me great leads to "hidden" research.

Dr. Tom Jenkins (University of California Sierra Nevada Aquatic Research Laboratories), Dr. Don Hall (University of British Columbia), and Dr. William Youngs (Cornell University) unraveled the history, evolution, and management of the brook trout.

Bill Flick, with thirty plus years studying the brook trout at Cornell University, graciously hosted my incessant questions from his home in Livingston, Montana.

Dr. Dick Baumann (Brigham Young University) and Dr. Allen Knight (University of California, Davis) spent untold hours nurturing my interest in aquatic entomology and guiding me through difficult taxonomic keys.

Phil Pister's unique blend of hard scientific data and soft philosophy permeate this book. Phil has left a very positive mark on this planet.

Ed Abbey, Phil Berry, Dave Brower, Dave Foreman, and David Gaines each contributed to the shaping of my "wilderness ethic." Thanks guys.

Frank Amato, Cal Bird, Joe Humphreys, Randall Kaufmann, Mel Krieger, Al Kyte, Gary LaFontaine, Brant Oswald, and Rusty Vorous contributed to this book in sometimes subtle, often profound ways, and Joyce Herbst for her creative and meticulous layout and design.

Thanks to Dave Hughes for his wealth of literary advice.

Dr. Peter Larkin (University of British Columbia) sent me original manuscripts and spent hours leading me through his prodigious works on aquatic biology and limnology.

Steve Zell MD, FACP, and Associate Professor of Medicine at the University of Nevada School of Medicine kindly walked me through the minefield of Giardia fact and fantasy.

Many thanks to Joe Tomelleri and Guy Ernsting, for instigating our hilarious whirlwind tour of the Sierra "in search of" genetically pure trout specimens for the illustrations.

Bob Golden, who Dave Brower feels is the finest ecologist on the Sierra Club's staff, spent untold hours reviewing and commenting on each and every lake and stream in the distribution charts. Bob's insights, based on many decades as a biologist and backpacker, touched many pages in this book.

Others who reviewed and edited the distribution tables were Jim Duffy, Cathleen Eagan, John Marcacci, and the folks at UC Davis, UC Berkeley, UC Santa Barbara, and Humboldt State University...Thank you.

And last of all, ultimate thanks to my wife and best friend Lisa, for keeping me on track and making this book a reality.

A dusting of fall snow signals the start of some of the hottest big trout angling of the year.

PREFACE TO THE
REVISED EDITION

In the ten years following research for the original edition of *Sierra Trout Guide,* an extraordinary number of changes have occurred. Floods, drought, wildfire, and human impacts have altered the Sierra.

There are more than 1,200 changes in the trout distribution charts alone.

Since the first edition, Sierra trout have had their proteins mapped through electrophoresis. Electrophoresis has given us a fascinating insight into the history and evolution of trout in the Sierra. This is the first book outside of technical journals to give an accurate depiction of Sierra trout evolution.

This edition includes information on 550 rivers and streams in addition to the 1,700 lakes.

The chapters regarding Productivity and the Trout's Environment should give the reader a basic grasp of fisheries biology and limnology in the Sierra realm. Understanding a trout's world will not only make one a better fisherman, but more importantly, will engender a certain degree of awe and respect toward the trout.

This book has the most comprehensive insect information available for California fly fishers to date. By comparison, the "Hatch" information in the 1984 edition was pretty vague and crude.

I've thrown in a chapter on backpacking and camping to help maximize your experience and minimize your impact in the Sierra. I've done a lot of walking around in the woods and have made plenty of mistakes...perhaps this chapter will save you some grief.

Finally, the chapter on Ethics was written as much for the reader as it was for myself. I feel strange teaching people how to stick a hook into some of my best friends; maybe this chapter will somehow balance that.

Ralph Cutter
Truckee, California

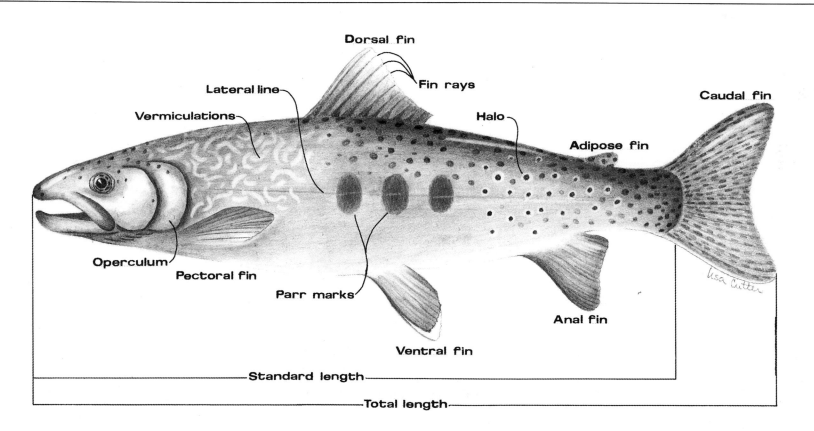

INTRODUCTION

The Sierra Nevada is a vast and formidable range. Rising to a height of almost 15,000 feet, the Sierra stand unchallenged as the tallest mountain range in the continental United States. Early pioneers feared the Indian, grizzly and deserts. They feared the unknown. But most of all early settlers feared the Sierra Nevada. Many would perish in the deserts as they attempted to skirt the Sierra by heading south. Others would die at the hands of Indians and overland gangsters as they tried to outflank the range to the north. Many others never bothered coming west at all. The Sierra were the nation's last bastion of pure, unadulterated, raw, inhospitable wilderness.

Not much has changed in the last 100 years. In fact, not much has changed in the last 20,000 years. Considering the tremendous land mass the Sierra encompass and that the range lies almost entirely within the most populated state in the nation, there are precious few civilized outposts among the granite, trees, lakes and streams. The Sierra still belong in large part to the wild animals that can endure the long frozen winters and the short frantic summers.

The Sierra trout is one of the select few who abide year-round in the Range of Light. The Sierra trout whose colors not only encompass all those of the rainbow, but also its pot of gold, is as tough and hardy an animal as evolution could build. From the jewel like golden who trustingly rises to any offering, to the wary brown who spurns the most seductive tie, all seirra trout are bound by the strength and tenacity to survive the absolute worst nature can offer.

Nature's worst doesn't compare with some of man's best. Through ignorance, greed, and apathy, man can and has done in a few years what nature hasn't been able to do in 20,000. This book will not only provide the reader with the knowledge that will place him in the "ten percent of the anglers who will catch ninety percent of the fish," it will also provide the insight that will allow him to truly appreciate and understand Sierra trout.

For convenience sake we will consider all trout living north of Lake Isabella, south of Butte and Plumas county lines, east of the 3,500 foot level of the Sierra foothills and west of the Great Basin as Sierra trout.

An angler examines his fly box along the banks of the East Carson River. Probably the only angler in miles.

CONTENTS

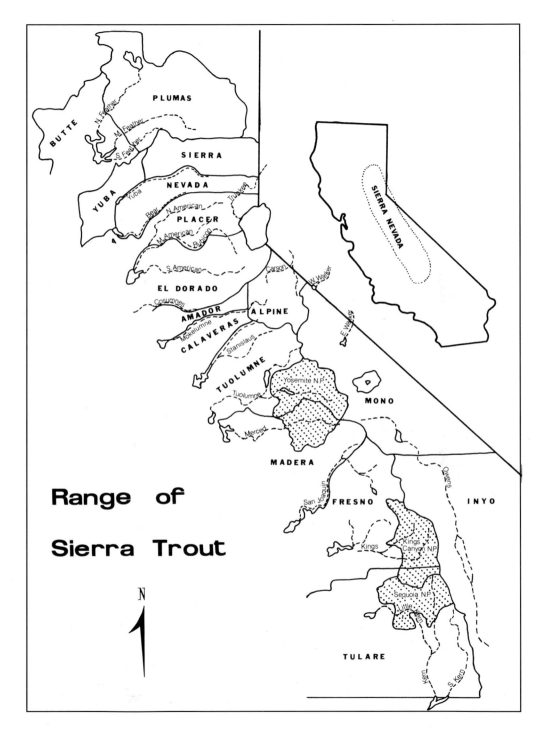

Range of

Sierra Trout

N

THE SIERRA TROUT

ONE

ONLY THE CUTTHROAT, GOLDEN AND KERN RIVER RAINBOW TROUT ARE NATIVE TO THE SIERRA. BEFORE TRANS- PLANTS BEGAN IN THE LATE 1800S, NO TROUT LIVED ABOVE THE 10,000 FOOT LEVEL.

CUTTHROAT TROUT

LAHONTAN CUTTHROAT
Oncorhynchus clarki henshawi

California record is 31 1/2 pounds. Lahontan cutthroat historically attained a size of over sixty pounds. A cutthroat today over ten pounds is considered trophy class. In most of the Sierra waters it inhabits, a two-pound cutthroat is a nice fish. The cutthroat can be readily identified by the red, orange or yellow "slash" marks under each jaw. The cutthroat is often called the spotted trout due to the profuse black spotting over its dorsal and posterior features. The base body coloration is olive-yellow with a rosy hue along its lateral features and the sides of the head are coppery-red.

Basibranchial teeth (sometimes referred to as hyoid teeth) are present as are vomerine teeth which are set in an irregular, zigzagging pattern on the roof of the mouth.

The cutthroat often interbreeds with rainbows and the hybridized meristics can be confusing even to trained fisheries biologists.

The cutthroat originated along the Pacific Coast, moved up the Columbia River system and migrated through interconnected prehistoric lakes until they established themselves as residents of Lake Lahontan. Lahontan was an enormous body of water (8,665 square miles) which covered much of Nevada as well as parts of California. Today's only remnants of this prehistoric sea are Walker and Pyramid lakes.

The cutthroat evolved into a distinct race of fish known as the Lahontan cutthroat or speckled trout. The cutts, having carried their anadromous genes with them into the inland environment, utilized the east slope rivers and streams as spawning grounds. Early in the spring hundreds of thousands of these massive fish (many weighed well over thirty pounds) would make their way up rivers to lay their eggs. Many of the migrants as well as their offspring adapted well to the mountain environment and became permanent residents of the east slope watershed.

The Lahontan cutthroat has been associated with the Sierran waters since the stone age. Fish traps and fishing spear points along the lower Truckee River and Pyramid Lake date back 4,000 years.

When Fremont found Pyramid Lake in 1844, he was dumbfounded by its fishery. Regarding the Lahontan Cutthroat his journal states, "Their flavor was excellent...superior in fact to that of any other fish I have ever known. They were of extraordinary size...about as large as Columbia River salmon...generally from two to four feet in length."

During the late 1800s and early 1900s, the Lahontan cutthroat of Pyramid Lake comprised one of the world's most commercially exploited freshwater fisheries. Hungry miners and high society gourmets alike demanded the flavorful meat. Countless thousands, perhaps millions, of fish were netted during their spawning runs. Over harvesting of the trout and pollution from upstream logging operations severely depleted the population.

Derby Dam delivered the coup de grace to the Lahontan cutthroat fishery. The dam was built across the Truckee River as a part of the Newlands Reclamation Project which was meant to deliver irrigation water to the Truckee Meadows. Built under specification number one, drawing number one, of

The Owens River, one of the major eastern Sierra waterways.

the Bureau of Reclamation, this, their first project, was destined to be the forerunner of such ecologically disastrous projects as Hoover, Grand Coulee, Shasta, and Glen Canyon dams.

During the inaugural celebration of Derby Dam, the Truckee River was abruptly diverted leaving thousands of ten- to thirty-pound trout flopping in the mud. Cheering spectators wallowed in the slime and clubbed the stranded fish.

Built with a poorly designed and unregulated fish ladder, Derby Dam blocked passage of Lahontan cutthroat as they attempted to reach their spawning beds in the Truckee River near Reno. Water diversions at the dam reduced downstream flows to the point where spawning became impossible. Unable to reproduce, the cutthroat of Pyramid Lake died. With one short sighted and ill conceived project, the Bureau of Reclamation destroyed the greatest freshwater fishery in the world. Today, the diverted Truckee is primarily used to grow low grade cattle feed; we've traded lunkers for Whoppers.

Luckily for the race of the Lahontan cutthroat, a few isolated pockets of fish were found in the years following the extinction of the Pyramid population. These trout were protected and managed in such a fashion as to provide a viable brood stock for the future.

The Pyramid Lake fishery was re-established (with Lahontan cutthroat X rainbow trout hybrids) and is still viable today due only to the intensive (and expensive) artificial propagation and rearing facilities run by the Paiute Indians. Derby Dam, subsequent siltation, and water pollution have cast severe doubt that the Pyramid fish will ever spawn again naturally. Each spring there is a cutthroat "run" up the channels of the Pyramid Lake hatchery where the fish are stripped of sperm and eggs, then released back into the lake. The fry are raised until they are large enough to feed on the tui chub that thrive in Pyramid's alkaline waters.

The Pyramid fishery is once again being threatened by upstream water users who are diverting the major portion of the water before it reaches the lake. As the water level drops in Pyramid, the alkalinity climbs, and in the near future the levels may reach a point incompatible with fish life. Interest groups ranging from fishing clubs to Congress have tried unsuccessfully to negotiate a treaty among the Indians, ranchers, and municipal water users of California and Nevada.

Lake Tahoe carried a population of Lahontan cutthroat and like its Pyramid Lake neighbor, provided an important commercial fishery. In the late 1800s up to 73,000 pounds of trout were harvested from Tahoe's crystalline waters on a yearly basis. Tons of fish were sent via railroads to markets in Chicago and San Francisco.

The major tributaries of Tahoe and the lake's outlet into the Truckee River provided spawning grounds for the large fish. Permanent traps and gill nets up to one half mile long were used to harvest the trout as they attempted to migrate to their spawning beds.

Due to over harvest and the Bureau of Reclamation's dam, which was built at Tahoe's outlet, the lake's cutthroat population dropped precipitously. Between 1922 and 1928 massive die offs of the remaining cutthroat annihilated the race. It is still uncertain as to the exact cause of the die offs but it has been speculated that some pathogen introduced into Tahoe's waters during plantings of non-native game fish was responsible for the kill.

Virtually all of the well known Lahontan cutthroat fisheries in the Sierra actually contain Lahontan cutthroat X rainbow trout hybrids. These cutbows are the "Lahontan cutthroat" found in Martis, Heenan, Marlette, and even Pyramid lakes. Most genetically pure Lahontan cutthroat are found in very small and secluded creeks.

Cutthroat thrive in the alkaline waters of the Sierra east slope and the Great Basin. Among the most gullible of trout, cutthroat can be easily over harvested if not managed with care and restraint. Even in the catch and release fishery of Heenan Lake, cutthroat that have been taken many times continue to make half hearted strikes at poorly presented flies that resemble nothing in their habitat. Woolly Worms on heavy leaders will take about as many cutthroat as will the finely presented imitation.

When hooked, the cutthroat will put up a dogged, albeit unspectacular fight. On the other hand, cutthroat/rainbow hybrids (cutbows) can be incredibly tough to bring to the net. "Hybrid vigor" is the term biologists use to describe the gamey nature often associated with crossbred trout.

When taken from alkaline waters, the meat of the cutthroat is remarkably rich. It was this flavorsome quality which helped lead the Lahontan cutthroat to the brink of extinction. Cutthroat are not particularly common anywhere in the Sierra; they compete poorly with other fish and are prone to over harvest.

The angler who has never tasted an alkaline water cutthroat can eat a fish every now and then (they really ARE tasty!), but of all Sierra trout, the cutthroat as a species will probably benefit most from catch and release.

PAIUTE CUTTHROAT
Oncorhynchus clarki seleniris

The Paiute cutthroat rivals the golden trout for beauty. It is a small (seldom exceeding 14 inches), perfectly proportioned trout. Other than its extreme rarity, the most distinguishing attribute of this fish is its coloration. The dorsolateral appearance is a light olive that gradually fades to a soft golden yellow as it nears the lateral line. Pure Paiutes lack the heavy dorsal spotting of most cutthroat. The scarlet lateral line is interrupted by about nine olive parr marks. These parr marks are evident even in adult fish. The scarlet fades ventrally into gold. The ventral surfaces are a stark cadmium. The opercles are apricot as are the distinguishing cutthroat slash marks under the jaw. Perhaps the most intriguing aspect of the Paiute is the iridescent sheen which envelopes its body. Iridocytes ("mirror scales") rich in crystalline guanine cause the Paiute to be bathed in a veil of shimmering coppery-purple opalescence. Even hard core scientists are beguiled by the beauty of the Paiute. The Paiute trout's scientific name, *seleneris*, means rainbow of the moon.

The only fish with which the Paiute might be confused is the golden trout. The Paiute lacks the white tipped dorsal, anal, and ventral fin sported by most goldens. "Pure" Paiutes have few if any spots on the dorsal/posterior surfaces. Goldens have spotting on the dorsal surface, dorsal fin and caudal fin.

Unlike the Lahontan cutthroat where only by intensive scientific manipulation has the fishery survived extinction, one strain of the cutthroat is alive today due to the whim of a Basque sheepherder. In 1912 near the headwaters of the Carson River a shepherd caught some particularly beautiful trout, put them in a can and carried them a short way up the stream and planted them above a waterfall. The waterfall had acted as a barrier to upstream trout migration, and the water above the falls was barren of fish. The shepherd's can of trout survived, bred and populated the river with its kind. The river is the Silver King, the falls are named Lewellyn and the trout, the Paiute cutthroat, is among the rarest in the world.

Within a few years of the transplant, rainbow and golden trout populated the waters of Silver King below the falls and interbred with the resident Paiutes. The falls which had originally prevented the Paiutes from populating the headwaters of the Silver King now prevented the exotics from gaining access to its waters and its pure strain of Paiutes.

Since 1937 the Paiutes have been transplanted into at least eight watersheds outside the Silver King drainage. Five of the transplants have produced tiny populations of reproducing fish.

Due to an incredible stroke of luck, the Paiute lives today. Its existence, however, is continually being challenged by human interference. An inadvertent planting of Lahontan cutthroat in one of the lakes which feeds Silver King nearly wiped out the Paiutes in the mid '50s. Even now biologists are attempting to cull the Lahontan/Paiute hybrids from the watershed. In the mid 1970s biologists working under the misconception that Paiutes with six or fewer spots were pure fish treated Silver King Creek and removed all "unpure" fish. Electroshocking surveys done in 1990 revealed many Paiutes with dozens of spots. The dominant spotting gene was carried by the supposedly pure fish. In 1991 the creek will be once again treated and planted with non-spotted Paiutes from nearby Coyote and Fly creeks.

Electrophoretic studies have raised the possibility that the Paiute may not be a subspecies of the Lahontan cutthroat, but simply a Lahontan with few spots. In fact, in 1933 when Snyder first described the Paiute as a trout "with no black spots," some of his collected specimens actually had up to nine spots.

Dr. William Berg of the Endangered Species Genetic Laboratory at the University of California at Davis says, "Through protein electrophoresis we cannot find a difference between the Lahontan and Paiute cutthroat. However, this method only samples 1% of the DNA. With 99% of the DNA untested, I'd be reluctant to throw in the towel and say there isn't a difference somewhere."

Through the efforts of biologists from California Fish and Game, the Toiyabe National Forest, and volunteers from Trout Unlimited the Paiute stands a chance of surviving into the next century.

Habitat destruction by beavers and range cattle are of serious concern. A full time stream-guard lives at Silver King to curtail poaching of the rare trout. A single fisherman who through ignorance transplants a few rainbows above the falls or a careless hunter who allows his campfire to escape and burn through the watershed may very well wipe out the Paiute cutthroat.

The Bureau of Reclamation which destroyed the entire Pyramid race of Lahontan cutthroat and helped launch the Tahoe race towards extinction is on record proposing to dam the Silver King.

COLORADO CUTTHROAT
Oncorhynchus clarki pleuriticus

The Colorado cutthroat is the most beautifully marked of the cutthroat family. The dorsum is a light olive which fades into brassy flanks through which runs a rosy lateral line. The opercles flash a rosy gold and the belly can be nearly as crimson as

that of a spawning brook trout. Sharply defined jet black spots are splashed over the entire fish.

The Colorado cutthroat has 38 or more scales above the lateral line which distinguishes it from any other Sierra cutthroat, and its lack of white tipped fins instantly separate it from goldens of the area.

In its historic range of the Colorado and Green rivers, the Colorado cutthroat is reported to have exceeded twenty pounds. Today, Colorado cutthroat seldom top ten pounds, and in the Sierra a two-pound fish would be a trophy.

In July of 1931 the Colorado Fish Commission traded 30,000 Colorado cutthroat eggs for 25,000 golden trout eggs. The cutthroat eggs were hatched at the Mt. Whitney hatchery and the fry were planted in a basin of lakes on the shoulders of the highest peaks in the nation.

Of all the lakes in the Sierra few are more remote or more difficult to approach. High elevation, unstable talus, and precipitous slopes bar access from all but the most single minded hikers. I've had to depend on crampons and ice axe to safely reach the basin as late as mid July during heavy winter years. The lakes are within the Bighorn Sheep Zoological Area which makes access a legal as well as physical barrier. To further protect the rare trout, Fish and Game biologists have requested that I not name the lakes.

For over fifty years this colony of trout inhabited an isolated corner of the Sierra all but forgotten by the rest of the world. Unfortunately, during that fifty year span, habitat destruction and interbreeding decimated the Colorado cutthroat in its home range. Electrophoretic studies during the eighties questioned the genetic purity of some of Colorado's native stocks.

In 1987 Colorado and California worked together in a complex multi-agency effort to extract 250 trout from their Sierra stronghold and transplant them back into a barren lake in Rocky Mountain National Park. Today, Colorado has a reproducing population of undisputedly pure Colorado cutthroat from which to re-seed their waters.

GOLDEN TROUT

The golden trout is THE trout of the high Sierra. Even though it is the California state fish, few people will see it in its native splendor. The brilliant colors which make the golden so distinctive fade and are quickly lost when it is brought to lower elevations. As a result, one must make the effort to reach California's high country to see this trout at its splendid best.

Though goldens can be occasionally found along a few of the east slope creeks after a heavy spring run off, there are no roadside waters which contain the golden in dependable numbers. Even if it's only the mile long hike from the Golden Trout Wilderness trailhead, the angler who wishes to see a golden must put in some effort.

The golden trout complex consists of the Little Kern golden, the Volcano Creek golden, and the Little Kern rainbow. Having common ancestors and the propensity to hybridize, these fish are difficult to consistently differentiate from one another. Biologist Dan Christenson who has extensive experience with goldens says, "Anyone who says he can accurately identify these fish outside of a laboratory is living in a dreamworld."

The best method for determining species is by watershed. The Little Kern golden inhabits the Little Kern, its tributaries and the Coyote Creek tributary of the South Kern. The Little Kern rainbow lives in the Kern River upstream of Forks of the Kern and in some of the Little Kern tributaries such as Peppermint and Freeman creeks.

Outside of this limited range the Volcano golden is widely disseminated.

Before the last ice age 20,000 years ago, rainbow trout migrated from the Pacific Ocean and inhabited much of the western Sierra. Except for the Kern River on the southern end of the range, all the Sierra became locked in a frozen ice cap which wiped out the rainbows. The rainbow trout which survived in the Kern and Little Kern river systems evolved into the Little Kern golden trout of today.

As the ice age ended about 6,000 years ago,

coastal rainbow trout once again found their way into the Kern and hybridized with the goldens to produce the Kern River rainbow trout. Little Kern goldens survived intact only in waters physically isolated from the rainbows.

Dave Hughes tricked this Little Kern golden to a soft hackle fly.

Before the return of the coastal rainbows, Volcano Creek (recently named Golden Trout Creek) became separated from the Kern River. Its population of goldens continued to evolve even more brilliant and spectacular coloration than the Little Kern fish.

Several thousand years ago, a lava flow split the headwaters of Volcano Creek near Tunnel Meadows and diverted its water into the barren South Fork of

Spotting a fish is always easier from an elevated position.

the Kern. The Volcano Creek goldens seeded the South Kern and established a strong population. Because this fish originated from Volcano Creek and was initially described by a specimen from Volcano Creek, it is properly known as the Volcano Creek golden trout rather than the common "South Kern golden." Roosevelt trout is a long defunct synonym for the Volcano golden.

The South Fork Kern has been infiltrated with rainbows which have altered the coloration of many South Fork fish, leading some to believe the South Fork fish is a different species from the Volcano Creek fish. The most pure goldens will be found in the South Fork headwaters near Mulkey Creek and increasingly impure trout will be encountered as the river descends towards Forks of the Kern.

Some immature lake bound goldens are a dull pewter with a pastel red lateral line. These fish can usually be distinguished from a rainbow by the distinctive heavy black spots that are found between the tail and dorsal fin—few if any are located below the lateral line. By comparison, the rainbow's spots are small, irregularly shaped and look more like freckles than the singular spots of the golden. The rainbow's freckles are scattered both above and below the lateral line.

Biologists are divided in their opinions as to how or why the golden developed its spectacular coloration. The most widely held theory is that the golden evolved its red and golden colors to achieve a camouflage compatible with the coppery colored gravels of its habitat. The argument against this theory points out that predators of the golden are far and few between and that selective harvest of the fish isn't a factor in its evolution.

Another theory states that the golden evolved its coloration to help protect it from the harmful solar radiation inherent in the high elevation of its habitat. A strong point used for this theory is that another high elevation trout, the Paiute, has developed the same brilliant coloration.

Yet another theory states that female goldens prefer to spawn with only the brilliantly colored males. Controlled experiments have lent some

credence to this theory. No one really knows for sure why the golden was chosen to be such an exquisitely colored fish, nor does the lack of such knowledge detract in any way from this wonderful little trout's beauty.

Recently, rainbows entered the domain of the golden when sportsmen began transplanting them in the '30s. Where the species mixed, they quickly interbred. The rainbow coloration generally predominates but the distinctive parr marks and yellow belly of the golden often remain. Within a few generations the golden's characteristics are completely lost.

Brown and brook trout were also planted into golden habitat and their intrusions were soon felt by the native population. The brook trout, being able to spawn in the most marginal of conditions, completely displaced the golden from many of its waters. The predaceous browns fed on the native goldens and severely reduced their numbers in several locals.

At the same time man was introducing exotic fish into the golden's territory, he was also extending the range of the golden. When man first entered the high Sierra, all lakes were barren and devoid of any fish life. Shepherds, prospectors, loggers, and anglers alike became enamored with the brilliant colors of the golden and transplanted them into the barren lakes of the high country. The golden was by nature a stream dweller but it quickly adapted to the lake environment.

One of the first recorded and most important golden trout transplants occurred in 1876 when Colonel Sherman Stevens caught about a dozen goldens from Mulkey Creek (which had goldens transplanted into it seven years earlier from the South Fork of the Kern) and planted them into Cottonwood Creek. From the Cottonwood Creek stock, transplants were made into Cottonwood Lakes. The progeny from these original, pure strain goldens is used today by the California Department of Fish and Game as brood stock for the high Sierra golden trout fisheries.

Due to its beauty, scarcity, and unique quality of being a truly California trout, the state legislature in 1947 designated the golden as the state fish. The

Fish and Game Commission, also enchanted with the golden's qualities, established the following "Golden Trout Management Policy."

1. Certain waters within the high mountainous areas of Madera, Fresno, Inyo, Mono, and Tulare counties may be designated by the Department as "Golden Trout Waters of California." Within that area, they shall include, if possible (a) all of the native golden trout streams, (b) any other stream or lake in which non-native but self-sufficient wild golden trout form the bulk of the population, and (c) waters in which the stocking of another species will endanger existing or potential golden trout population. Within these waters golden trout will be preserved and maintained in as pure a state as possible. A reasonable number of barren lakes in this area may be reserved by the Department for future stocking of golden trout.

2. Artificially reared fingerlings shall be used for initial stocking in barren waters and for a limited program in lakes designated by the Department. No fingerlings shall be stocked to maintain populations in streams. In other lakes containing other fish populations the fingerlings shall be of such size that a reasonable survival may be expected. Brood stock shall be acquired and placed in lakes set aside for the sole purpose of natural propagation. Whenever practical, the range of golden trout shall be extended through wild fish or fingerlings planted in waters possessing adequate spawning grounds.

In 1939 the state legislature enacted a law prohibiting the exportation of golden trout eggs or fry. During the ten years preceding the ruling, goldens were sent to Colorado, England, New York, Montana, Washington, and Wyoming. In only a few areas did the goldens thrive. The Beartooths of Montana and the Wind River Range of Wyoming are notable exceptions. The world record golden, a staggering 11 pounder, was taken from the waters of Cook Lake, Wyoming.

LITTLE KERN GOLDEN TROUT
Oncorhynchus mykiss whitei

The Little Kern golden is an uncommon, small trout that seldom exceeds thirteen inches. The Little Kern golden is a beautiful fish by any standards, but doesn't quite have the brilliance of its sister species the Volcano Creek golden.

At first glance the dorsal aspect looks dark olive, but when turned in the sun, brilliant golden scales appear and sparkle like glitter. These gold flecks rapidly disappear when the fish has been kept out of water for a few minutes. The back and sides are usually profusely spotted to well below the lateral line (I've seen them with NO spots). The flanks are usually deep gold with a vermillion splash along the lateral line. Nine to eleven olive par marks spaced along the lateral band are retained through maturity. The belly and lower fins are reddish orange and the fins are tipped with white.

The coloration of the Little Kern Golden is so variable that until recently it has been broken into several different strains of golden known as the Soda Creek golden, the Coyote Creek golden, and the Gilbert golden. Electrophoretic mapping has identified these trout as one in the same.

The Little Kern golden evolved in the Kern and Little Kern rivers during the last ice age. After the ice age rainbows migrated into the Kern and hybridized all but the most isolated populations of Little Kern goldens. By the late 1970s interbreeding with introduced trout and competition from brook and brown trout reduced the Little Kern golden to five isolated populations within a total range of eight miles.

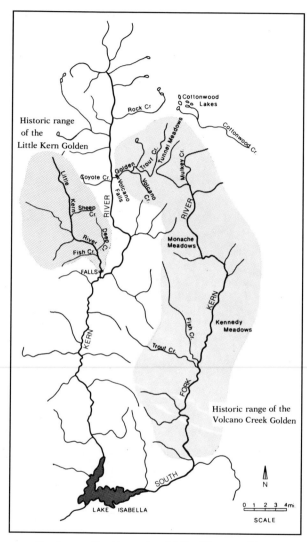

Facing extinction, the Little Kern golden was listed as threatened under the Endangered Species Act and a concerted effort was initiated to save the little fish.

State and Federal personnel as well as volunteers from Trout Unlimited chemically removed all exotic fish from many of the streams which historically harbored Little Kern goldens. They then built fish barriers to prevent upstream migration

and subsequent repopulation of exotic fish. Since 1975, 44 miles of streams and four lakes have been treated and protected. Pure Little Kern goldens from Deadman and Fish creeks were trapped and reintroduced into the cleansed waters.

It has been long, slow, and arduous, but so far the program seems to be an unqualified success. Eric Gerstung says that the project has been one of the most successful and gratifying of his career. This is no small statement from a man who has been on the forefront of the Threatened and Endangered Salmonid Rehabilitation Program and who has twice been voted the Sierra Club's conservationist of the year.

The Little Kern golden trout is a perfect example of how we can restore a natural resource if only we are willing to spend the time, money and effort. Along with the sea otter and the gray whale, the golden trout comeback must be placed among the top environmental Cinderella stories of the past few decades.

VOLCANO CREEK GOLDEN TROUT
Oncorhynchus mykiss aguabonita

California record—nine pounds, eight ounces.

The Volcano Creek golden is among the most beautiful fish in the world. It has a light olive back which suffuses to gold then crimson at the lateral line. Olive parr marks are evenly spaced along the lateral line and remain visible in all but the oldest fish. The golden yellow flanks meld to a brilliant orange ventral surface. The operculum are of the same fiery orange as the belly. The orange ventral and anal fins look as though the tips were dipped in snow white paint. Bold black spots spatter the dorsum and become profuse at the base of the caudal fin. On most Volcano Creek goldens spotting is absent or minimal below the lateral line.

Volcano Creek goldens are found in over 300 Sierra waters and are the golden typically encountered by high country anglers.

RAINBOW TROUT

Oncorhynchus mykiss ssp.

California record—27.4 pounds. (This was a sea-run fish there are no landlocked rainbow records kept.)

Rainbows run the color gamut from the richly hued specimens of the smaller streams to the mirror-like creatures taken from the waters of deep lakes. Like other trout, rainbows have the ability to change their coloration over a relatively short period of time. When planted into lakes, brightly colored hatchery fish, often within weeks, lose their colors and become chrome hued. Many people mistakenly believe the platinum rainbows taken from Lake Tahoe are of a special strain of "royal silvers" or "bluebacks."

The bright finish of a deep water trout is caused by a contraction of the pigment cells which expose the highly reflective "mirror scales" (iridocytes). The reflective coloration is the ultimate in camouflage in an open water environment where cover is non-existent.

A trout's internal coloration is as changeable as its external hue. Hatchery fish which subsist on fish meal pellets have a creamy colored muscle. Wild trout whose diets include insects and fish also have a pale meat. When the diet changes to crustaceans such as crayfish, scuds, or copepods the trout's flesh quickly transforms into a pink or orange. The color change results from the beta carotene present in crustaceans. Most people consider trout with colored flesh more palatable than those with pale flesh.

The "typical" rainbow has a gray/green, often bluish back speckled with black freckles. Its flanks are suffused with hues of crimson and the belly is cadmium white. The opercula are the same shade of red as the lateral lines and the head is profusely speckled.

When most people hear the word "trout" visions of a rainbow instantly pop into mind. The rainbow is *the* trout of roadside lakes and streams. The rainbow has been domesticated to a higher degree and transplanted into more waters than all other trout species combined. The rainbows found in Sierra waters are usually hybrids that might include genes from the coastal rainbow (*O.m. gairdneri*), Eagle Lake rainbows (*O.m. aquilarum*), the McCloud River rainbow (*O.m.ssp.*), and the red band trout (*O.m. gibsi*). [The famous "Kamloops" rainbow is a type of red band.] Rainbows have been mixed and matched so often throughout the range that there is little sense in trying to differentiate the species.

The rainbow, though definitely a western native, was not introduced into the high Sierra until the mid to late 1800s. It was a widespread practice among mountain men and prospectors of the era to catch rainbows and plant them into waters previously barren of trout.

The coastal rainbow was an abundant fish in the western watersheds up to the 4,000 foot elevation where their upstream migrations were halted by un-breachable waterfalls and cataracts. A large percentage of these rainbows were anadromous (living their adult lives at sea yet returning to fresh water to spawn).

Some rainbow populations, most notably those of the Kern and McCloud rivers, became inextricably landlocked behind geological barriers which formed between them and the ocean. The sea-going urge that was inherent in their downstream cousins became exorcised as the landlocked populations genetically adapted to their environment.

As rainbow transplantings became increasingly widespread (eggs packed in ice were shipped as far away as Europe, South America, and New Zealand) it was found, to the dismay of many, that once the trout approached maturity they would migrate to the ocean and disappear.

The answer to the migrating problem was found in the landlocked trout of the McCloud River. California's first hatchery was built on the McCloud, and the captive bred trout were disseminated throughout the world. The McCloud offspring were content to stay in their planted waters, but when trout from anadromous stocks were mixed with the McCloud rainbows, the offspring developed the urge

to migrate to sea. The anadromous instincts are still found in many contaminated landlocked rainbow populations today.

With the advent of the rainbow trout hatchery, high Sierra plantings began in earnest. By rail, mule, backpack and aircraft, rainbows were planted haphazardly through the range. It has been estimated that at one time or another over ninety percent of the Sierra watershed has been planted with rainbows. A good number of plantings were successful and rainbows were able to sustain viable populations. These fish have become as wild as the native trout with which they co-exist.

Generally the rainbow was a welcome addition to the Sierra landscape. The wild trout grew tough and strong in the harsh environment and their fighting qualities became legendary. In heavily fished waters the rainbows grew wary and selective and ranked as equals with brown trout for cunning and wiliness. The Sierra rainbow had become a game fish to be reckoned with.

Ecologists and fisheries biologists were less than enthused with some of the rainbow's side effects. Sharing the same genetic origin as both the cutthroat and golden trout, the rainbow quickly and easily interbred with the native fish. Many stocks of native fish were irreplaceably lost due to hybridization. Pathogens foreign to the Sierra were widely disseminated as both infected hatchery fish and the disease infested water they were contained in were dumped into "clean" watersheds.

The rainbow is here to stay, but today's sophisticated fishery managers seed rainbows into new territory only after long thought and deliberation. Or so they'd like us to believe.

KERN RIVER RAINBOW TROUT
Oncorhynchus mykiss gilberti

The Kern River rainbow trout is an uncommon subspecies of the rainbow which inhabits a small section of the Kern River and a few of its tributaries.

Kern River rainbow usually retain their parr marks into maturity and have golden flecks sprinkl-

ed over their bodies. Usually they are well spotted on the dorsum and flanks to below the lateral line. More often than not Kern River rainbows will have a distinctive blue or purple sheen over much of the body. Most Kern River rainbow have pale yellow or orange fins with white tips. The overall impression of a Kern River rainbow is that of a rainbow X golden trout hybrid which isn't too surprising considering that's exactly what it is.

Some Kern River rainbow trout look identical to Little Kern goldens. I asked Dr. William Berg of the Endangered Species Genetic Lab if there was a sure fire way to differentiate the two in the field. He said, "Sure, carry a portable electrophoresis unit. You'll find that the Kern River rainbow is a dead intermediate between a steelhead and Little Kern golden. But morphologically, there is no dependable difference."

The Kern River rainbow is considered to be a rainbow which hybridized with Little Kern golden trout immediately following the last ice age. As the ice sheets disappeared and the rivers subsided, barriers developed which kept the Kern River rainbow

separated from the coastal rainbows which filtered back into the Lower Kern River.

Because the Kern River rainbow is now surrounded by waters planted with domestic rainbows, it is inevitable the Kern River rainbow will become hybridized into extinction. Some Fish and Game biologists say that the falls north of Forks of the Kern will prevent planted rainbows from penetrating the headwaters of the Gilberti's range. I feel this is flawed logic considering that brown trout have already breached the falls and have populated the headwater region.

If it is truly necessary to plant the Kern, it would seem prudent to raise pure Little Kern rainbows and use those instead of foreign strains of trout. Hatchery managers tell me this would be "too expensive."

To knowingly extirpate an entire race of trout seems pretty expensive to me. For this to be done by the agency entrusted to protecting our wild fisheries seems especially repugnant. If you feel as I do, write to the California Fish and Game Commission, 1416 9th Street, Sacramento, CA 95814.

BROWN TROUT

Salmo trutta

California record—28 pounds. The brown trout is a lover of undercuts, brush piles, and deep, slow water. In keeping with its habits, its coloration is typically dark and somber. The back is an olive brown which lightens to a pale shade of the same color as it nears the lateral line. The lower flanks run from cinnamon brown to dull coppery yellow. Some individuals will be almost a lemon yellow with an aqua tinge suffused around the bases of the ventral fins. Many young browns have orange or red adipose fins. Large, well defined black, brown, and red spots adorn the body. The brown is the only Sierra trout with both brown and red spots. Many of the spots are set in pale halos.

Browns which inhabit deep lakes turn a bright silver and the back takes on a greenish opalescent hue. Even though lake dwellers attain the chrome plated appearance, enough heavy spotting around the head remains to differentiate the fish from a lake rainbow. A lake bound brown trout looks strikingly similar to its close relative the Atlantic salmon.

When in spawning form, the males develop a well hooked, tooth studded jaw (kype) and the coloration becomes vivid.

In 1883 brown trout eggs from Germany were brought to the United States packed in wet, iced down moss. The following year eggs from the Loch Leven region of Scotland were shipped to Canada. It was not until 13 years later that fish from these initial eggs were planted into the Sierra.

In 1896, 500 young "Loch Levens" were planted in a branch of Alder Creek near Wawona. Because Loch Levens were larger and more silver than the German brown trout they were considered two distinct species. In 1906 David Starr Jordan examined fifty Loch Leven progeny from Alder Creek and found, to his great surprise, that they looked exactly like the German brown.

From these findings and by comparing reports from England, he surmised that the Loch Leven and the German brown were the same fish. In time Jordan deduced that the eleven different species of browns from around Europe were the same fish and coloration was influenced not by genetics but by environment.

Because of its ability to survive in a wide range of conditions, the brown was planted throughout the Sierra during the early part of the century. It was only after the brown became well established that fishermen and fisheries biologists alike realized that the brown, though hardy and strong, wasn't quite the game fish they had planned on. Though no more piscivorous (fish eating) than any other trout, the brown earned a reputation as a cannibal and destroyer of fisheries.

In 1940 Paul Needham published a classic study that showed when trout of equal size were compared, rainbow and brook trout actually consumed more fish than the brown trout. Browns do consume more fish than their cousins simply because they outlive and outgrow other trout in heavily fished waters.

Young browns routinely feed on surface insects. As the trout approach a foot in length they tend to shy from exposed water and prey mainly on subsurface fare such as nymphs, crayfish, and fish. At night or under cover of darkness, browns will cruise the shorelines in search of shrews, ducks, and anything else that will fit in their mouth. One twelve-pound brown taken from Stampede Reservoir near Truckee contained two adult chipmunks!

Being chiefly nocturnal and naturally wary, brown trout have earned a well deserved reputation for avoiding the angler's hook. In one survey of a Sierra stream, browns outnumbered rainbows five to one. A creel census of the same stream showed anglers were catching four rainbows to every brown.

A study in Sequoia National Park indicates that brown trout populations actually increase with moderate angling pressure. As rainbows are harvested, the browns can occupy more choice ecological niches without competition from the rainbows. Sequoia is considering an open limit on brown trout to try to increase the success of the native rainbows.

Joseph R. Tamelleur
© '86

BROOK TROUT

Salvelinus fontinalis

California record—nine pounds, twelve ounces. The brooky is not a true trout but a char. They share this family with the arctic char, bull trout, Dolly Varden and lake trout. A distinguishing characteristic of all char is the presence of light spots on a dark background (trout have dark markings on a light background). The dorsal fin and back of the brook trout are covered with vermiculations (squiggly patterns) rather than the typical spots of a trout.

The back and flanks of the brook trout are dark olive, the vermiculations are an off amber color. The flanks are spattered with gray and red spots, many of which are set in blue halos. The belly of a brook trout can range from a pale yellow to a brilliant crimson orange in spawning males. The pectoral, ventral and anal fins share the coloration of the belly. The leading edges of the pectoral fins are snow

white...a characteristic foreign to true trout.

The scales of a brook trout are small and more numerous than a true trout. On the lateral line 154 to 254 scales will be found, 37 when counted from mid lateral line to mid back, and 30 when counted from mid lateral line to the belly.

The caudal fin (tail) is squared off, hence the common name "square tail." The square tail easily differentiates the brook trout from our other Sierra char, the lake trout, which has a deeply forked tail.

The original and most popular strain of brook trout which inhabits Sierra waters was developed by Seth Green. Green was a noted fish culturist of the late 1800s who introduced both the striped bass and American shad to the Pacific coast.

The wild brook trout of Pennsylvania naturally reached maturity at about four years. With declining habitat, few brook trout were living long enough to spawn so Green set out to make a strain of trout that would mature in one fourth that time. Green would find perhaps fifty trout from a population as large as 10,000 that would meet his early matura-

tion criteria. By inbreeding these fish and selectively culling their progeny over many generations he produced a strain of fish that would consistently produce brook trout that would mature in little over a year.

Green's "super" trout were disseminated through New York hatcheries and from there, in the 1870s, to the San Bernardino mountains of southern California. Progeny from these fish were quickly seeded throughout the Sierra.

The brooky is well suited to the many lakes and tarns of the higher mountain reaches where tributaries are non existent. Unlike most trout, the brook trout is able to spawn in the gravel of underwater springs and even along the shores of wave swept beaches and gravel bars. Many otherwise barren lakes have large, self-sustaining populations of brook trout. If the brook trout has a fault, it is in its propensity to over populate the waters it inhabits. When planted with less competitive fish such as golden and cutthroat trout, the brook trout can, and often does, displace the native populations with sheer numbers.

Authorities are divided in their opinions as to why the brook trout so readily overpopulates and becomes stunted. Some, such as Cornell's Bill Flick feel the problem can be directly traced back to the brook trout's highly manipulated genetics. Others such as Dr. Tom Jenkins of the Sierra Nevada Aquatic Research Lab (SNARL) feel that habitat and a lack of population feedback are the culprits.

Many animal species reach certain population densities then self limit further density through cannibalism, lack of reproduction, or other means. Dr. Jenkins found that brook trout don't have a feedback response and will simply grow smaller as the population density increases. Brook trout smaller than four inches were found to be sexually mature. (In some Sierra waters brook trout eight inches long were found to be in excess of twenty years old.)

[For more detail on the population dynamics of the brook trout and attempts to modify their behavior see the chapter titled "Sierra Trout Fisheries."]

Though brook trout can be taken from every

conceivable Sierra water type, the true sport of brook trout fishing belongs to the small brooks and sun-dappled beaver ponds hidden among the quaking aspens. In these clear, cool waters the brooky is caught and played in the intimacy of a one on one experience. Almost always the fish is spotted before it takes the fly. The fly rod is played like a delicate and beautiful musical instrument. A light rod, a fine tippet, and a dainty quarry makes fly fishing for brookies fishing at its very finest. In comparison a spinning outfit is simply an instrument of war.

Although it has caused irreparable harm to many of the native fisheries, the brook trout has become a beautiful and welcome addition to the Sierra waterscape.

LAKE TROUT

Salvelinus namaycush

California record—37 pounds, 6 ounces. The lake trout (mackinaw), is a member of the char family. Like the brookie, its back and dorsal fins are patterned with pale vermiculations on a darker background. The lake trout is the least colorful of all Sierra trout. Its body is shades of gray. The gray can be almost black near the dorsum, but grows progressively lighter as it nears the belly. The entire body is flecked with yellowish gray speckles. During spawning time the belly and lower flanks turn a brighter shade of yellow and the fins become yellow or orange hued.

The lake trout is unlikely to be confused with any other Sierra trout except for maybe its cousin the brook trout. The lake trout has a deeply forked tail while the brook trout has a square tail. The most outstanding feature of the lake trout is its massive size. Every year twenty to thirty pounders are taken from lakes Tahoe and Donner and ten-pound fish are common.

The lake trout is found primarily in the headwaters of the Truckee River drainage. This giant fish was first introduced into Lake Tahoe in 1889 by the Nevada Fish and Game Commission. Several years later the mackinaw was planted in other lakes of the

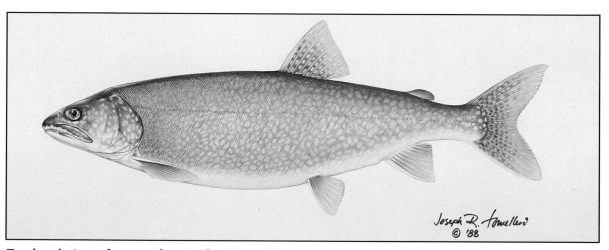

Joseph R. Tomelleri © '88

Truckee drainage from stocks raised in Sisson Hatchery near Mt. Shasta.

Because of its "poor" sporting qualities, fish eating nature, and need for deep, cold water, the lake trout has not been introduced into a wide range of Sierra watersheds.

The lake trout was mistakenly held responsible for the extinction of Lake Tahoe's cutthroat fishery. In reality the decline was due to over harvest, lumbering practices, habitat destruction, and the introduction of foreign pathogens into the watershed.

In retrospect, some biologists believe the lake trout was an ideal fish for Tahoe and Donner lakes because it is the only Sierra trout which does not require gravel spawning beds for reproduction. The mackinaw scatters its eggs over the rocky lakebed and lets nature take its course. In an area where logging practices, mining and damming has destroyed most spawning tributaries, the lake trout has thrived where other trout might have suffered for lack of spawning habitat.

If we continue to destroy and disrupt the spawning areas of more desirable trout, the lake trout may, through default, become a wide spread inhabitant of the Sierra.

The lake trout needs icy cold waters to thrive. During winter months lake trout can be found in the shallows, but most of the year they dwell in water between 50 and 600 feet.

Commercial party boats locate the huge trout with sonar then dredge the depths with downriggers and lead cannonballs or let out many hundreds of feet of steel line. A lake trout caught by such means provides as much sport as a waterlogged inner tube. Winching up a lake trout from great depths causes the air bladder to expand until it sometimes distends out the fish's mouth. These fish are all but dead by the time they reach the boat.

Most people swear that lake trout are poor sporting fare because they "don't know how to fight." These same people would quickly change their minds if they played an eighteen-pound lake trout on a fly rod or light spinning gear. On nice winter evenings you can cast large streamers to visible lake trout, and anytime of the year drifting a live minnow on one to two hundred feet of six-pound monofilament can put you into fish. A large lake trout has no problem pulling you and your canoe around the lake for a quarter of an hour while you struggle to bring in line.

Some may debate the sporting quality of a lake trout, but none debates the table quality of these fish. The white flesh is firm and flaky and has that delicate flavor only found in cold water trout. A fresh lake trout simmered in a foil boat with a little white wine, garlic, butter, dill, salt and pepper over a bed of glowing mountain mahogany coals will convert even the most rabid hater of fish.

THE TROUT FISHERY

TWO

THE WIDESPREAD, RANDOM HATCHERY PLANTS OF THE PAST CENTURY HAVE GIVEN WAY TO FISHERY MANAGEMENT PRACTICES WHICH EMPHASIZE ENHANCEMENT OF EXISTING STOCKS RATHER THAN THE CREATION OF NEW ONES.

> *"Happily, there is reason to hope that these (fisheries) conditions are not going to grow worse..."*
> -George La Branche. 1914

Fine tuning of trout populations by controlling hybridization and species displacement by exotic fish is a growing endeavor. Habitat construction and rehabilitation are gaining increased attention as we realize there are finite limits to the resource and the amount of abuse we can bestow upon it.

State biologist Russ Wickwire recently illustrated the graphic improvement a fishery can make if habitat alone is creatively managed. An electroshocking survey revealed only one catchable trout for every hundred yards of the Little Truckee River. Wickwire determined that lack of cover and holding habitat were partially responsible for the dearth of fish. He contracted with the Department of Transportation and the U.S. Forest Service to dump rocks and boulders into the river. Two years after the rocks were in place another electroshocking survey was conducted. Where there had been only one fish per every hundred yards there was now over one hundred catchable trout.

In many Sierra lakes tui chubs seveerely compete with trout stocks. Because of their ability to reproduce in great numbers, tui chub eventually displace a large segment of the trout population. Kokanee salmon, being filter feeders like the tui chub, directly compete with the chubs. Some species of trout, most notably the Eagle Lake rainbow specialize in feeding upon tui chub. Utilizing kokanee salmon and Eagle Lake rainbows as measures against tui chubs are perfect examples of biological control.

Many Sierra waters have fine habitat but are being put to the wrong use or under utilized. With proper fisheries management the resource can be operated at maximal productivity. Intelligent multi species mingling is one method for increasing fishing opportunities. Lunker Lake (a pseudonym to protect the lake from over use) has long been known for producing large brook trout. When the water warmed in the summer, the brook trout would seek the cool springs deep within the weedbeds and become inaccessible to anglers. Lahontan cutthroat, which are less apt to seek the weedy springs, were put into the lake to provide summer action in the open, fishable waters of the lake.

The most recent and profound change in management of Sierra trout has been the decreasing reliance on hatchery plants. Hatchery fish, though essential in the original seeding of Sierra waters, have not proved to be the panacea they originally seemed. The problems of introduced trout are widespread.

Hatchery fish have been raised as a monocultured agricultural product for almost 100 years. The fish have been specifically bred and raised to produce the most poundage for the least investment. Bred and nurtured in an environment devoid of predators and other naturally occurring threats to their existence, hatchery trout have evolved through generations where the instincts for survival were not necessary to procreate. Many survival tendencies were consciously and systematically bred out so the fish would grow fatter faster in a hatchery.

Trout in a natural environment have developed a crude yet effective means of communication. When a small fish enters the domain of a larger fish, the large fish reacts in a number of agonistic ways. Brook trout will elicit a brightening in their coloration and all trout will, to some degree, display aggression through posturing. In one display the trout opens its mouth, arches its back and flares its fins. The effect is that of the fish suddenly growing

In terms of knowledge gained, a day of underwater observation is worth a season of fishing.

larger. If these displays of aggression fail to elicit an immediate exodus by the intruder, the dominant fish will chase and bite the other.

Hatchery raised fish don't understand the language of wild trout. When planted into an ecosystem inhabited by wild trout, hatchery fish raise havoc. Undaunted by even the most aggressive posturing, the plants will move, en mass, into niches occupied by native trout. Confused, the wild fish will flee from the mob. Studies have repeatedly shown that within two weeks of planting hatchery fish, up to forty percent of the wild fish have vacated the area. The displaced trout crowd into lies of other trout and the confusion leapfrogs throughout the system.

Long Lake in the Golden Trout Wilderness.

Factory trout not only displace natives and directly compete for prime habitat and food, they can cause long term trouble when interbred with wild fish. Fewer than five percent of hatchery raised fish live long enough to spawn in the wilds. Those that do attempt to spawn compete for often scarce spawning habitat. Many hatchery fish are sterile, and of those that do breed, the progeny are often mutant. When hatchery trout breed with wild trout their offspring lose many of the genetic traits crucial to survival that had been passed on to them from their wild forefathers.

Diseases such as whirling disease and parasites like *Epistylis* thrive in many hatcheries. Whirling disease, virtually unknown twenty years ago, is now encountered in epidemic proportions in many Sierra waters. The disease attacks the nervous system of trout, causing discoloration in fry and spinal and cranial deformities in adult fish. Such deformities can result in a tail-chasing, spinning behavior as the trout attempts to swim. Probably 100 percent of the rainbow trout in the Truckee River drainage are now infected with whirling disease. Due to the expense of raising fish, many infected trout which should be destroyed are simply planted into waters known to already harbor the disease. The Truckee River system routinely plays host to diseased lots of fish. Even if justified on biological grounds, esthetically the practice is repugnant.

In light of the considerable harm that can result from stocking, hatchery plants should be considered only after a rational, calculated decision has been made. A few fisheries managers of old are still apt to dump fingerlings or catchables into a system whenever angler success is low.

Because of growing data indicating how harmful hatchery plants can be, many have condemned hatcheries as outdated management tools. It must be remembered that starting with the McCloud facility in 1897, hatcheries are responsible for the Sierra fisheries we have today. Without hatchery seeding and inter-watershed transplants, virtually all of the High Sierra waters would be devoid of trout.

Most hatchery fish are bred with one goal in mind: grow the fish in the least amount of time and on the least amount of food. When hatchery trout with "grow fat fast" genetics, are planted into benign, food rich waters, they quickly outgrow and displace wild stocks; however, these trout have a tendency to burn out at an early age and die. More research needs to be directed toward creating hatchery fish that will assimilate with the environment for the long term, will self propagate, and will be cost effective to plant.

Robert Behnke, among the nation's more progressive fisheries biologists, made this statement, "...by the wise use of specific pre-adapted forms of wild trout to better fill certain niches, by the use of combinations of forms to initiate ecological segregation and by the use of sterile hatchery trout, I believe trout production could be increased by 50 percent in millions of acres of lakes and reservoirs, thereby relieving the pressures and demands for stocking streams supporting wild salmonid. The increased angling opportunities in lakes and reservoirs should greatly facilitate a rapid increase in special regulations management of wild trout." (Paper presented to the American Fisheries Society, February 21, 1982).

Hatcheries have a very important place in the management of our fisheries both present and future. Without hatcheries, studies of trout disease would be crippled. Without hatcheries there would be no hope for the many rare species of fish that need to be artificially bred and studied if their kind is to survive. Without hatcheries almost all of what we call fisheries management would be adversely affected. When used wisely, hatcheries are an integral and powerful tool in fisheries manipulation.

There will always be a need for put and take waters in our mountains. Many anglers have grown to expect, and rightfully deserve, the privilege of being able to go to certain waters where they can fish and come home with a mess of nice trout. Not all anglers are concerned with a trout's origin, many simply want to fish with a realistic chance of catching a few.

In the seventies, a management system called the California Wild Trout Program was implemented on a few of the state's richest waters. Modeled after a similar program in Pennsylvania, California took a major step away from its dependency on the hatchery program. By: A). reducing catch and kill limits, B). encouraging catch and release practices, and C). mandating minimum size limits to allow trout to reach sexual maturity before being harvested.

The first water to be tested in the Wild Trout Program was Hat Creek north of Mt. Lassen. Hat Creek was a classic case of a river being overharvested and overwhelmed with non game fish. Through the efforts of Trout Unlimited volunteers and the Department of Fish and Game, a fish barrier was placed at the lower end of Hat Creek so that fish couldn't migrate from the Pitt River into Hat. Hat Creek was poisoned to remove all fish then the river was planted with rainbows of local origin as well as brown trout. In 1978 a catch and keep limit of two fish of eighteen inches or larger was imposed. To facilitate the release of unwanted fish, only barbless flies and lures were allowed. Bait was not allowed because of the high mortality associated with released bait-caught fish (trout tend to swallow bait much deeper than a fly).

In 1978 1,989 trout were electroshocked from Hat Creek with a total weight of 1,098 pounds. Five years later a similar electroshocking was conducted with results that astounded even the most ardent supporters of the wild trout project. Over 6,200 trout were caught with a total weight of over two tons. There was nearly an eight fold increase in the numbers of fish in the 12 to 16 inch range. Browns were netted that weighed over ten pounds. [Note: Since the first edition was printed in 1984, Hat Creek has become horribly abused. Overuse, combined with an influx of silt has reduced Hat Creek to a memory of its former self.]

The beauty behind the Hat Creek project in particular and the Wild Trout Program in general was its simplicity. As project manager John Dienstadt eloquently understated, "We just let the trout do their own thing."

The Wild Trout Program was off to an incredible start. The State Fish and Game Commission

A Lahontan cutthroat with a trace of rainbow in its ancestory.

legislated that every year twenty five miles of river and at least one lake be considered for management as a wild trout water. Some of the outstanding Sierra waters that have been blessed with wild trout status are: North Fork of the American, East Fork of the Carson, Middle and North Fork of the Feather, Kings River, Martis Lake, East Walker River, Truckee River, and Owens River.

The management of fisheries so that wild trout can self populate has come of age. Due to the quality of angling and the extreme cost efficiency of such management, the Wild Trout Program will be the model of resource managers for years to come.

An offshoot of the Wild Trout Program has been a heightened awareness of the limited yet potentially renewable resource wild trout can provide. Many anglers who used to measure their success by how many fish they could bring home, now use barbless hooks and release most if not all of the trout they catch... even on waters NOT under special management. With a growing population of large, wild trout, fishermen are now becoming acutely aware of the differences of catching and landing a pampered hatchery clone versus a wary and frighteningly strong wild trout. A real trout.

Catch and release is by and large a good ethic to

fish by; however, like everything else, it must be tempered with common sense. Catch and release is NOT indicated in all situations. Brook trout have a propensity to overpopulate many of their waters. Brookies can spawn under marginal conditions and the result can be lakes filled with stunted fish. Even the most rabid catch and release fanatic would be hard pressed justifying returning a stunted and starving fish back to an overpopulated system.

Year after year golden trout are planted by aircraft into brook trout lakes in the vain hope that somehow the goldens will dislodge the brookies. According to Don Hall a PhD. fisheries biologist who has spent years studying brook trout of the High Sierra, this practice is not only very expensive but ludicrous. "These aerial plants provide a few anglers a chance to catch a few hatchery goldens before the goldens are eaten or displaced by the resident brook trout. The money and effort could be much better spent on other resource projects."

In a few lakes brown trout have been introduced to cull the huge brook trout population. The results have been unspectacular; a few of the browns consistently feed on brook trout but most simply compete with brookies for existing food stocks.

Biologists electroshock trout from a river to study its population dynamics.

Dr. Hall experimented with the brook trout population in one lake by severely reducing their numbers. Day after day he would pull out gill nets filled with brook trout and within short order the population rebuilt itself. Dr. Hall compared brook trout populations from heavily used roadside waters with backcountry waters that rarely saw a rod...there wasn't much difference. He concluded that fishermen were not making a dent in the brook trout population.

Dr. Tom Jenkins studied a brook trout lake in Sequoia National Park where spawning conditions were good and fishing wasn't allowed. Year after year the population grew and the size of the trout shrunk. Toward the end of the study, sexually mature brook trout less than four inches long were common.

In the early 1980s a "new" brook trout was introduced in several Sierra locations. Unlike its Sierra cousin, this Canadian trout was of pure unadulterated wild stock. According to Bill Flick of Cornell University, typical hatchery brook trout of the U.S. have their origins in the artificially manipulated brood of Seth Green. Mr. Green's trout were bred so that they would reproduce at an early age. (Some male Sierra brook trout are sexually mature at nine months.)

Mr Flick contends that the Canadian (Assinica) brook trout grows at the same rate as the typical Sierra trout, but it doesn't become sexually mature until at least its third year, and it can be expected to live for six or more years ("Instead of dying after the fourth year like most typical Sierra brook trout.") He further states that instead of expending all their energy growing gonads, the Canadian brook trout put on meat.

Dr. William Youngs of Cornell University and Dr. Tom Jenkins of the Sierra Nevada Aquatic Research Laboratory feel that habitat has more influence on brook trout size and longevity than genetics. This is easily demonstrated in the highly productive Sierra lakes where brook trout numbers are controlled by planting rather than natural reproduction. In these waters brook trout commonly exceed three pounds in their third year.

Both Dr. Youngs and Dr. Jenkins feel that a short growing season and typically low productivity along with the brooky's proclivity to reproduce combine to produce stunted populations.

Dr. Jenkins further refutes Mr. Flick's assertion that Sierra brook trout seldom lives longer than four years. He says, "Many brook trout in the Sierra exceed ten years of age and brook trout well over twenty years old have been documented."

By the late 1980s, due to drought, winter kill, and an inability to import eggs, the experiment with the Canadian brook trout came to an inconclusive close. With public pressure perhaps the Department of Fish and Game can renew its efforts to provide a better Sierra brook trout sport fishery.

Since the late seventies virtually all Sierra waters enclosed in National Park boundaries have ceased being planted. Almost half the lakes in the Sierra are under Park control and the vast majority cannot sustain viable populations naturally. The effect has been profound. This book was originally researched in the late seventies. When researching the revision 12 years later I found almost 1,200 changes in Sierra lake fisheries. Many, but of course not all, of these changes were attributable to the Park's management policies.

The Parks are mandated to operate under a policy of "naturalness" where exotic animals such as trout are to be discouraged because of their untoward effect on the environment. (See the chapter on ethics.)

Trout HAVE effected the Sierra ecosystem in many ways that we can recognize and probably in many ways we have yet to discover. A very profound difference in human impact can be seen around lakes which have trout compared to those which don't. Fire rings, lack of woody vegetation, pounded banks, and litter are commonly associated with lakes that receive a lot of human pressure...fishless lakes rarely sustain this type of impact.

Barren lakes are only barren of trout. In many instances, lakes without trout are more biologically diverse than those that support fisheries.

Mountain yellow legged frogs used to be very common throughout the range. Trout prey heavily on tadpoles and in lakes where fish have been introduced, the yellow legged frog has all but vanished. Lakes too shallow to support trout are usually too shallow to support frogs through a severe winter. Now that the Park Service has ceased planting its lakes, the yellow legged frog is making a slow comeback, in some parts of its historic range. In Sequoia National Park the once common Mountain Yellow Legged Frog is now extinct. The precise cause is unknown, but air pollution and or acid deposition are highly suspected.

Trout can impact the environment in very subtle fashion. Large zooplankton such as Daphnia feed on algae. When introduced trout feed on the large zooplankton, the algae grows unchecked. Algae reduces penetration of sunlight which in turn measurably reduces the water temperature and the depth that photosynthesis can take place. I won't say this is good or bad it is simply an altered ecosystem.

Virtually every lake in the Sierra has, at one time or another, been planted with fish. Through ignorance we have irrevocably altered the Sierra lakes' ecosystem. At this point in our evolution it would be criminal to plant fish into any virgin water...no matter how potentially spectacular the fishery might be. We have altered enough ecosystems in our time; give future generations the chance to play with untouched waters.

Phil Pister, a respected fisheries biologist who has spent a lifetime working with trout in the Sierra says, "If I were granted one wish, that wish would be to have a magic button I could push that would undo all the fish plants ever done in the Sierra. With our current state of fisheries management and ecological awareness, wouldn't it be wonderful to have a clean slate from which to manage the Sierra? Not just as a consumptive use fishery, but as an ecologically healthy and well rounded environment."

Although trout were undeniably imported into the scene, they have become as much a part of the Sierra as the waters they inhabit. I feel the Parks could supplement fish stocks in lakes where natural reproduction continues to produce enough fish to disrupt the natural scheme of things, but doesn't

produce enough fish to make them viable sport fisheries.

The Park Service is walking a fine line between preserving nature in its primitive state while serving it on a platter to the public. Compromises are made every day. If the Park Service feels selling designer tee shirts in the center of Yosemite Valley is compatible with their mission; why can't they supplement marginally self sustaining fish stocks?

In one of man's many attempts to improve upon nature, beavers were introduced into the Sierra. It was soon realized that the beaver was incompatible with the Sierra flora and fauna. Beavers naturally subsist on softwood trees such as aspen and cottonwood. In the Rockies, the beaver's traditional home, willows keep pace with the beaver population. In the Sierra the beaver's appetite quickly outstrips the growing ability of the native softwoods.

A typical evolution is as follows: A beaver moves into a Sierra valley and dams its stream. Fry trapped above it are unable to reach their nursery. Trout downstream are unable to breach the barrier and reach spawning grounds. Summer droughts and winter freeze often kill fish trapped by the dam. With streamside trees gnawed down, banks destabilize and, lacking shade, water temperatures rise to intolerable levels.

After the beaver eats all of the softwoods in the valley, it moves to a new valley to begin the cycle anew. Unattended, the dam washes out in spring floods and the silt trapped behind the dam flushes into and destroys much downstream habitat. All that remains of the beaver's presence is a stand of dead conifers that drowned in the beaver pond and a depleted trout population.

With government encouragement and approval a new type of dam is now being found on many Sierra rivers and streams. In a move to harness energy, the federal government is subsidizing the cost of small hydroelectric dams. The incentives are great and an epidemic of dam building is spreading throughout western watersheds. Esthetics aside, damming streams can create long term damage to fisheries. Fish migration routes become blocked, abrupt flow changes kill aquatic life, regulated

releases create "armored" streambeds from impacted silt...The environmental list of concerns is long.

One small dam on one small creek is arguably harmless to the ecosystem. The cumulative effect of hundreds of such dams can be devastating. Unfortunately, the dam approval process only considers one dam at a time and the ruling is invariably in favor of the builder.

Of growing concern is the threat of acidification of Sierra waters. "Acid rain" has laid waste to hundreds of fisheries in the northeastern U.S. and Canada. As bad as the situation is in the East, the problem is potentially much worse in the Sierra Nevada. Unlike the eastern environment where carbonates are naturally found in the soil (carbonates combine with the acids to produce a neutral compound), the High Sierra are devoid of any buffering agents.

From the populous areas of California over 990 tons of nitrous oxides and sulfur dioxides are pumped into the atmosphere every day. These compounds are carried in westerly winds over the Sierra where they transform into nitric and sulfuric acids and precipitate in the form of acid rain and snow. Virtually all of California's exhaust emissions (both auto and industrial) end up in the granite catch basins of the Sierra. The result has a very direct and measurable impact on the Sierra watershed. Between 1954 and 1974 acidity has doubled in many lakes.

Solid grounds for the wise use of our fishery resources have been established in the recent past. In the history of fisheries management we have made tremendous progress and committed grievous errors. Presently we are not making the best use of our hindsight and the future is rapidly approaching.

THE TROUT & ITS ENVIRONMENT

THREE

WATER IS EVERYTHING TO A FISH. A TROUT CANNOT PACK ITS BAGS AND VISIT ANOTHER STREAM, SO THE WATER INTO WHICH IT WAS BORN MOLDS THE TROUT'S DESTINY. RICH QUIET WATERS WILL PRODUCE FAT AND SELECTIVE TROUT AND SWIFT LEAN WATERS WILL PRODUCE SLENDER, YET STRONG FISH. POLLUTED WATERS MAY PRODUCE NO FISH AT ALL.

"The bottom has a rocky reputation"
-Rod Stewart

Because of water's buoyancy, fish have evolved with weak bones and connective tissues. A fish is tough and durable when in water but becomes extremely vulnerable to internal injury when removed from its supportive medium (i.e., try not to remove a fish from water as you release it).

Trout have adapted well to water's density. Computer models show that the streamlined profile is nearly perfect...even a trout's eyes are covered with a rubbery membrane that reduces turbulence around the eyeball and socket. The skin is covered with a slimy film that provides a slippery interface between the trout and the water. This slime sheds as a trout swims which further reduces friction. As a trout breathes it expels water from its gills which adds a measure of "jet propulsion" to its movement, and envelopes the trout in a slipstream of water that allows the fish to travel with reduced resistance.

The resistance of trout is directly proportional to the surface area of the fish; a small trout has a relatively larger surface area than a large trout. A larger trout not only has a smaller percentage of surface area, its greater length gives it added leverage against the water as it beats its tail. The speed of a trout can be calculated by multiplying a trout's length by the number of tail beats...a large trout is much faster and stronger than a small one. A trout can dart to 20 mph but the average speed of a fast moving trout is only about 8 to 10 mph.

It is interesting to note that "velocity barriers" can effectively weed out fish below a certain size. A famous example is the Smith River of northwestern California. To reach the spawning beds of the Smith, steelhead must pass through a velocity barrier created by a series of violent rapids. Only the largest fish can penetrate the barrier and spawn, thus the Smith River strain of steelhead is among the largest in the country.

Water is a chemical soup which a fish is continually absorbing through its skin, breathing through its gills and swallowing into its digestive tract.

Osmosis is where the concentration of particles on either side of a semi-permeable membrane try to balance each other out. Due to the high concentration of salts and proteins in the fish, it takes considerable energy on the trout's part to keep from getting waterlogged.

Where the concentration of particles in the water (total dissolved solids or TDS) is about equal to the concentration inside the fish, the trout can spend energy growing and reproducing rather than expending energy on maintaining homeostasis. Hatchery managers have known for a long time that by adding salts to brood ponds, trout growth will increase dramatically.

The makeup of the TDS is very important to trout growth. For instance, if the TDS has a high percentage of calcium compounds, trout can absorb the calcium ions and put those to use building bones, forming eggs, and performing a variety of other functions. Waters rich in calcium support such trout foods as scuds and snails which use great quantities of the mineral in their shell (exoskeleton) development.

A brown trout hugs the river bottom.

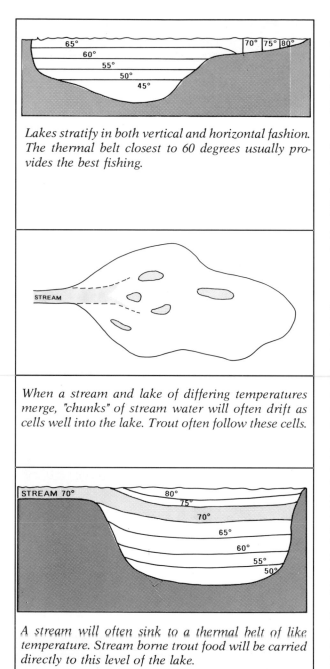

Lakes stratify in both vertical and horizontal fashion. The thermal belt closest to 60 degrees usually provides the best fishing.

When a stream and lake of differing temperatures merge, "chunks" of stream water will often drift as cells well into the lake. Trout often follow these cells.

A stream will often sink to a thermal belt of like temperature. Stream borne trout food will be carried directly to this level of the lake.

THE most important element of a trout water is oxygen content. Trout can survive on levels of dissolved oxygen (DO) as low as 3 parts per million (ppm) but usually require concentrations of 5 ppm or greater. As water warms it sheds oxygen until at about 80 degrees F. the DO concentration falls below the survival threshold of a trout.

As the water warms and the *available oxygen is decreasing*, the trout's metabolism is working faster and its *oxygen demand is increasing*. The optimal temperature for a trout is between 58 and 64 degrees F. This is the range in which trout eat the most and grow the quickest. As temperatures fall below this range, trout take longer to digest their food, eat less frequently and don't grow quite as quickly. At temperatures above 64 degrees trout go into a survival mode where they must seek water of richer oxygen content or go into a state of torpor.

Trout ACTIVELY seek water closest to the 58 to 64 degrees F. range. During periods when water temperature is in the thirties and low forties, trout will be found huddled over spring heads where the water is maintained at a relatively warm fifty degree range. Trout will pack warm water tributaries when main stem streams are frigid. Trout will be found over areas of dark, heat absorbing rock, or within inches of a lake shore where the shallows have gained a few degrees over the rest of the lake.

When water warms above the magic 64 degrees F. trout will once again be found in the relative cool of spring heads, deep pools, and cool tributaries (tail waters from the bottom of cold reservoirs are notorious for holding great numbers of trout during hot summer months). Warm water can become supercharged with oxygen if it is well aerated...trout will seek the turbulent white water of rapids and fast riffles. During periods of hot weather, aquatic weed beds will attract trout as the plants give off oxygen during photosynthesis.

Photosynthesis is the foundation of a trout's food chain. Where sunlight penetrates the water, plants convert water and carbon dioxide into organic simple sugars...food. The primary aquatic plants responsible for photosynthesis are the algae. In shallow waters algae will coat the rocks in a nutritious scum that literally crawl with small grazing organisms. The small grazers are fed upon by bigger organisms which are in turn the food of even larger animals like trout.

Riffles are considered the food factories of a river. The water in a riffle is shallow enough for sunlight to reach the river bed and drive photosynthesis. Riffles churn air into the water as it cascades over rocks and splashes through the cobbles. This "white water" is not only super saturated with oxygen, but the broken surface hides organisms from terrestrial predators.

The rocks and gravel which form the riffles provide a multitude of nooks and crannies in which organisms can live while feeding on algae and each other. The range of ecological niches found in a riffle is staggering; the caddisflies are only one of a number of riffle loving organisms, yet this one order alone fills dozens of unique niches.

The *Glossosoma* caddisfly larva builds a little hut of gravel over itself then seals this hut (called a test) to a rock so that it may graze on the algae underfoot in relative protection. Another caddisfly, the *Rhyacophila*, rappels from stone to stone on a silken thread as it searches for food. Yet another caddisfly larva, the *Hydropsyche*, builds a little net then waits for the riffle's current to fill it with debris. Once the net is filled, the *Hydropsyche* sorts through the net and picks out bits of food. The *Macronema* lives in pockets of still water in the riffle and builds a pitot tube which sticks into the moving water and draws in organisms drifting with the current.

Pools are on the other end of the environmental spectrum. Being too deep for photosynthesis to occur at a blockbuster rate, pools are generally the residence of scavengers such as crayfish and burrowing insects like midges and some mayflies. These organisms feed on organic debris which settles out of the current. Trout use pools as areas of refuge from predators and strong currents.

Runs can be any depth but as a rule have a strong laminar flow and lack the frothy, musical white water of a riffle. Runs can be restless areas with nervous, jumpy wavelets, or they can be silky smooth and gurgle and hiss. Runs are often deceptively strong and with this strength carve out deep undercut banks and scour deep (treacherous) channels. Where the riverbed is composed of large or durable substratum (such as granite boulders), a run can be a very richly populated river section. If the run occurs over an area of soft riverbed, the strength of the flow will scour any available habitat and the run will be virtual desert.

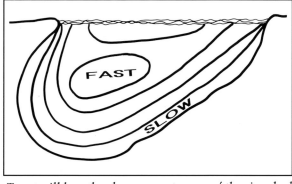

Trout will hug the slow current zones of the river bed and undercuts. The surface of the river flows considerably slower than its core.

Current, like water density, can be a two edged sword in the life of a trout. A river trout is continually exercising to maintain his position in the stream, and unlike its slothful lake brothers, rarely attains obese proportions. In trade for not providing the angler such a large "trophy," a river trout will invariably fight harder and longer than the same trout taken from a lake.

All currents are not created equal. Friction from streambed and banks dramatically slow the current along its edges. The slowest currents occur in undercut banks because of the friction from the streambed, bank, and overhanging roots draggin against the surface. At the actual water/streambed interface the current is nonexistent. Directly above this zone of zero current, a smooth film of water glides by in a laminar flow. In this calm, micro environment insect nymphs and larva scurry about even beneath the most terrifying rapids.

The friction of the atmosphere slows the cur-

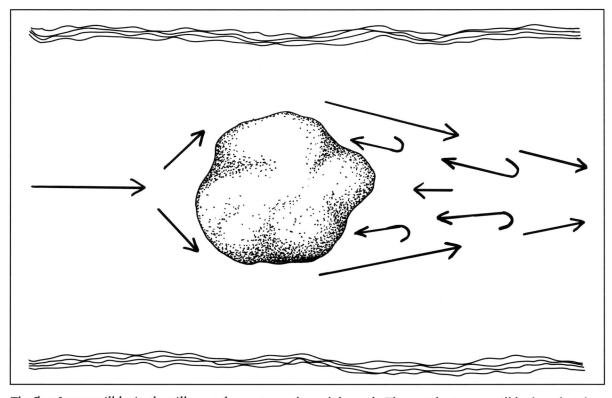

The "best" trout will be in the pillow at the upstream face of the rock. The next best trout will be found at the downstream edges of the rock where the eddy begins.

rent at a stream's surface and the friction along the streambed slows it further still. The quickest portion of a river is its core (visualize the river as a long bone...the fastest current would be the marrow).

In a nutshell: *the strongest current is in the core, the slowest current is along the streambed, and the medium fast current is on the surface.* This diversity of currents helps explain why it can be so frustrating for the novice angler attempting to obtain a drag free drift with a sub surface pattern.

Obstacles in and under the water cause currents to speed up and slow down. Water must get around the boulder that sits mid stream. As the water hits the boulder, it attempts to climb the face of the boulder then falls back on itself to form a bulge or

pillow on the upstream side of the boulder. *The water underneath the pillow is almost dead calm.*

The boulder mid stream constricts the flow and acts like a nozzle. The constricted flow speeds up around the boulder just as water does when you constrict the flow coming out of a hose with your thumb. As water increases in speed, it increases its propensity to carry debris. The accelerated current plucks at the riverbed and trenches around the sides of the obstructing boulder.

The current reverses direction to fill the void behind the boulder. This reversal in direction is called an **eddy.** As the current spins behind the boulder it slows and drops its sediment load. This deposition of debris creates surprisingly shallow zones on the downstream side of boulders, often creating safe haven for anglers attempting to wade a rapid.

The interface between the downstream current and the upstream eddy is called an **eddy line.** In large rapids, eddy lines can be immensely violent zones that can overturn river craft. In more typical trout waters, eddies will be seen as stationary, foamy banners that trail downstream from both sides of a boulder or other obstacle. On slow moving spring creeks and even on wind swept lakes, eddy lines are often nearly invisible; however, they *always* occur when an object breaks a current, and they are *always* suspiciously fishy places.

A trout has to find refuge from the current or it will expend lethal amounts of energy trying to hold its position in the river. This place of refuge from the river is called a **resting lie.** Typical resting lies would be in the eddy line, along the river bed, or tight against an undercut bank.

A **protective lie** is a place a trout can find refuge from a predator. A *relative* protective lie would be found in the depths of a shadow or in a curtain of bubbles. These relatively protective lies don't give physical protection to the fish, but hide it from enemies. An *absolute* protective lie would be amidst a tangle of roots or deep inside a log jam. An absolute lie provides a physical barrier between the trout and its predators.

A **feeding lie** is a position a trout takes to obtain food. On a lake the trout will have a *travelling* lie as he moves to the food. On a windy day a lake bound trout will swim in a straight line directly into the wind, and on a calm day the same fish will usually make long circular foraging patterns (remember this when trying to guess where a feeding trout will make his next rise).

It is common to find trout cruising lake edges during windy conditions. Terrestrials are often blown into the water along a lake's windward edge and the lee side will accumulate the bugs swept across the surface of the lake. Trout often take stations on the leeward edge of points and islands in a lake to take insects caught in the eddy.

River trout will position themselves in a spot to intercept insects ferried to them by the current. As in lakes, eddies are favorite places as are pinch points where wide areas of river become constricted and the volume of food is concentrated. As mentioned earlier, shallow riffles are the "food factories" of a river and trout will often actively work the riffles in search of prey. The shallows expose trout to enemies so the fish will usually work these areas under cover of darkness.

Trout taking insects from the drift are masters at conserving energy. They let the food come to them or allow the current to ferry them to the food. A trout will take up position and as the insect drifts toward the fish, the trout will cock its pectoral fins against the current and allow the river to push it to the surface. (It's just like holding your hand out the window of a car. When the hand is held flat it will stay put; however, when you angle the hand, the wind pushes it in the direction of the angle.) The rise of a river trout is invariably well downstream of where the fish first saw the insect (put your imitation well upstream of the rise form, not on it).

Prime lies combine the properties of resting, protective, and feeding lies. These zones are in high demand and are usually occupied by the dominant trout. If the occupant of a prime lie is removed, another dominant trout will quickly take up residence. A classic prime lie is the pillow on the upstream side of a rock. The calm water provides a good resting position, the overhead turbulence as well as the undercut trenches along the sides of the

During ice-out trout will lay in the shadows just beneath the ice's edge.

rock afford excellent protection, and any insect drifting into the pillow becomes trapped in the folding water...easy prey for the trout.

Another prime lie is in the undercut at the outside of a river's bend. As explained earlier, the current in an undercut is dramatically reduced, outstanding cover is immediately at hand, and the centrifugal force of the water will carry drifting food into the undercut.

The successful angler will always keep in mind the physical requirements of his quarry. By continually looking for factors that are favorable for trout, the observant fisherman will invariably take more fish than the average angler.

Where a riffle shelves into deeper water you should automatically think trout.

LOCATING PRODUCTIVE WATERS

FOUR

THE RICHNESS OR PRODUCTIVITY OF A FISHERY IS DETERMINED BY A COMBINATION OF WATER CHEMISTRY, TOPOGRAPHY, AND CLIMATE. THE ANGLER WHO UNDERSTANDS THE SYNERGY OF THESE INGREDIENTS CAN OFTEN PREDICT WHERE THE BEST TROUT WATERS WILL BE BEFORE EVER LEAVING HOME.

> *"As certainly as some pastures breed larger sheep, so some rivers, by reason of the ground over which they run, breed larger trout."*
>
> -Isaak Walton
> *The Compleat Angler, 1653*

Throughout this chapter don't lose sight of the fiact that fishing is a good excuse to be there and the lack oif fish shouldn't stand in the way of having a perfectly fine day of fishing.

CHEMISTRY

The foundation of the food chain is built on tiny plants called phytoplankton (free floating algae) and periphyton (attached algae). These algae feed the simple grazing organisms which in turn are fed upon by larger creatures. It makes sense then, that the most important nutrients in the system are plant nutrients.

The most important plant nutrients are phosphorus and nitrogen. These nutrients must be in equilibrium with one another or plants are unable to utilize them. For instance, water flowing through a phosphate deposit may still be relatively infertile if nitrates are unavailable. Even when both minerals are present, micro nutrients such as iron, copper, and molybdenum must be present for optimal plant growth.

The concentration of plant nutrients is determined largely by the soils through which the water flows. All soils contain some nutrient, but those originating from volcanic and marine formations are the "mother lode" of productive trout water. Volcanic and marine deposits tend to weather easily and contribute a wide range of dissolved minerals to the water.

The length of time water is in contact with nutrient bearing soils will also determine produc-tivity. Water which has had an extended "residency time," whether it be in a lake or underground aquifer, will tend to accumulate more minerals than water which flushes quickly through a system.

Lakes with high rates of evaporation are among the richest trout environments because minerals are super concentrated in their waters. Evaporative lakes have high concentrations of ions (in the form of salts) which encourage insect and trout growth by narrowing the osmotic differences between the organism and its environment and by contributing directly to the mineral uptake of the animal.

The measure of relative acidity or alkalinity is called pH. A pH level of 7 is neutral (distilled water). A pH level lower than 7 is considered acidic, and a pH level higher than 7 (to a maximum of 14) is alkaline. Alkaline (hard) waters usually have elevated levels of calcium or magnesium associated with carbonates. Calcium is not only vital for the development of bony skeletons, but is important for many physiological processes including neuro transmission and reproduction.

A classic example of the effect of alkaline water on trout growth is seen on the Liffey River of Ireland. The upper section of the river runs through acidic peat pastures and the pH drops as low as 4.6. About midway through its course, the river flows through a region of limestone where calcium carbonate is dissolved into the water and the pH jumps to an alkaline 8.4. The trout in the calcium rich stretch take only two seasons to attain the size of five year old trout in the acidic section.

The best trout waters in the world share pH levels from 7.5 to 9.5. Since high (alkaline) pH is almost always associated with waters that have a high mineral content, the angler can take a quick pH measurement of a trout water and make a good estimation of its productivity potential.

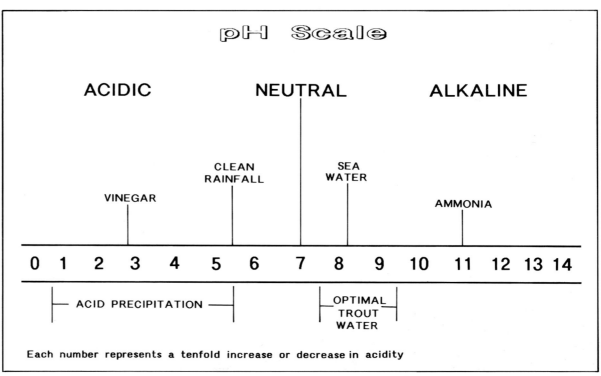

TOPOGRAPHY

The topographic profile of a trout water has a dramatic effect on its productivity. A river or stream which runs for many miles will have entrained more nutrients than that same river at its head. As a rule, the longer a stream, the greater the diversity of minerals it has contacted and the more productive the water will be.

Tumbling freestone creeks are oxygen and bug rich.

In areas of erosional deposition (alluvial plains and glacial moraines) even short water courses can be highly productive because the act of erosion has brought a large variety of nutrients to a localized region. This is a key thing to look for when prospecting for rich waters along the slopes of the Sierra.

Moving water tends to carry a load of debris. The greater the velocity, the greater the tendency to pluck material from the bed and transport it. The debris carried by a stream is called **seston.** Some aquatic insects such as *hydropsyche* caddisflies spin nets to capture the seston, then pick through it and eat the edible items.

A stream is always changing in character, digging out the bed in one spot and depositing it in another. When the mound of deposition reaches a point where the water plunges over the downstream side, the increased velocity carves into the berm and redeposit the load a little farther downstream. In this manner the river is continually slowing down then speeding up; excavating pools and laying down riffles in the classic "riffle run" configuration of a freestone trout stream.

As a river bends, centrifugal force increases the velocity against the outer edge of the turn where a great deal of cutting and erosion takes place. Conversely, the water on the inside of a bend slows and drops its load. River bends are favorite places for trout. The deep dark undercut at the outside of the bend provides excellent shelter for the fish and the rich, food producing riffles on the inside of the bend are always close at hand.

A plunging (freestone) stream continually scours its bed and provides little foothold for plant growth. Silt is kept clear of the cracks and crevices which provides a myriad of hiding places for insects and crustaceans adapted to the turbulent environment.

A freestone stream entrains great quantities of air as it churns and spills over rocks, as a result it has very high amounts of oxygen available for its residents. Silt free gravel beds and highly oxygenated water are vital for trout egg incubation.

When a stream flattens and slows, it deposits its sediment load and allows for plants to take root.

Aquatic plants, particularly stonewort and watercress, supply not only food but tremendous habitat for organisms such as scuds, snails, and midge larva. A river will, on an average, increase its productivity three fold when it meanders through a meadow.

A plunging stream interspersed with slow meadow sections will provide the greatest potential for excellent trout reproduction and growth.

LIGHT PENETRATION

A key ingredient of plant growth is sunlight. Through photosynthesis, plants convert sunlight into usable energy and produce oxygen as a byproduct. Water which is silty or discolored reduces the amount of sun energy available to the system and productivity rapidly diminishes.

As water increases in productivity, a concomitant decrease in light penetration occurs due to the heightened levels of plankton and algae. In extremely rich waters, the light scattering effect of plankton can establish the upper boundary of productivity.

Being translucent, ice allows enough sunlight to penetrate to keep aquatic plants photosynthetically active. If a heavy blanket of snow covers the ice, sunlight cannot penetrate and photosynthesis stops. Not only do the plants die and stop producing oxygen, but the bacteria which multiply as they devour the dead plants rapidly consume what available oxygen is in the lake. The trout suffocate and die in a classic case of "winter kill."

TEMPERATURE

Whether it be the simple dissolving of minerals into water, the act of photosynthesis in a plant, or the metabolic activity of a trout, temperature directly influences the outcome. As temperature climbs, photosynthesis and metabolism increase and water loses its ability to carry oxygen.

In cold water environs, plant and animal growth tends to be slow; for instance, a brook trout egg will hatch in fifty days at fifty degrees F. but won't hatch for one hundred days if the water is only ten degrees F. cooler.

Moving water takes longer to freeze than water which is calm. The water that moves right along the bottom and edges of a stream is the slowest so it usually freezes first and attaches to the riverbed. As this "anchor ice" grows thicker it becomes increasingly buoyant until it finally bobs to the surface, carrying with it a chunk of the riverbed. The anchor iceberg drifts with the current and the abrasive sand and rock affixed to its bottom scours the riverbed causing extensive environmental damage.

Heavy snows usually bridge western rivers with an insulating blanket before the bitter cold of mid winter can create anchor ice.

Warm water can be extremely productive, but its inability to carry much oxygen can reduce or eliminate trout populations. A few desert races of cutthroat trout have adapted to the extent that they can survive in creeks that routinely reach eighty degrees. To most trout however, waters with sustained temperatures over seventy five degrees are beyond the limits of tolerability.

PUTTING IT ALL TOGETHER

Granite "catch basin" lakes usually don't harbor tremendous biomass.

The factors of productivity are in a constant state of flux and as one aspect changes, the others are effected. The combinations of factors are infinite but the results are fairly predictable. Lets look at several trout waters and determine how productive they might be.

Gem Lake is nestled in a granite bowl amid the highest peaks of the High Sierra. Gem's water source is nearly on its shoreline, and the steep topography rushes snow melt into the lake giving little chance for the water to capture any minerals from the surrounding granite (granite gives off precious few nutrients in the best of times). Even though the clear waters allow maximal sun penetration, the lack of nutrients prevents much plant life

from forming, and Gem is nearly sterile.

Lunker and Frog lakes are tucked against the flanks of Mount Pluto, a dormant volcano. In every sense these lakes have the same components as Gem Lake; however, instead of granite, these lakes are built on soils of volcanic origin. The waters are rich in phosphates and nitrates as well as numerous trace minerals. Because the waters are nutrient rich, billions of drifting plankton and algae give the water a murky tinge.

Though these lakes are only separated by a few hundred yards and look nearly identical, Lunker is filled with large trout and Frog Lake is fishless. Lunker Lake straddles a pass where winter winds keep the frozen lake swept of snow. Frog Lake is on

the leeward side of the ridge and the same winds that scour Lunker, eddy behind the ridge and deposit thick quilts of snow onto Frog causing winter kill.

With a bit of imagination, a topo map, and a minerals map, the savvy angler could browse Gem, Lunker, and Frog lakes from the comfort of his kitchen and make a pretty good estimate of their big fish potential.

It's like a treasure hunt, and once you've discovered a couple of secret Henry's Forks, you'll never be happy with crowded "famous" waters again. With a little effort you can find more rich water in a weekend than the average angler will find in a lifetime.

TACKLE AND TECHNIQUES

FIVE

To enjoy Sierra trout doesn't mean you need to catch and eat them or even catch them at all. One of my favorite pieces of "tackle" is a face mask and snorkel that allows me to settle in with the fish and quietly observe them.

Most Sierra trout fishing is done with spinning or fly gear. Bait fishing can be very productive but with a little practice, one will find that flies and lures are far more effective.

Flies and lures can cover much more water than bait, and artificials catch the larger, more wary fish because they imitate the foods that the trout are used to feeding on. The average Sierra trout hasn't had many meals of marshmallows, corn, or Powerbait.

Bait has the disadvantage of being swallowed deeply and fish often get hooked in or near the gills. Trout taken on bait usually die which is a problem even for the angler who wants to eat his fish.

The maximum limit in the Sierra is five trout. The fisher looking for breakfast doesn't want to be limited to five, three-inch fish. He wants the flexibility catch and release allows so that he can release the small fish and take some pan sized trout home.

BASIC TACKLE

A nine foot, five weight, graphite rod is possibly the best all around Sierra trout rod.

The relatively long, nine foot rod is more effective than a short one for four important reasons: 1). A long rod keeps unnecessary fly line off the water for enhanced drag free drifts. 2). A long rod lifts lots of line effortlessly during mending. 3). A long rod helps keep backcasts high which is a plus when deep wading or when fishing from a float tube. 4). A long rod is great for small creek fishing because it allows the angler to stay well back from the banks as he daps his fly into pockets and along undercuts.

A five weight has enough backbone to punch a good sized fly into a breeze yet is still light enough to make gentle presentations and get a great fight out of a pan sized trout. If you routinely fish streamers perhaps a six weight would be a better rod, and if your forte is smaller creeks get a four weight.

Rod "weight" is determined by the line size that optimally loads the rod when thirty feet of line is in the air. Since most Sierra fishing is done with considerably less than thirty feet of line I'll usually load my reel with a line size or two heavier than the rod designation.

Graphite is the overwhelming favorite rod material of the '90s. Graphite is very strong and light and has a remarkable damping ability (the rod quickly stops wriggling after a cast is made). Competition has driven average rod prices down from the early eighties when graphite was reserved for the elite. Fiberglass, boron, and cane rods are available, but steer clear of them unless you have a very specific reason for doing otherwise.

When this book first came out I castigated pack rods for their poor action. Since then I've been introduced to the four piece rods made by Larry Kinney of Scott Powr-Ply. They're not only incredible travel rods, they've become my favorite rod of any kind. One lives behind the seat of my pickup.

If you can't rationalize spending the money for a Scott travel rod, stick with your favorite two piece . . . they're not that big of a hassle to tie to your pack

Trout reels tend to be over engineered and far too expensive. I just saw an ad for a trout reel that

A long rod will help keep backcasts off the water when fishing from a float tube.

Fly shops are far and few between in the high country.

boasted of all its springs and bearings; just more things to go wrong as far as I'm concerned. Ultra close tolerance reels may be works of art but they jam on bits of sand...usually when a nice fish is on the line. Many of the newer reels have disc drags which are silent. A big part of fishing to me is the sound of a screaming reel as a hot trout leaves town.

Scientific Anglers makes a sensible, affordable line of reels. On the higher end of the economic scale I'd consider one of the Sage 500 reels; they're similar to Hardy Marquis but are machined from solid

aluminum barstock rather than cast like the Hardys (cast reels are brittle and break when dropped just right).

I prefer weight forward fly lines over double tapers because they're great for firing off a quick cast with a minimum of effort. Double tapers roll cast easier and deliver a gentler cast than a weight forward, so they may be preferable for the angler who haunts brushy creeks and beaver ponds.

Cortland lines cast farther than Scientific Angler's because they're stiffer and don't sag between the guides. This same stiffness works against the Cortland when it's on the water because it tends to drag the fly rather than wrinkle with the water as the softer SA lines do. The choice is yours, but I'll give up distance for a softer presentation any day.

Leaders for small creeks and streams can be as short as seven or eight feet and a leader for selective lake goldens might need to be as long as eighteen feet. A good all around Sierra leader would be about ten feet tapered to a 5X or four-pound tippet.

Most modern pre-tapered leaders are excellent when compared with those of only a decade ago. I have yet to find an extruded leader with a tippet soft enough to pile nicely so I ALWAYS add a few feet of tippet to my pre-tapered leaders.

Tippet material has undergone radical changes, and there isn't much difference between the better brands. The ultra strong copolymer tippets are technical marvels. Don't be fooled into believing strength to diameter ratios are the only measure of a tippet's value. Some brands are abrasion resistant but stiff, while others are limp but kink terribly when a knot is drawn up. Experiment and decide which brands you prefer. My current choice lies with the Orvis SS and Dai Riki.

TIP: Hard copolymer tippets will cut through softer monofilaments so don't mix brands. Copolymer tippets are very slick and knots tend to slip. Use extra turns when tying clinch or blood knots better yet, use duncan and triple surgeon's knots.

When buying tippet be sure to avoid those which have been displayed under fluorescent lights or in window displays because the UV light rapidly

degrades the monofilament. Likewise, always store tippet spools and extra leaders in a dark zipped vest pocket. Heat weakens tippet so avoid storing your vest in a hot car and never use rubber faced "leader straighteners."

VEST

A fishing vest should be above all else, comfortable. A vest that pulls on your neck or feels like a shirt worn backwards can make a day on the river downright unpleasant. Get a vest that hangs squarely on the shoulders and is loose enough to wear over a sweater, but not so loose that it becomes unwieldy while casting.

Many vests have liners, piping around the pockets, and lots of eyewash that has nothing to do with fishing. I like my vests as lightweight and quick drying as humanly possible (I fall in a lot). The Patagonia mesh vest fits this bill perfectly.

Most vests have far too many pockets. I've never known an empty pocket that stayed empty for long. To keep from carrying the kitchen sink, buy a vest with a minimum number of intelligently sized pockets. Most vests have a large pocket in the back for a raincoat or lunch. I've yet to see a vest that was comfortable after the lunch pocket was filled...a fanny or day pack makes a better lunch box than a vest.

A fanny pack often doubles as a very capable vest, but isn't practical when deep wading. Glue a fly patch somewhere on the outside of the fanny pack so that you're not tempted to drop slimy flies back in their box.

WADERS and FLOAT TUBES

THE wader for backpacking is the Red Ball ST. Simms made a short run of excellent nylon waders with Seal Dri type feet but for some reason quit making them (I've written Simms several times to find out why, but all I get in reply is one of their catalogs. Makes you wonder how good they are at fixing defective waders). When my pair of SIMMS wears out it's back to the trusty Red Balls.

Nike Aqua Socks look funky but make great wading and float tubing shoes. They're inexpensive, feather light, durable and dry in seconds. What more could you ask for? Lighter than sandals or sneakers, Aqua Socks are also excellent for general camp wear.

Float tubes are a pain anyway you look at them. They're heavy, bulky, require waders and fins and the good ones require a pump. Lunker Hunter has a float tube which inflates by a "pump" made from its stuff sack. It's a pretty ingenious set up. A major fault of the Lunker Hunter is that the inflated pressure is so low that you wallow around like a pig in quicksand. Even with this fairly serious short-coming, it's the tube I use and will continue to use until something better hits the market.

New for the second printing of this book: Something better hit the market! Bucks Bags has a front entry float tube called the Bullet. This is a deluxe tube with all the trappings one could hope to find (I wish they'd cut the weight by making a trim-med down backpacker's version). Unlike other front entry tubes this one has a strut that holds the blad-ders apart and allows for very comfortable and ef-fieient kicking. It is not only a dream to fish from, it has a very lightweight internal bladder that can be inflated by mouth. Needless to say, my Lunker Hunter is sulking.

Another new item is the high volume, nearly weightless pump made by Sabe. The pump is ridiculously inexpensive and makes a perfect travel companion to the bullet.

To have a top-performing float tube you'll have to carry it inflated or bring along a pump.

A bicycle hand pump takes about forty minutes to fill a standard Caddis float tube and a foot pump takes about half that long. A light hand pump weighs 12 ounces compared to a foot pump at two pounds. The choice is yours.

Tiny Silver King Creek holds the world's rarest trout; the Paiute cutthroat.

Small rafts weighing five or six pounds are used by some backpacking anglers. The weight isn't so bad when you figure that with a float tube you'll need to carry fins, waders, and maybe a pump. Small rafts are awkward to fish from and even a slight breeze can send one to China.

FLIES

Fly selection probably causes more confusion than any other aspect of fly fishing. An easy way to eliminate the need to sort through dozens of possible patterns is to begin with only a few patterns in the box. Start with a basic selection and learn to effectively fish those patterns before adding to your collection.

A freshly emerged (teneral) damselfly patiently waits for its wings to harden.

For the angler venturing into the Sierra on his first fly fishing trip I would suggest six flies: Elk Hair Caddis, Ant, Adams, Gold Ribbed Hares Ear, and Royal Trude. Pick up a few of each of these patterns in size 12, 14, and 18. Get a couple of brown number 6 Woolly Bugger streamers to complete the selection. Stick with these patterns and try a variety of presentation techniques rather than swapping flies when fish are uncooperative. With a little prac-

tice and patience, you'll be amazed at how effective your offering can be.

The Elk Hair Caddis mimics all sorts of common Sierra insects like caddisflies, stoneflies, moths, grasshoppers, and midges. This is the fly I would tie on when in doubt of what to use. Start off fishing it treated with floatant so that it drifts on the surface. Give it a twitch every now and then. If fish aren't interested, let it sink and retrieve it just under the surface. If fish still aren't too impressed, crimp a split shot about a foot up the leader and fish it right along the river or lake bed like a nymph.

The Adams is a standard dry fly which is a good choice when insects with upright wings (probably mayflies) are on the water. Mayflies are common on both still and moving waters and during a hatch trout will sometimes take these to the exclusion of all other food forms. Try to match the size of the real insect with your Adams but don't be too concerned if the colors don't match...proper size, silhouette, and presentation are far more important.

Ants are common around all Sierra waters throughout the season. Trout are accustomed to feeding on them and will often take an ant imitation without hesitation. Favorite places to fish ants are on smaller brushy creeks and along the edges of ponds and beaver pools. A neat trick is to fish an ant underwater with a split shot. Few anglers try this, yet during scuba surveys, I've seen many drowned terrestrials drifting along the river beds.

If you tie your own flies or can get a friend to tie a few, make some Perfect Ants: Tie a clump of black deer hair so that it sticks out past the bend of the hook. Starting from the bend dub black Antron forward, over the tied-in deer hair, to a point about mid shank of the hook. Pull the hair that extends beyond the bend over the Antron, humpy style, and tie it down just in front of the Antron. Post the deer hair and trim it about a half-inch tall. Parachute wrap a brown hackle around the post then dub an Antron head in front of the post. Whip finish and cut the thread. Trim the post just above the parachute hackle and drip a glob of head cement into the post to secure the hackle.

The natural ant looks black in the hand...that's

why all artificial ants are black. However, from underwater the ant is silver because of the air bubbles sticking to the tiny bristles that cover the ant. The Antron on the Perfect Ant also traps air bubbles and looks very much like the real thing. The deer hair shell is buoyant and helps float the ant in the film and the hackle bends the water around the fly like the legs and (sometime) wing of the real ant.

The Gold Ribbed Hare's Ear imitates a great variety of nymphs and can work wonders on otherwise snobbish trout. Buy unweighted nymph patterns when possible. If fish are rising and you can't catch them with an Adams or Elk Hair Caddis, try dressing your leader with fly floatant and fish the nymph just under the film; very often trout are actually taking the emerging nymph rather than the adult insect on the surface.

TIP: If a fish leaves a bubble in the rings of its rise, it took an insect from the surface; if the fish rises and doesn't leave a bubble behind, it took the imitation just underneath the film. Many fish which expose their head and entire backs are taking insects under the surface...watch for the bubble.

The way to fish a nymph is with a split shot crimped about a foot up the leader so that it drifts along the river bed. The biggest mistake people make when nymphing is trying to fish too far away; one or two rods length's distance is as far as you want to cast. Hold the rod high in the air so that there is almost a taught line between the rod tip and the nymph. In this manner the current will exert a minimum of drag on the line and takes will be easily detected.

The Royal Trude is a fly that goes against my philosophy of trying to imitate specific food items; however, it is such an effective pattern that I don't leave home without it. The commercial patterns work well, but if you tie your own flies a few simple changes will markedly increase its fish catchability. Use fluorescent white calf's tail or better yet polar bear rather than normal calf's tail for the wing. The standard tail is made from hackle which isn't stiff enough for tumbling Sierra streams. I prefer Micro Fibbets laced with a few golden pheasant tippets.

The Woolly Bugger not only does a good job imitating dragonfly larva, crayfish, and baitfish, it has an appealing action that makes trout just want to bite the thing. There is really no wrong way to fish a "Bugger." Cast it out and bring it back fast, slow, near the surface, or right along the bottom. Buggers can be deadly when fished along the edge of weedbeds and the edges of beaver dams.

Remember that bait fish (a bait fish is any fish smaller than a hungry fish) swim downstream when scared or injured. For this reason a Woolly Bugger or any other streamer is generally most effective when cast upcurrent then retrieved downstream. A killer technique is to leave several inches of line on the tag end of the knot that holds the Woolly Bugger. Crimp some shot onto the tag and slowly feed the Bugger downstream so that it backs into under-cuts and along the edges of boulders. Let the line out slow enough that the Bugger flutters in the current. If the shot become snagged, pulling the Bugger free only results in some lost weight.

Crayfish are common in most Sierra rivers and the Woolly Bugger is as good an imitation as any for this crustacean. I've spent a great deal of time underwater watching crayfish and people trying to imitate crayfish with a fly. I've yet to see the action of a crayfish properly imitated in moving water. The best technique is to drift the bugger close to the streambed without any action at all.

In still water an effective crayfish retrieve is to quickly strip in two or three feet of line then let the Woolly Bugger sink to the bottom. As soon as the fly is on the bottom strip in another few feet and repeat the action over and over. On muddy lake beds puffs of silt will erupt when the fly touches down and attract fish from a considerable distance. Often, a trout will curiously follow a bouncing Bugger to the shoreline. If this happens, immediately cast the Bugger beyond the fish and retrieve it in fast jerky strips; chances are good the trout will hammer your fly.

The experienced fly fisher will undoubtedly have his favorite selection of flies as he enters the Sierra. The following are a few flies and techniques I've found particularly useful:

Hanging valleys carved by glaciers often hide seldom visited waters.

Immediately following ice out the rainbows, goldens and cutthroat will be spawning. This may be your best shot at getting a large golden because they have left the sanctuary of the deep lakes and are pretty vulnerable in the feeder tributaries. Stray trout eggs will be trickling along the stream beds and trout of all sizes will eagerly gobble them up. A bit of pink or pale orange yarn on a size 16 hook can be deadly. The best imitation is a Mini Egg made by buying some 3mm pompoms from a craft store and spearing them on a hook. Drift the egg with just enough weight to keep it near the bottom.

Midges (Chironomidae) are the single most important aquatic trout food throughout the year. When fish are rising to "nothing" they are probably onto midges. A handful of midge pupa or emergers (color is not important, just have a few light and a few dark ones) can be the difference between a frustrating outing and a bountiful one. Most high elevation midges will run from size 18 to invisible. My favorite commercial pattern is Kaufmann's Chironomid Pupa.

Grease the leader and tippet but not the midge. Cast out to the rising fish and let the midge sink; the greased tippet will suspend it just under the film along with all the natural midges. Watch for a boil and simply tighten to the trout; sharply setting the hook will only result in broken tippets or missed hookups.

Stoneflies

Stoneflies are prehistoric insects with very simple gills that require well oxygenated water to survive. They thrive in cool Sierra creeks and streams. The most common stoneflies in the Sierra are the so called little yellow stoneflies because they are little (half an inch to an inch), and yellow (a few are greenish, and many have orange abdomens). Any generic nymph pattern will mimic the nymph, but the most fun stage to fish is the egg laying adult.

The female little yellow stones hang out in the streamside vegetation during the day and at dusk fly out to lay eggs. They do this by crashing into the water to break the surface tension then releasing a few eggs. The little yellow stones flutter up off the water and repeat this again and again until they've beaten themselves senseless. After one too many crashes the females are no longer able to fly away so they flutter a bit in the film and get swept away as

These trout are actively feeding on emerging caddis pupa.

trout food.

The best way to imitate ovipositing little yellow stones is to smack your imitation against the water to make its presence known, then allow it to drift downstream with an occasional twitch. Elk Hair Caddis work alright but they don't float after much of this abuse. I use a little yellow stone imitation that is basically an Elk Hair Caddis but its body is made out of clipped deer hair so it's extremely durable and floats like a cork (deer hair is filled with tiny air chambers). I call this pattern the Perfect Little Yellow Stone and it has become a standby for many Sierra fly fishers.

Big trout are attracted to big bugs and some of the biggest bugs are the large stoneflies. The golden stonefly which is abundant in most Sierra rivers can be as large as three inches. Unlike most aquatic insects which undergo the transition from inception to adult in one year, the big stoneflies take several years to develop. This means that trout are used to

seeing stonefly nymphs winter, spring, summer, and fall. One of the best imitations of the large stonefly nymph is the Simulator. The Simulator's kissing cousin (both developed by Randall Kaufmann) is the Stimulator, a great imitator of the adult golden stone.

Caddisflies are important on almost all moving waters, and in many timberline lakes cased caddis larva are a mainstay. See the HATCHES section for more definitive information on the various caddis species, but there are a few techniques which are great for caddis in general.

Undoubtedly the most accessible caddis for trout in moving water are those of the uncased variety. These "rockworms" move from rock to rock by rapelling on thin silken threads. The protective coloration of these larva hide them exceedingly well but their threads are highly visible. Trout key in on these strands and inhale the larva dangling from their ends.

These rapelling caddis are easily imitated by running the last foot of tippet across a square of typewriter correction tape. Squeeze a split shot about 18" up the leader from the fly and cast it up and across stream. As the fly drifts downstream the shot will hang up on the bottom and the imitation will dangle downstream of its opaque tippet in a seductive fashion.

Emerging caddis pupa drift or swim to the surface to hatch into adults. These emerging caddis generate air bubbles between themselves and their pupal membrane probably to add buoyancy and to help separate the adults within from the shuck.

Many adult caddis swim or crawl to the streambed to lay their eggs. As they slip into the water, a solid bubble of air forms around them and clings to the insect as it makes its underwater journey. The air bubbles of both the pupa and adult caddis glisten and twinkle in a very characteristic fashion that trout recognize as food.

A pattern called the Sparkle Caddis imitates these air encrusted insects, but the more effective way to go is to spray a fuzzy nymph such as a Bird's Nest or Hare's Ear with Osprey's Fly Magic (don't use paste floatants, they gum up the fuzz). The floatant repels water and air bubbles cling tenaciously to the nymph just as they do on the caddis (and water beetles, backswimmers, midge pupa, and a host of other trout foods). Dry the nymphs with false casts between each drift and shake the insects in a desiccant like Siedel's 800 or Cortland's Dry-Ur-Fly every few minutes.

Don't slap the nymphs through the water or much of the bubble will shed. Cast as gently as you would a dry fly. A few split shot on the leader will overcome the buoyancy of the air encrusted nymph. This is a pretty amazing way to catch trout. It's the deadliest method I know of.

Cased caddis in lakes provide an important trout food source throughout the summer. Special imitations like the Peeking Caddis and the Strawman are great, but are too specialized for the hiker who needs to keep his fly selection down to a minimum. The Pheasant Tail Nymph is a great general nymph pattern as well as being a credible imitation of a cased caddis larva. On lakes with sandy or granite bottoms it is a simple and deadly matter to crawl the nymph along the bottom with a slow, hand twist retrieve.

Unlike mayflies which spend considerable time drifting on the water as they wait for their wings to harden, caddisflies get into the air almost immediately after emerging through the film. The exception to this is the caddis who gets trapped in its pupal shuck. These so called crippled caddis are easy prey and even very large trout will be on the lookout for them.

After watching trout capitalize on crippled caddis emergers, I experimented and developed a pattern that closely imitates the silhouette of the real thing. Called the EC Caddis (Emergent/Crippled caddis) it is easy to tie and fish. I often use this as a searching pattern even when trout aren't rising because it looks natural enough to bring even spooky fish to the surface.

To tie the EC Caddis attach a piece of rust colored Antron or Zelon yarn so that a frayed end extends about a half an inch beyond the hook bend. LOOSELY wrap the yarn forward to about half the hook shank and tie off. Dub some bright green, olive,

or brown fur on the thread and wrap that forward two or three turns and tie off. Lay a clump of deer or elk hair over the hook so it extends to the bend and tie down like the wing of an Elk Hair Caddis. Post the butts of the hair and parachute wrap a brown, dun, or grizzly hackle around the post. Trim the post, then whip finish and cut the thread.

Little yellow stonefly nymphs hug the rocks of quick water sections.

Fish the EC Caddis by dressing the wing, hackle and tippet with floatant so the fly rests IN the film rather than on top of it. The fly can be hard to see so make an overhand knot about two feet up leader from the fly and slide in a small piece of yarn as a fly locator. This overhand knot without the yarn would be called a wind knot and would make the leader pretty weak, however; the yarn will cushion the leader and prevent it from cutting into itself.

During the short days of autumn, the giant "October caddis" emerges from almost every mid-elevation Sierra stream. These huge, brown winged, orange bodied caddis look more like small hummingbirds than insects. Fall trout, fat and strong from a long summer of feeding rise eagerly to these huge morsels.

During the day the best bet is to bounce a split shot and large orange pupa along the riverbeds. My

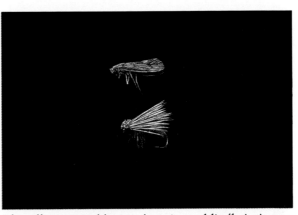

The Elk Hair Caddis is a favorite caddis fly imitator for obvious reasons.

favorite pattern is called the Tangerine Dream and is extremely easy to tie. Take a size six 2X long hook (Tiemco 200 is perfect) and dub a creamy orange body, a little thicker than a crayon, the entire length of the hook. Now take a dark brown speckled hen feather and wrap it soft hackle fashion just behind the eye of the hook three or four times. Whip finish and trim.

As the shadows lengthen in the late afternoon, the adult caddis start returning to the river with their characteristic herky jerky flight patterns. They soon start dipping into the water to oviposit and the trout are there to meet them. Splat a large Stimulator or Bucktail into a pool, twitch it around and hang on!

Mayfly

The *Callibaetis* mayfly is common on almost all still and slow moving waters in the Sierra. It is easily recognized by the white veins on the grayish wing which gives it a speckled appearance. The nymphs live in and around aquatic weeds.

An excellent way to imitate this nymph is to cast a Pheasant Tail over a weed bed then slowly count as the nymph sinks. Stop counting when the nymph hits bottom. Let's say you counted to ten when the nymph bottomed out. On the next cast start *slowly* retrieving the bug on the count of nine. By doing this

A pure Volcano Creek golden trout—silver phase.

The Bivisible Dun has a white and black post of calf tail for the wings. The trout don't seem to mind this odd color combination yet the angler is given the great advantage of being able to easily see the fly. As the fly drifts into the shadows the white post is visible, and when it floats into bright glare, the black post creates an easily identifiable silhouette.

THE APPROACH and "SIZE UP"

Catching a fish begins before the water is ever reached. It is easy to spot the pro at the trailhead because the pro will *maximize his time by minimizing redundancies.*

Where the casual angler may put on his waders, string up his rod, then unhitch his waders because he is over-heating; the pro will put on his waders at the very last moment so that he doesn't go through the redundant motions of unhitching then re-hitching them. This sounds like a very little thing but little things add up, and in the final analysis, the pro will spend considerably more time fishing than the average guy.

The casual angler will invariably tie a fly to his leader before walking to the water. If he finds he tied on the wrong fly, he will have to go through the wasted effort of retying a new imitation or he will just try to make do with the original fly. The pro will simply wait until he is at the water's edge and has a good idea what fly is best before ever tying one.

As the pro approaches the water he will be looking for clues. Swallows or nighthawks working above the tree tops very often indicate mayfly spinners are mating and that a spinner fall is going to occur in the near future. The sparkle of mayfly wings above the trees is another sure sign of a spinner fall to come. Swallows skimming the water's surface can indicate a hatch in progress.

The pro will stand in the shade and look almost directly at the sun...back lit insects are easily detected where the same insects can be nearly invisible when in direct sunlight. The Pro will kick the grass and shake the streamside vegetation with the hope that yesterday's hatch will become dislodged

you can work your fly in the productive zone along the weed tops without snagging.

One of the more common fastwater mayflies of the Sierra are members of the Heptageniidae family. Called the clinger mayflies, these nymphs are found clinging to the bottoms of stones in fast, cold water. They are easily recognized by their flat appearance and shovel shaped head.

For several hours before hatching, the nymphs will cling to the downstream edges of rocks and inflate with air. The nymphs can become inflated to the point where they look like little golden/black grapes. When the buoyancy of the entrapped air overcomes the nymph's ability to cling to the rocks, the nymph will ascend through the water column. As the nymph rises the air expands and breaks open the nymphal shuck whereupon the adult struggles out. Many Heptageniidae adults are completely free by the time they reach the surface. This unique method of hatching has probably evolved because the turbulent waters in which these mayflies live

would mangle an ordinary slow emerging mayfly.

The Zug Bug is a nymph made almost entirely of peacock herl which has a purple/green iridescence and does a great job of imitating the air filled clinger nymphs. As many experienced Sierra anglers will attest, the Zug Bug can be a highly effective fly on tumbling streams and rivers.

The Soft Hackle fly not only resembles the emerging clinger mayfly, but just about any other insect caught in the current. I carry Soft Hackles in sizes 6 through 22 and use them almost as often as the Elk Hair Caddis. In swift water the soft hackle is most effectively fished in a dead drift, but in still waters, a slow stop-and-go retrieve will pulse the Soft Hackle enticingly.

Two of my favorite dun imitations are the Sparkle Dun and the Bivisible Dun. The shiny trailing tail of the Sparkle Dun represents the shuck of the nymph still clinging to the mayfly adult. These emerging duns are sometimes preferred by selective trout.

and reveal itself. Spider webs, streamside foam, even radiator grills will often reveal the more abundant insects in the area.

Streambed rock rolling is an honored tradition among fly fishers. Not only will the observant angler get a good idea of the spectrum of insects in the river, but by looking for insect nymphs with dark, well developed wing pads, the angler will get an indication of the insect that will be hatching in the immediate future. Mayflies of the Heptagenidae family will usually cluster on the downstream edge of rocks just prior to hatching. Nymphs of the Siphlonuridae family will congregate at the waterline of emergent vegetation and river rocks immediately before hatching.

Once the pro has decided what imitation to use, he will still NOT tie on his fly until he has watched the water for rises. The way a trout rises (or the fact that there are no trout rising) will tell the observant angler a lot. Very subtle sipping, slurping, or gulping type rises are a sure sign that fish are taking a prey that is not trying to get away—like an emerging mayfly, a trapped spinner or drowned terrestrial insect.

Rolling or porpoising fish are often taking nymphs or emergers just under the surface. If a fish leaves a bubble in the ripple or "ring" of his rise, it is an indicator that the fish took the fly from the surface. [A trout doesn't bite a fly, it inhales the fly with a gulp of water. If the fly is on the surface, air gets trapped in the gulp and is immediately expelled out the trout's gills.] If the trout does not leave a bubble in the ring of the rise, the prey was taken subsurface...REGARDLESS HOW MUCH OF THE TROUT WAS EXPOSED WHEN IT TOOK THE BUG!

Splashy or aggressive rises indicate the prey was moving and the trout was making an effort to catch the prey before it escaped. Scuds, baitfish, damsel nymphs, swimming caddisfly and midge pupae are often responsible for splashy rises.

When a trout leaps out of the water it is often taking the same prey as splashy trout however, if damselflies are about, have a high index of suspicion that the trout are intercepting damsels in mid air...try a spent damsel in the film.

When fish are rising, the pro won't simply "covey shoot" the rises, he will work the fish in a manner which maximizes his efforts. If he wants to take several fish from a pod, very often he will work the most downstream fish first and will immediately pull it away from the rest of the fish so it doesn't spook the entire school.

If he wants to catch the largest fish, he will observe the method in which that fish is feeding. Fish, like people, are right and left side dominant. If an abundance of food is on the water, often a fish will ONLY take prey on his left or right side. He will keep in mind that fish prefer to rise away from the sun. Often a fish will rise in a very predictable rhythm and the pro will count cadence with this rhythm to make sure his fly is drifting over the trout during the rise cycle.

In calm lakes a trout will cruise in a large circle, rising to insects as he goes. If a stiff wind is blowing over the water, the trout will swim a straight line into the wind. In rivers, a trout will drift downstream and towards the surface to take an insect; the rise form is usually well downstream of where the trout first saw the bug. The pro is aware of these facts and will place his fly accordingly.

If fish are not rising, the pro will not put on a dry fly...no matter that the water is carpeted with insects. The pro will look for fish feeding underwater...it is not nearly as difficult as it sounds. It takes only a little practice to look through the water rather than at it. He will look for subtle glints of silver or copper as the fish bend to pick up prey in the drift. The pro will often position himself so that he is looking directly downstream all the better to see the white flashes of the inside of a trout's mouth as he opens it to take a bite.

Fish are masters at camouflage. A trout in the riffles will look like an elongated silver or gray blob. The pro will not dismiss a good looking "blob" without closely observing it for AT LEAST a minute. If it is indeed a fish, sooner or later it will sidle up or down current or it will drift to one side or the other as it intercepts a drifting bit of food.

A trout can blend so well with its background that it is impossible to see. A trout's shadow is not nearly so invisible. The pro often looks for fishy looking shadows rather than the fish itself.

Very often a trout will take up residence in a well defined territory. The constant swishing back and forth of his tail will sweep silt and algae from the surrounding streambed and the tell tale glow of relatively clean and pale rocks will be a dead give away of his location.

The Kern River serves an abundance of trout in one of the Sierra's most beautiful canyons.

Spotting fish is always easier from an elevated position. Experienced anglers sometimes go to a good deal of trouble scrambling a steep bank or climbing into a tree simply to get a better angle of vision on the water. Boats are profoundly better fishing vehicles than float tubes because they allow the angler to look down into the water rather than out across it.

Polaroid glasses are a must, and even the novice usually wears a pair; however, it is the rare person who utilizes his shades to their optimal potential. Gray is an oft-touted color because it doesn't alter color perception, however color perception isn't really very important in 98 percent of fishing situations (especially when you realize trout perceive colors far differently than humans).

Amber lenses are the color of choice because they screen some of the blue wave lengths. This filtering increases depth and definition perception (notice that sharp shooters and skiers in flat light always wear amber).

Polarized lenses work because they only allow parallel light rays to penetrate the glass. The savvy angler will often be seen bobbing his head up and down and tilting his head from side to side to "catch" the parallel rays most advantageous to his viewing situation.

All too often the casual fisher will walk right up to the bank or even into the water then start casting

to hot looking spots. As the pro nears the water he will keep in the shadows and use available cover to screen his approach. When the pro finally rigs up and begins to fish, he begins his fishing up close and gradually lengthens his casts. If at all possible, the pro will cast sidearm rather than telegraph his presence by waving a flashy rod tip nine feet in the air.

The pro will maximize his efforts by making every cast count. A sloppy cast that doesn't land precisely where he wants is fished and retrieved with the same amount of effort and concentration as the perfect cast. The fly that drifts past its quarry will not be ripped off the water but will be allowed to float into a discrete location or will be lifted deftly from the surface with a roll cast.

Often it is best not to attempt a pin point cast where the fish might be spooked if the cast isn't perfect, but to cast upstream and beyond the trout. Once the line is on the water it is an easy matter to drag the fly directly up current of the fish and allow the fly to drift right into position.

The expert will minimize the amount of drag the current exerts on his fly by using any of a number of tactics. The finer and/or longer the leader, the less influence the current will have on it. The less line on the water, the less line that is available for the current to drag around. The fewer current paths that the line crosses the lower the chance is that any or a combination of those currents will cause drag. Hold the rod high to keep line off the water; get in position to fish almost directly downstream to the fish; and don't try to fish more than several rod length's distance.

A final bit of advice: KEEP THE FLY ON THE WATER. Whether you're wading from one point to another, are picking through the fly box, or merely taking a break to watch the moonrise, leave the fly on the water...it is amazing how often the fish gods will surprise you with their benevolence.

THE MIND SET

Many people will think this is corny, but most

A large golden such as this one won't ignore the incautious angler.

experienced fishers I know will cautiously admit to "thinking" the fish to their fly.

First and foremost think positively and be receptive to subconscious ques regarding your tactics and strategy. I can't begin to count the times I've thrown a cast into a most unlikely spot because "something" told me to do it. That something might be as subtle as an incongruent ripple on the water or a subliminal glint off the side of a feeding trout. Usually I don't know what that "something" is but I go with the feeling.

When swimming a streamer or drifting a nymph I'll force myself to visualize the fly and direct its actions like a wire guided missile. That nymph is not just a hook on a line but an extension of myself; a marionette on a string directed by my conscious and not so conscious actions.

Spending time underwater observing the interplay of trout and trout foods helps immensely to correctly visualize the scene.

As the nymph approaches your target, visualize the trout as it responds to your offering. Its throbbing tail imperceptibly quickens, its fins slightly flare, and the fish's entire demeanor perks as the nymph drifts ever closer. He WANTS your fly.

Visualize the nymph coasting just off the cobbles then gently swim it upwards as it enters the foraging range of the fish (don't ask me how, you'll just know when you've penetrated the feeding zone).

The trout ever so slightly shifts its position, bends to the nymph, and barely altering its breathing rhythm, gently inhales your fly.

NOW!

You don't set the hook as much as you simply tighten to the fish. No fish? Oh well, there usually isn't, but it was good practice. With time he will come.

The twin peaks of mounts Ritter and Banner are a familiar landmark to the North Sierra traveler.

ANGLING
ETHICS

SIX

Nine out of ten people who pick up this book will skip this chapter. Maybe I should salt it with a couple fishing tips or a few secret places to fish. I won't do that though. Even if no one reads this chapter, I'll feel better for writing it.

"I still don't know why I fish. Perhaps fishing is, for me, only an excuse to be near rivers. If so, I'm glad I thought of it."
— Roderick Haig-Brown,
A River Never Sleeps.

Fishing for Sierra trout is a special thing. Rare is the person not affected by the beauty, splendor, and solitude of the Sierra angling experience. The air is crisp and clean (As Mark Twain wrote, "Why shouldn't it be, it's the same air which angels breath."), and the water is cold and clear. Sierra trout are hardy individuals who eke a meager existence from the beautiful yet harsh environment. Long after the hiker and angler leave the mountains the fish abide. Unlike the human who can come and go as he pleases, the trout must exist with whatever surroundings it is given. If we leave oatmeal, soapsuds, and other refuse in the mountain waters, the trout have to live (or die) with our trash.

Sierra trout are as special as the mountain range in which they live. There are only a finite number of habitats in which these fish can live and only a finite number of fish to inhabit them. Killing and eating the trout one catches is often an integral part of a pack trip. As a hunting predator, man has an instinctive urge and possibly a defensible right to kill and eat the trout he catches. However, as an advanced animal who has morals and holds the value of life in high regard, man has an obligation to kill his quarry quickly and cleanly and to utilize every fish he kills (leaving a trout to flop in the sand is not quick and clean, rapping it on the head with a rock is).

In this day and age when even the most remote back country trail resembles a cattle path, it must be clear to even the most ignorant person that if everyone kills his limit of fish, there will not be enough fish to go around. Limiting one's kill rather than killing one's limit is to be encouraged. *Catch and release has come of age.*

A trout can be inadvertently killed during any one of three phases of catch and release: Hooking, playing and releasing.

The easiest way to prevent killing a fish during hookup is to AVOID THE USE OF BAIT. Bait tends to be swallowed deeper than flies or lures, and the trout gets stuck in a vital area.

Hooks larger than a size 8 can be deadly because they can easily reach major vessels or the brain. Most successful Sierra anglers use size twelve or smaller hooks.

The clarity of high Sierra waters dictates that fishing line be of small diameter. The fineness of the line should be a compromise between fish hooking ability and fish landing ability. The largest Sierra trout, with a bit of luck, could be landed on one-pound tippet—that same trout will probably die if not carefully revived over a very long period of time.

Using tippet lighter than 6X (three pound) is rarely indicated. The angler who consistently finds he needs to use tiny diameter line to fool a trout is a poor fisherman. I've heard many fly fishers brag about how light a tippet they use, these guys may as well be saying, "I can't fish worth a damn."

Improper handling probably kills the majority of trout. This is absolutely inexcusable. Common sense should tell you that laying a fish on dirt or holding it out of water for several minutes to take a picture isn't in its best interest. Less apparent, but just as deadly, is lifting a fish out of water during a

A genetically pure Lahontan cutthroat from a tiny Sierra brook.

Gently cradle the fish, and keep it out of the water only a minimal amount of time.

high wind or when the air temperature is below freezing. Handling a fish with dry hands can cause the protective slime covering to scrape off (wet hands also keeps slime and fish smell down to a minimum).

If there is a need to take a photo, grasp the fish firmly at the base of the tail and cradle the fish under the belly with the other hand. Lift the fish out of the water, have someone snap the picture, then quickly set the fish back. Fifteen or twenty seconds should be ample time to fire off a few frames. It goes without saying that the cameraman should get his light readings and gross focus prior to having the trout taken out of the water.

While handling the trout *never ever* allow anything to slip behind the gill coverings. Having a finger in a trout's gills is comparable to having someone shove their hands into your lungs.

Handling time can be greatly reduced if you use barbless hooks. It has been proven over and again that barbless hooks have a greater holding power than barbed hooks. Many commercial anglers use barbless hooks exclusively. A barbed hook faces increasing resistance as it forces its wedge deeper into tissue a barbless hook easily slips through the hole made when the hook is initially set. Unlike a barbed hook that is continually enlarging its hole, the barbless hook doesn't become increasingly loose as the fish fights.

A barbless hook is easily made by smashing the barb on your fly or lure with a pair of needle nose pliers.

When unhooking a fish on a barbless hook, simply grab the hook shank and twist the hook upside down. Many times you can release the fish without handling it.

A huge portion of the Sierra is contained within National Park boundaries. Under a very clear and specific mandate our Parks are to "protect and preserve the biotic associations as nearly as possible in the condition that prevailed when the area was first visited by white man" (paraphrased from the Leopold Report of 1963).

Under Park Service Management Policies of 1975 the waters of Yosemite, Sequoia, and Kings Canyon can no longer be stocked with fish (unless to reestablish native species). *The next logical step is to prohibit fishing within Park boundaries.*

Parks, unlike National Forest lands, are managed for their intrinsic wilderness values rather than consumptive resource value. In National Forests trees, minerals, and even water are used to the point of being used up. In Parks it is illegal to pick a flower much less log timber. It has been illegal to hunt "wildlife" in Parks since 1883 and as early as the 1920s park managers suggested that the distinction between fish and wildlife was pretty arbitrary. I must agree...if trout aren't wildlife, then what are they?

As environmental awareness grows, so does the perception that fishing in National Parks violates every principal under which the Parks operate. As Paul Schullery observed in *A Reasonable Illusion*, "These people are not basing their objection [to fishing] on a moral repugnance to the sport itself...they are confining themselves to the interpretation of the Park Service's mission."

It is only a matter of time before animal rights groups grab this ball and run with it. In court they very possibly could win. Mountain lion hunting is now outlawed in California and numerous hunting closures have been instated by court order.

In 1967, *Man and Nature in the National Parks* was published by the Conservation Foundation. In what may prove to be a prophetic observation it pronounced, "We would put the point of view at this juncture that the privilege of fishing in national parks is one that needs radical reconsideration...Fishing is surely one of those out worn privileges in a national park of the later 20th century."

This is an issue that will not go away. Forty years ago it was inconceivable that "perfectly good" Park waters would be allowed to go barren (naturalists will correctly point out that these waters are only barren of trout). Be what it may, I predict that forty years from now fishing in Yosemite, Sequoia, and Kings Canyon National Parks will be outlawed.

Minimize your impact on the river by staying away from the edge of the water. Trampling streamside vegetation and collapsing banks are two very efficient methods of reducing a stream's productivity (two excellent reasons to keep cattle out of riparian corridors).

People wade far more than necessary. Wading not only scares fish but crushes aquatic organisms and destroys habitat. I know it seems like a little thing, but there are hundreds of years and thousands of people following you.

If you've read this far, thank you. As your reward I'll share a secret with you: I'm a life long angler who has guided fly fishers on some of the finest trout waters in the world. I teach people how to catch fish. I lecture and write about fish. I design fishing flies. You'd think by now hooking fish would be the thing in life I like best. Not so. I fish a lot, but as often as not I don't use a hook. I fish for the grab.

Instead of hooking fish, I spend an inordinate amount of time underwater just watching them. They're incredible creatures as are all the other things that have evolved in mountain streams. I've learned more about fishing in the past ten years of observing than I could in a lifetime of catching.

A face mask is a cheap ticket into another world. Witness a golden trout slide up to another and spawn the next generation. Watch a brook trout ride the current and glide to the surface like an eagle on a thermal. Laugh as tiny fry, brilliant as any tropical fish, try to catch a butterfly twice their size. See the terror and confusion in a mountain pool when a trout feels the sting of a hook.

I am *NOT* trying to convert anyone to hookless fishing or even catch and release, that's an individual decision. I'm only trying to spread the word that there's more to a trout than a tug on the line.

Only lift the fish from the water after the photographer has prepared the shot.

Dry Flies

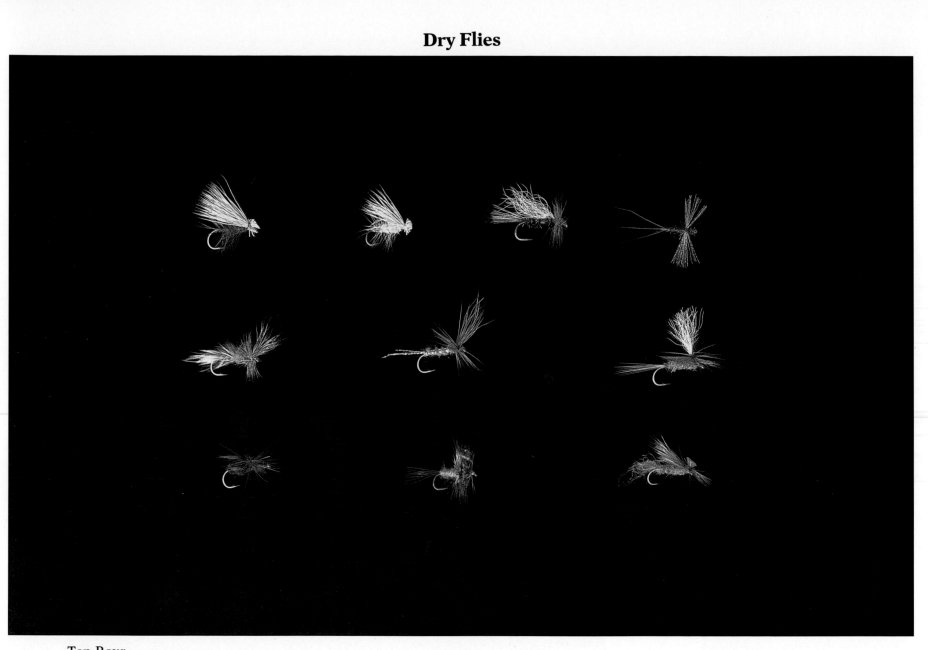

Top Row:
   Elk Hair Caddis
   Perfect Little Yellow Stonefly
   Royal Trude
   Polywing Spinner

Second Row:
   Cripple Mayfly
   Martis Midge
   Bivisible Dun

Third Row:
   Perfect Ant
   Moosetail Adams
   Emergent/Cripple Caddis

Wet Flies

Top Row:
  Bird's Nest
  Green Rockworm
  Gold Ribbed Hare's Ear

Second Row:
  Tangerine Dream
  Mini-egg
  Pheasant Tail

Third Row:
  Goblin
  Woolly Bugger

INTO THE BACKCOUNTRY

SEVEN

A TRIP INTO THE SIERRA BEGINS WITH PLANNING AT HOME. USE A CHECKLIST TO MAKE SURE YOUR EQUIPMENT IS PACKED: IT'S NO FUN IMPROVISING TOILET PAPER ON THE SECOND DAY OF A TWO WEEK TRIP. THE LIST IN THE APPENDIX IS A GOOD START BUT IT CERTAINLY ISN'T THE HOLY GRAIL.

THE FEET

Unless your trips include a lot of off-trail talus scrambling with a pack, heavy full grain leather boots with cleated soles are definitely out. As the saying goes, "A pound on the foot is worth five in the pack." Lug soles shred the landscape without adding any appreciable traction.

Nike, Asolo, Hi Tech, and Technica make excellent medium weight boots which provide adequate support and protection for most back country users. When fitting boots be sure to wear the socks you'll be hiking in.

A thin polypropylene liner sock under a heavier sock helps keep your feet blister free. I strongly recommend Thor Lo socks. Thor Lo's are extremely well padded and conform to the foot which reduces blister.

Clean feet and dry socks keep blisters to a minimum. Many experienced hikers change into a fresh pair of socks at lunch. Don't wait for hot spots to evolve into blisters which can turn an otherwise wonderful hike into a nightmare. Moleskin placed on a hot heel or toe almost always stops a blister from forming. If a blister does occur, wash the area and cover it with Spenco's Second Skin. The Second Skin not only reduces the pain of a blister but seems to help speed the healing time.

THE LEGS

Long pants should be worn if you anticipate off trail hiking through snow, brush and manzanita.

Early season hiking usually necessitates crossing snowfields which can be highly abrasive as you plunge through the crust. Stout pants or at least high gaiters are a must.

Shorts are almost a trail uniform during the Sierra summers. Nylon gym shorts are light and dry instantly but abrasive granite quickly rips holes in the butt. Sportiff stretch shorts are worn by many hikers but I find them to be pretty binding when taking large steps over talus. Patagonia and Cabela canvas shorts are durable and time proven.

An excellent "legs" combination that minimizes weight and maximizes versatility is a pair of shorts, a pair of pile sweats (I particularly like Patagonia's stretch Synchilla tights, they don't bunch up under waders or rain pants), and a pair of light rain pants. Mix and match these as conditions dictate.

A beautiful Kern River rainbow trout.

THE UPPER BODY

Out of vogue but highly versatile is the fishnet tee shirt. During hot summer afternoons, the netting keeps pack straps from chafing and allows air to circulate between the pack and your back (makes an interesting tan too). As the weather cools, the fishnet tee shirt adds a surprising amount of dead air warmth to any shirt. For an item that weighs so little, it serves a lot of purposes.

Cotton, canvas and chamois shirts are nearly useless when wet, but everyone including myself seems to live in them just fine. Wool or pile shirts are the sensible alternative to cotton. A down jacket was considered de rigueur for any Sierra traveller until polypropylene pile proved to be as comfortable, as light, and more effective when wet. Polypro doesn't compress worth a darn which might be a

consideration when a multi week trip is bursting the seams of your pack.

HEAD AND FACE

A brimmed hat of some sort is almost mandatory. During a long day in the sun, a shadow cast across the face will be appreciated. When in rain or snow, a brimmed hat under a rain jacket's hood will keep the worst of the weather away from your glasses and camera.

Cowboy style hats blow off in every breeze and are impossible to wear with a backpack. Baseball caps sort of protect the face but leave the ears vulnerable to sunburn.

The most functional hat I've worn is the up-downer style popularized by flats fishermen. The wide bill keeps the sun from sneaking behind your glasses and the floppy side and back brims stay away from the pack while keeping sun off your ears.

Racoons are always more than happy to share the food you so painfully carried in.

If a brimmed hat is almost mandatory, sunglasses are *absolutely mandated*. Even under hazy conditions the glare of stark granite will keep you squinting all day. UV light is much more intense at altitude than at sea level. The word is out that UV rays are bad for the eyes, so get glasses that block out the UV spectrum. I would imagine that most people reading this fish, so it only makes sense that your glasses be polarized to help see through the water.

Mirrored lenses are great when crossing snow fields or miles of white granite. While the glasses are protecting your eyes from the sun they are frying your nose as effectively as a parabolic oven. Use plenty of sun screen.

Side shields are highly recommended by the people who manufacture them but most people who buy them throw them away. I like my peripheral vision.

A string of some sort to hold the glasses around your neck is invaluable when taking photos or using binoculars. It's all too easy to drop your glasses in the dirt when a good picture leaps up from the trail. It's even easier to forget just where the glasses were dropped a half hour later.

RAIN/SNOW GEAR

It can and does snow every month of the year in the Sierra. If this is the trip of a lifetime, expect it to snow. Actually, snow isn't as bad as it sounds as long as you *stay dry*. Keeping dry means putting on foul weather gear before getting soaked and then not sweating up a storm.

Gore-Tex is a hoax. I've been given third generation, high tech Gore-Tex with taped seams, ergometrically fitted hood, etc.. and it worked just fine in gentle rain and snow but failed miserably when the chips were down. Sierra storms can be torrential and accompanied by cyclonic winds. The only stuff that *always* works is good old non-pervious plastic or rubber.

Patagonia and Helly Hansen make state of the art ventilated raingear which costs a lot less than the "breathable, waterproof" stuff. Buy a coat and pants; ponchos always leak and cagoules are miserable to hike in. A raincoat should be at the very top of the pack even (especially) if you *know* it won't rain. At the least it might help seal your pack in the event of a swim.

BACKPACK

Get a good *external* frame pack with a sensible one piece waist belt. The frame carries the load slightly away from the back which means more than you think when a reel handle or fuel bottle is jabbing

An external frame pack allows you to easily strap extra gear to your back.

into your spine. The frame is invaluable for lashing rod tubes and wet shoes onto, and in camp the frame will hold the pack upright and open for easy access and packing.

Frameless and internal frame packs are excellent for skiing and mountaineering where balance is of utmost importance. To the typical backpacker however, frameless packs are unwieldy sweaty things that are only slightly more useful than a rucksack.

When carrying a pack, most of the weight should ride on the hips rather than shoulders. Heavy gear should be loaded near the bottom of the pack which will lower its center of gravity and reduce that top heavy tipsiness.

SLEEPING GEAR

Synthetic sleeping bag filler, like polyester and dacron, is great when it gets wet because it retains its loft and most of its warmth. Synthetic fill is also nice on lumpy ground because it doesn't compress like down and herein lies a problem; there are times when you'd really like the stuff to compress. Synthetic bags take an inordinate amount of space on the pack.

Down is very light, and compresses into microscopic stuff sacks. Nothing comes close to the comfort of down, plus I like the idea that a goose can make something better than any technical engineer. Be sure the bag label specifies down and not just feathers or you'll end up with pin feathers poking through the nylon. Down is sold by lofting ability. Loft equals warmth and money. An ounce of down which lofts to 500 cubic centimeters is said to be 500 fill. It is obviously better to have an ounce of down fill 650cc's rather than 400cc's.

When hiking in Alaska or other equally soggy environment it would be crazy to carry anything but a synthetic bag, but with some foresight you can keep a down bag dry in the relatively arid Sierra. I cheated and got a Gore-Tex/down bag. I feel protected against everything up to a moderate dew (see Gore-Tex under RAIN GEAR).

TIP: Leave a cozy pair of socks in your sleeping bag. They will always be clean and dry and waiting for you.

The best sleeping bag will be neutralized without some sort of pad. A pad not only helps soften pine cones but keeps a sleeping bag's insulating loft from being completely squashed. Ensolite has long been a favorite among Sierra hikers but is slowly being pushed out of the picture by the clearly superior and vastly more expensive Thermo Rest. Thermo Rests are open celled slabs of foam encased in coated nylon. When inflated (they almost self-inflate) they insulate and pad unlike anything else I've ever used. Highly recommended.

SHELTER

Most of the time a Sierra shelter is a refuge from mosquitos and frost, but when push comes to shove, a tent can be a life saver. Four season mountain tents such as North Face's VE-25 (my current favorite) are heavy, expensive but bullet proof. The ubiquitous Eureka Timberline tents are about one third the cost, half the weight and provide fine shelter for the summer camper...I wouldn't want to be in the high country in late fall with one.

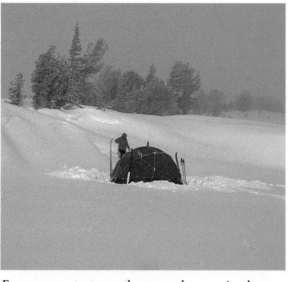

Four season tents are heavy and expensive but are worth their weight in gold when needed.

Solo shelters have come a long ways since the days of rolling up in a poncho. For about three pounds and a hundred bucks, a solo shelter such as Eureka's Gossamer is the nicest thing you would never wish to spend the night in. These claustrophobic little coffins are a godsend when the mosquitos are on the war path or when a midnight thunderstorm rolls through. When packing with a solo shelter don't forget to bring a groundcloth to cover your gear.

COOKING STUFF

In the high country don't even consider cooking over a cozy little camp fire. I mean it. Building a camp fire seems like a simple thing, but the impact can last for centuries. The thin soil of the mountains provides precious few nutrients and most of these are stored in the plants rooted in the soil. Through photosynthesis plants build nutrients which are returned to the earth when the plant dies and decomposes.

When a log is thrown into the fire, accumulated nutrients that took perhaps centuries to develop are exhausted in a few minutes. Backpacking stoves are lightweight, efficient and dependable...use them.

Butane stoves are convenient, but performance can suffer at altitude and in cold conditions. Empty butane cartridges must be packed out and are non-recyclable.

Small white gas stoves such as Coleman's Peak 1 and MSR's Whisperlite are perfect. Don't forget the matches as I once did. Tip: carry several sets of matches or butane lighters in Zip Lock bags and spread them among the members of your trip or at least through different pockets of your pack.

When in wooded areas, simply assume bears are also, and hang food high.

Only male deer bear deciduous antlers.

Leave the tin Sierra Club cup at home and bring a large insulated plastic mug with a handle. Your cup will be your plate, bowl, and insect catcher so make sure it's large and durable. It doesn't hurt to mark half cup increments on the side before leaving home.

Aluminum cookware supposedly causes some disease that I forgot the name of so I bought a copper bottomed stainless job that boils water like a champ. Don't get a pot so large that it won't fit inside the windscreens that come with the pack stoves. Make sure the pot handle stays upright by itself so you don't have to brand your fingers trying to lift it from the stove.

Spoons are useful and can do just about everything a fork can so don't bother with a fork. A *small* Swiss army knife will always be put to use as will a cloth bandanna or hand towel.

WATER

Flopping onto your belly in the prickly grass and sucking water from a creek is an experience not long forgotten. I'm always amazed at the wonderful world there just inches under my nose. Nothing tastes better than a long draught of cold water straight from a pure mountain stream. I consider it one of the neatest bonuses the Sierra have to offer.

By now you're reeling in your chair thinking, "I know better than THAT. He could catch the 'G' word."

Yeah, I know. But the risk is slight. Instead of being the rampant pathogen popular dogma would have it to be, *Giardia lamblia* is NOT commonly found in backcountry water.

Coyotes play an important part in the high Sierra ecosystem.

Desolation Wilderness is the most heavily used Wilderness area in the country, yet researchers there have to filter hundreds of gallons of water to get a sample of five or ten cysts. No one really knows the infective dose of Giardia, but the chance of getting infected from your pot of water IS statistically small.

It is known that many animals including beavers can carry and spread *Giardia;* however, there is strong belief that the three known species of *Giardia* are each host specific and perhaps only one species causes untoward effects in humans. It is probable that "Beaver Fever" doesn't exist.

Giardia is transferred via the oral fecal route. Most cases of *Giardia* are found in day care centers and nursing homes where personal hygiene is suspect. Relatively few *documented* cases of *Giardia* are attributed to contaminated water supply. You stand a much better chance of contracting *Giardia* from your child or institutionalized grandmother than you do from backcountry water.

The widespread public outcry, fueled by unknowing outdoor writers and the Federal Government, has led to a whole generation of backcountry hydrophobics. As of March 1, 1993, neither the U.S. Forest Service, the National Park Service, the Center for Disease Control, or the Environmental Protection Agency, have data from scientific research regarding *Giardia* in the backcountry. Every piece of "advise" published by the government has been purely anecdotal.

Should you chemically treat, boil, or filter your water? I don't bother, but the choice is personal.

Chlorine (Halazone) and iodine taste like the chemicals that they are. A study in the *American Journal of Public Health* reports that when used as directed, neither chlorine or iodine inactivate *Giardia* cysts. When placed in a known concentration of cysts, the chemicals had to have a contact time in excess of eight hours to be effective.

Boiling water at 212 degrees F. is very effective for killing micro organisms, but remember, at altitude water boils at cooler temperatures than at sea level. The official U.S. Forest Service stance is that water should be brought to a "rolling boil for 15 minutes." That sounds like a lot of time and fuel to me; plus, boiled water tastes flat. If you are really intent on ridding your water of bacteria, viruses, and *Giardia*, prolonged boiling is the way to go.

Filtering make sense if only for the placebo effect. Remember though, as you're pumping away on that little handle, many bacteria can slip right through the filter.

Use common sense about your water source. *Giardia* isn't the only thing out there. *E. coli* and *Campylobacter*, are fecal contaminants that may be more common than *Giardia*. Get water from springs and creeks that come from low use areas, i.e. upstream of campsites and trail crossings.

If you get diarrhea, oh well, you got diarrhea.

Bacterial diarrhea should be suspected if accompanied by fever, chills, and bloody stools. Ciprofloxacin and Norfloxacin are the preferred antibiotics for bacterial (traveler's) diarrhea because of the low side effect profile.

Viral diarrhea has a rapid onset, but is always self limiting (it goes away by itself). It is not normally accompanied by fever. Immodium is an excellent narcotic antimotility agent for symptomatic relief of viral diarrhea. Anti biotics have no role in the treatment of viral diarrhea.

Giardiasis usually takes at least ten days to become symptomatic. Stools are not bloody and there is no fever; bloating and cramping are common symptoms. Because of the long incubation period, *Giardia* is only an issue of discomfort when on a prolonged trip. Quinacrine or Flagyl are effective antimicrobial drugs.

Just as a note: Yes, I have had *Giardia* and it's not terribly pleasant, but by the same token it's not so awfully terrible either.

However you treat your water, *drink plenty of it*. As a rule, one should have to pee at least once every two hours while at altitude. The high dry air saps moisture from your lungs at an incredible rate. Dehydration is an insidious thing, even low grade dehydration can cause or exacerbate hypothermia, muscle cramps, and fatigue.

FOOD

"Back packing food" is whatever one puts in his pack, not necessarily what the manufactures tell you is "trail mix." On one or two day hikes, food can be anything out of the cupboard, but on extended trips the choice of foods is important. The ideal food would have lots of carbohydrates, protein, fat, be chock full of calories, be non perishable and weightless. Chocolate covered peanuts come close.

Freeze dried meals are, on the whole, excellent. A cup of Mountain House shrimp cocktail chilled over snow is wonderfully decadent after a long hike. Many dehydrated foods such as macaroni and cheese and Top Ramen aren't nearly as exotic but are satisfying and less expensive than "backpack" food.

Backpacking is the time to ignore the "rules" and eat lots of fat. Fat is what keeps you satiated and provides fuel for the long run. It is amazing how much fat can be burned on a two week trip. Great for trimming the jelly roll, but it does present problems to those too dependent on dehydrated foods.

Porcupines will chew hiking boots to shreds while they feast on the salt from your sweat.

Salami, cheese, bacon bars, margarine and nuts are relatively non perishable fatty foods that will tame that incessant gnawing in the gut so many hikers grumble about. TIP: Pack fatty foods inside your sleeping bag to insulate them from heat.

Fiber, particularly during the early days of a hike will help overcome the irregularity that often accompanies a change in diet and exercise. A 50/50 mix of Fiber One and your favorite dry cereal with a generous splash of Milkman powdered milk is a simple and fairly palatable breakfast.

A cony gathers straw for the long winter ahead.

Lunches should be nibbled throughout the day rather than at one sit down, pig out at noon. Hard candies, M&Ms, dry fruit, fruit rolls, granola bars, and the fatty foods listed above make great trail food. Chewing a stick of gum throughout the day will keep your mouth moist and diffuse the effects of trail dust. Many people like powdered flavorings in their water...I enjoy the mountain water as it is.

Big breakfasts and lunches don't seem to settle very well when one has a lot of miles to pound immediately after eating. Dinner is the time to enjoy a full meal. Freeze dried fruits and vegetable salads are great. Beef stroganoff and spaghetti are perennial favorites as are instant puddings. Choose meals that are simple and easy to clean up. Most of the "back pack" meals can be cooked in their own mylar packages.

As a rule, divide the "serves X meals" found on the packaging in half. If the dehydrated lasagna says, "serves four," it probably serves two. Most people crave spicy foods after sweating on the trail for a few days. Salt, pepper, oregano, and garlic powder are worth their weight in gold.

TOILETRIES

Everyone has to decide for him or herself how socially acceptable they want to be. On the trail I don't shave or carry a comb, but I wouldn't be caught dead without my little solar shower.

A small solar shower weighs only 3.5 ounces and I swear to god it's the best 3.5 ounces I have on my back. The two liter black and silver bag heats in about two hours of afternoon sun (you can cheat and warm the water on your stove) and will provide the most memorable shower of your life. A must have!

A snug timberline campsite.

Castile soap works as a pot cleaner as well as a general body soap and shampoo. Castile is "biodegradable" which means it's okay to dump the suds *at least* 100 feet from the nearest water.

Pre-moistened towelettes are nice to have when tent bound. The witch hazel and Sea Breeze models can make you feel clean even when you're not.

Don't forget the toilet paper! Any old stuff will do, but unroll it from the tube and fold it into a Zip Lock bag. When nature calls, get well away from water and places water might be when spring run off occurs. Ridge lines are a favorite place of mine because I can enjoy the view. Bury your feces and toilet paper under several inches of dirt then place a log or rock on top of that to keep curious animals from immediately digging it up.

Tooth powder is lighter than toothpaste but I stopped using it when moisture got into the container and turned it into a brick. Little travel tubes of toothpaste aren't too heavy. One backpacking author recommends cutting the handle off your toothbrush to save weight, but that seems pretty neurotic to me.

Hands can get pretty chapped and raw so a tube of good lotion is nice. Sunscreen and Chapstick are mandatory.

ODDS 'N ENDS

One of my more valuable possessions is a tattered copy of Storer and Usinger's *Sierra Nevada Natural History*. This treasure trove of information is available from UC Press and can be found in most book stores. I DON'T leave the trailhead without it.

A small pinch type flashlight can be handy for untying shoes in the dark.

I would feel naked without a USGS topo map of not only my immediate vicinity but of adjacent areas as well. I like to identify distant peaks and valleys and dream of future pack trips. Fifteen minute maps are more practical than 7.5 quads and Forest Service maps are best left at home. I hate to say a compass is useless in the Sierra but I can't ever remember carrying one on a summer hike. It is always possible to pick out a few landmarks and align the maps to them (in winter when everything looks the same, I live with a compass).

Insect repellent can save a trip when the mosquitos get bad. I've worked as fishing guide in some of the most notorious mosquito country in Alaska and can honestly say the Sierra can be every bit as buggy. Despite all the health warnings I use Muskol liquid (95 percent DEET) on my skin and spray Cutter's (21 percent DEET) on my hair and clothes. Skin So Soft has received a lot of publicity as a bug repellent, but a double blind study performed by Smithsonian showed it to be only slightly more effective than nothing and much less effective than DEET.

CAMP

Selecting a good campsite is as much an art as a science. Some people are willing to pitch camp where ever they drop their pack. I'm forever on the lookout for the perfect spot.

The perfect spot should get early morning sun and have a good view but be hidden from view. Everything else is a distant second. The books say a good campsite should be near water but some of my favorite spots are on mountain tops and among sand dunes far from water. I guess since this is a fishing book I'll capitulate and say that the perfect campsite is not only near water, but near water with trout in it.

When camping near water, camp close enough to hear the gurgling but not much closer. The experts say camp at least 100 feet from water, which is okay for people who need definable limits, but I'd prefer to use common sense. There is nothing wrong with sleeping thirty feet from a brook as long as you camp discreetly and don't defecate next to your sleeping bag. On the other hand, 100 feet is intolerably close to a watering hole in bighorn territory.

Don't even think about camping within sight or sound of another campsite. People come to the mountains for a lot of reasons and one of them is not to be near you. You are perfectly within you rights to tell someone to keep marching if they start nest building on your doorstep.

A few things to consider when choosing a camp-site: Cold air settles into valleys at night and ridge lines tend to be windy and lightning prone. Rockfall is a very real danger in the mountains; don't camp at the base of cliffs. Fir and pine trees drip sap which is nearly impossible to remove from tents and sleeping bags; camp among the trees but not directly under them. Absolutely flat ground tends to hold puddles while a gently sloping campsite drains.

A few things to consider while camping: Discard fish guts into the water...the rangers are going to hate me for that one! When a trout dies, it settles to the bottom where it feeds the planaria, caddisflies and other consumers. If you yank the fish from the water and toss its viscera into the woods you are robbing the aquatic system of nutrient. This is NOT an excuse to dump your oatmeal in the creek, cast all exotic food into the bushes.

A few things to consider when leaving a camp-site: Pick up all trash of course. If you made a fire (shame) scatter the fire ring and make sure the rocks settle char side down. Scuff up the soil and kick some pine cones and duff over the flattened area where the tent was. Make a quick walk around the area before leaving. You'll be amazed at how often you find a spoon or pair of glasses lying just out of sight.

HIKING

Don't ruin the entire week by over-doing it on the first day. The pack is at its heaviest and you are the least acclimated to the altitude on the first day. Overexertion can lead to mountain sickness and un-necessary aches and pains that will last the entire trip.

It is an excellent idea to spend the night at the trailhead prior to hiking in. A night at altitude will give your system a head start generating extra red blood cells and otherwise becoming acclimated.

Five miles the first day followed by a layover day sounds like a lot of wimp factor, but I guarantee a better trip than if you attempt fifteen miles a day from the get go. Ten miles a day is a comfortable rate for most physically fit people. Walk at your own pace. It is just as hard for a person with a long stride to walk slowly as it is for a person with a slow pace to race alongside a faster walker.

It is much better to stop several times an hour for a moment or two than stop once an hour for fif-teen minutes. Lean against a rock to take the pack's weight from your shoulders, have a couple swallows of water then continue on.

Unless going cross country, use the trails and don't cut across switchbacks. When meeting pack animals, stand quietly well off the downhill side of the trail.

Don't leave monuments to your passing. Go out of your way to erase the monuments of others. Knock over Boy Scout forts, scatter fire rings, and pull up surveyor's stakes. Especially, pull up surveyor's stakes.

PACK ANIMALS

I've guided a lot of commercial horse pack trips into the Sierra and can say from first hand ex-perience that stock are hard on the alpine environ-ment. Horses pound trails, destroy the vegetation, and their dung breeds flies. Even the most conscien-tious packers can't always keep their horses out of soft meadows or prevent them from stripping trees.

Horses do allow people, who are otherwise unable, to get into the Sierra. Pack animals can carry impossible loads into the mountains and they do cover a lot of miles quickly. Riding is enjoyable in its own right. Horses do have a place in the back-country but they should be limited to areas that can sustain their impact with a minimum of damage.

When dealing with horses there are a few things

Riding horses into the high country is a time honored tradition.

The hiker can access remote waters that pack animals could never approach.

Neither crowd the horse in front of you or let such a gap develop that your animal wants to run to catch up with the string.

An irritated or uncomfortable horse can paw and trample the soil enough to cause serious damage. Use insect repellents and keep the animals well fed. The quantity and quality of feed is dependant on the region of the Sierra you're visiting as well as season and elevation. In many areas you must pack in feed. Contact the local ranger for grazing information.

Never tie a horse by its reigns. A 5/8" or thicker halter rope should be used to secure the animal, smaller diameter ropes tend to cut into the bark. Don't tie the animal to small green trees, the rope WILL girdle and kill the tree. When tying a horse for any length of time it is best to secure it to a hitchline strung between two trees. This keeps the animal from damaging tree roots by pawing or trampling.

It is the responsibility of every rider to minimize his horse's impact. A few irresponsible riders have caused portions of the Sierra to be closed to all stock.

MOUNTAIN BIKES

Though mountain bikes are excluded from all wilderness areas and most parks, there are huge sections of the Sierra where bikes are allowed.

Bikes can cover a great deal of territory quickly and quietly. When used responsibly, mountain bikes cause much less environmental damage than pack stock. Bikes don't breed flies, graze on wildflowers, or girdle trees. The biggest problem with bikes isn't environmental but social. A biker quietly coasting down an old logging road can quickly sneak up on the hiker lost in meditation. Even a polite "Hello" from the biker can scare the daylights out of the hiker and cause a hostile reaction.

Of course there are those Neanderthal bikers who delight in scarring trails and scaring stock. These are the same throwbacks who would shred a meadow with their horse, cut switch backs and carve their names into aspen trees.

Mountain bikes are severely limited, particular-

you can do to make the trip safer and more comfortable for both yourself and the animal.

Riding a horse is a lot like riding a motorcycle; lean forward when climbing and lean back with your weight in the stirrups on downhills. Carry your weight and maintain balance on your feet and inner thighs.

Horses will spend as little time as possible on areas of unstable footing so expect a few lunges or crow hops when crossing mud, snow, or loose gravel. Pack animals often jump over creeks and puddles rather than walking through them. Horses don't do well on slick granite so prepare for a quick dismount.

When your horse has to urinate, stand lightly in the stirrups to keep your weight off its kidneys. Let the horse drink as long and deeply as it wants but don't let it rip mouthfuls of browse from the trailside vegetation.

Don't hang cameras or day packs from the horn and let them bang against your horse. Even mellow horses can spook when a rider flails with a poncho; avoid changing clothes in the saddle. Keep fishing rods in aluminum tubes and stuff some cloth in the tube to keep the rods from rattling and irritating the stock.

It's a real hassle attempting to get good photos from a horse; it's usually worth the effort to dismount. I had one moron get thrown from his horse when he used a flash bulb.

ly when laden with fishing or camping gear. When frequent encounters with rocks, stream crossings, or loose gravel cause the biker to spend as much time pushing as pedaling, mountain biking quickly loses its appeal.

Bikes come onto their own on logging roads which have been closed to motor vehicles. It is no big deal to bike to a lake some ten miles distant, inflate the float tube and fish until dark then cruise back to the trailhead.

Because bikes can get you into remote country rather quickly, it is imperative that the bike be of good quality and reliably maintained. No matter how bullet proof the bike, the rider should never get farther into the wilderness than he is prepared to walk out. A friend recently rode thirty miles into the American River canyon then broke his headset. Two days later, tired and hungry, he pushed his bike out of the canyon.

Riding with a backpack is uncomfortable and at times unsafe. Bikers who chose a pack should stick with a slim profile internal or frameless pack. Some of the new high volume fanny packs can carry a surprising amount of stuff and still be comfortable to carry.

Panniers are really THE way to carry gear. Balance is much more important on the trail than on a road so stick with low slung saddle panniers rather than handle bar bags. The "experts" say to evenly balance front and back panniers; I prefer putting the heavier gear in the rear bags.

I tape my rod tube to the top tube and let it extend out over the rear tire (beware on rapid dismounts...you have to raise your leg higher than usual!) I use a standard two piece because its tube is relatively skinny. The tube for the four piece pack rods are half again as wide as the normal tubes and rub on my thighs.

Toe clips are essential for good control. Clips allow you to pull as well as push on the pedals, but far more importantly, they keep your feet attached during bumpy going.

You *will*, at some time, have to carry your bike through brush. One of the most infuriating things that happens during a "hike" through brush is that

the bike pedals get caught in the branches, spin around, and catch you in the heel...over and over again. Carry a piece of Velcro and secure a pedal to the bike frame.

Two big bike bottles filled to the brim will make you very popular when lost in a maze of firebreaks on a hot summer afternoon. Light colored bottles absorb less heat than black ones.

When numerous stream crossings are made, the bike frame can get filled with several pounds of water. Drilling a couple of small drain holes at low points in the frame will eliminate this problem. It is probably a good idea to check with your local bike shop before drilling to make sure your frame won't be unduly weakened.

A neat and sanitary gadget is an aluminum clamp that unobtrusively bolts to the handlebars and holds a Mini Mag flashlight. Headlamps (the kind you wear on your head) are fine until you look at your partner and blind him or her. This is a sure fire way to ruin a relationship.

Another gadget I politely put on my bike after receiving it as a father's day present is a cheap little mirror that sticks into the end of the handlebars. That was two years and many crashes ago. The little mirror "keeps on keeping on" and has been pretty useful. Not only is it nice to see logging trucks sneaking up on you, it helps keep track of trailing bikers so you don't inadvertently ditch them when the trail splits.

A repair kit should include at the very least a pocket knife, spare tube, patch kit, tire irons, air pump, chain breaker screw driver, crescent wrench, mini vise grips, and selection of hex wrenches.

Paiute trout. This Sierra inhabitant is the rarest trout in the world.

Last but not least is a good helmet. Sure, you're tough and don't need a brain bucket, but take pity on the poor paramedic who might have to carry you out.

SAFETY

The only reason I mention safety is because I'm forever answering letters asking me, "Just how dangerous IS it out there? Do you really hike alone? What REALLY happened to the Donner Party?"

The Sierra are as safe as you make them.

Shooting stars.

Elephant Heads.

I work as a paramedic adjacent to one of the most heavily abused wilderness areas in the world and backcountry calls are a rarity. The most common calls are the infrequent heart attack or fall. These same guys probably would have had a heart attack on the golf course or would have fallen from their roof if they weren't in the mountains.

Rattlesnakes are abundant in the Sierra. I've seen them as high as 11,000 feet and was once bitten at 9,000 feet (Immediate use of a snake bite kit removed much of the venom and allowed me to backpack out of the mountains on a painfully swollen, but intact foot). Don't be overly concerned about snakebites, but do keep your eyes peeled and carry a snake bite kit. Rattlesnakes were here long before us...don't bother them.

Bears can be a nuisance but rarely cause injury. If a bear challenges you over your food or pack, try to scare it by banging some pots together but be prepared to surrender the goods if the bear isn't readily intimidated.

Bubonic plague is endemic in the ground squirrels of the Sierra. The disease is usually transmitted to humans through fleas which have dined on infected squirrels. Don't set up camp in the middle of a squirrel colony. Initial plague symptoms include severe fever of rapid onset and swollen lymph glands. Untreated, the plague can be deadly.

Columbine.

Hypothermia, mountain sickness, and lightning are the three factors hikers seem to be least informed about. Hypothermia generally results from hanging around in cool breezy weather in wet clothing. It's easy to avoid...stay dry and if you do get wet, get out of the wind. Surprisingly, most hypothermia cases occur in relatively nice weather when people take it for granted they'll warm up. Hypothermia is rare in winter because people are dressed for the cold. Don't try to walk the hypothermic patient out of the mountains, warm them up where they are.

A hypothermic victim has a difficult if not impossible time generating body heat. Simply wrapping the patient in a sleeping bag will not cause him to warm up. Be it a fire or body heat through skin to skin contact, the patient needs an external heat source.

Acute mountain sickness (AMS) can effect some people as low as 6,000 feet and about one in three will feel the effects at 10,000. There is no way to tell who will get it...physically fit people are just as susceptible as couch potatoes. Most people with AMS get headaches, malaise, nausea, and loss of appetite. A few cases progress to vomiting, pulmonary edema, altered mental status, and incoordination (ataxia). AMS usually goes away after a day or two.

Aspirin or acetaminophen should alleviate some of the headache and Compazine can control nausea and vomiting. Diamox and Procardia have been shown to prevent or reduce the effects of AMS (see a physician before using). Dropping altitude is the absolute cure to AMS and those who continue to climb after onset of AMS run the risk of developing severe symptoms such as pulmonary and cerebral edema.

Lightning is common during Sierra summers and every year someone gets fried. The best course is to seek shelter near a grove of trees during a lightning storm. Common sense would tell you to avoid the open or ridge lines where lightning is most apt to strike. Never hide in a cave or under an overhanging rock because electricity can jump the gap and burn everything in the arc. Only throwbacks fish during a lightning storm.

The best advise I could give regarding safety in the Sierra is to use common sense. I would strongly urge everyone who ventures into the backcountry to take an Emergency Medical Technician course. Many fire departments and most junior colleges offer EMT training. The classes are almost free and the information is priceless.

In remote country, safety is a matter of common sense.

TROUT
FOOD

EIGHT

Insect emergence dates in the Sierra are highly volatile. As a general rule, the higher the elevation, the more unpredictable the hatch. Cottonwood Lakes at 11,000 feet sport a fairly predictable caddisfly hatch around June 20. On some years though, the lakes are covered with ice into July.

> *"Small yellow stoneflies skitter and hop enticingly across the water, yet I've never seen a trout take one. They must taste like cod liver oil."*
> —Leonard Wright,
> *The Ways of a Trout.*

Latitude changes (differences north and south) have a profound effect on Sierra weather conditions. For a given elevation in the southern terminus of the range, the maximum temperature will be about ten degrees warmer than the same elevation in the northern Sierra. Precipitation greatly increases as the latitude becomes more northerly.

Altitude has like effects. For every thousand feet of altitude gained, the temperature cools about four degrees. For every three hundred feet of elevation gained, annual precipitation increases two to four inches. After about 6,000 feet most of the moisture has been released and the effect of altitude on precipitation lessens.

Longitude (differences east and west) effects Sierra weather primarily because of the moisture trap the mountain range provides. Western slopes tend to draw most of the moisture from the eastwardly moving air, creating dry desert-like conditions on the east slope. For any given elevation (at the same latitude), east and west slope temperatures are generally quite close. However, east slope temperatures, due to the drier air, are apt to fluctuate more quickly than the west slope counterpart.

Due to the "thinness" of the air at higher elevations, the effect of shade can have profound effect on a local environment. Shadows can create temperature differentials of 20 degrees and more. A patch of snow may outlast the rest of the snowpack by several months if protected from the sun.

The net effect of all this is extremely complex insect emergence cycles. At 3,000 feet in the Kern River canyon, *Callibaetis* typically go through their first emergence in late April or early May. (*Callibaetis* cycle through several generations in a season.) At White Rock Lake, north of Tahoe, the same mayfly may not hatch until July or even later. The angler who ventures into the Sierra for the first time expecting to find hatches occurring on pin point dates will be disappointed.

Instead of being frustrated, the knowledgeable angler can use the mountain environment to his advantage. If one wants to exclusively fish the green drake hatch, he can locate a suitable habitat at a low altitude or southern location. As the hatch begins to taper, he can simply move north or increase his altitude and fish the hatch again.

Use the **TRUCKEE RIVER HATCH CHART** as a gross basis for predicting hatches throughout the Sierra. The Truckee River at Truckee (6,000 feet) is located near the far northeastern edge of the Sierra range. With some exceptions, the insects of the Truckee are pretty typical of those found in a mid elevation, moderate sized river. For every thousand foot drop the hatch will be two days earlier than what the chart conveys. Again, this is a gross generalization.

The most coveted trout to rise to a fly—the Volcano Creek golden.

TRUCKEE RIVER HATCHES

SCIENTIFIC NAME	LOCAL NAME	SUGGESTED IMITATION WET / DRY	HOOK SIZE (Tiemco)	EMERGENCE DATES (Approximate dates of fishable hatches at Truckee)						
				MAY	JUN	JUL	AUG	SEP	OCT	NOV
MAYFLY										
AMELETUS	BROWN DUN	BIRD'S NEST / SPARKLE DUN	12-14	1-31						
HEPTAGENIA	BLUE WING OLIVE	ZUG BUG / ADAMS	14-18	1-31	1-30	1-15				
RHITHROGENA	MARCH BROWN	ZUG BUG / ADAMS	12-14	1-31	1-30	1-15				
CINYGMULA	RED QUILL	ZUG BUG / RED QUILL	18-20	1-31	1-21					
EPEORUS	SULPHER	ZUG BUG / LIGHT CAHILL	14-18		1-30	1-31				
BAETIS	BLUE WING OLIVE	P.T. NYMPH / SPARKLE DUN	14-22	1-31	1-30	†	†	†	1-31	†
PARALEPTOPHLEBIA	MAHOGANY DUN	P.T. NYMPH / RED QUILL	14-16	1-31	1-21	†				
DRUNELLA GRANDIS	GREEN DRAKE	BIRD'S NEST / PARADRAKE	10-12		10-25					
D. DODDSI	GREEN DRAKE	BIRD'S NEST / PARADRAKE	10-12		15-30	†				
EPHEM. INERMIS	PALE MORNING DUN	HARES EAR / SPARKLE DUN	18-20		1-30					
E. INFREQUENS	PALE MORNING DUN	HARES EAR / SPARKLE DUN	16-18			10-30	1-15			
E. TIBIALIS	CREAMY ORANGE	P.T. NYMPH / RED QUILL	16-18			15-30	1-31			
E. FLAVILINIA	LTL. GREEN DRAKE	BIRD'S NEST / PARADRAKE	12-14			15-30	1-31			
STONEFLY										
SKWALA	GOLDEN STONE	SIMULATOR / STIMULATOR	6-8	†						
CALINEURIA	GOLDEN STONE	SIMULATOR / STIMULATOR	6-8	15-31	1-15					
ISOPERLA	LTL YELLOW STONE	B NEST / LTL YELLOW STONE	12-18	15-31	1-30	1-20	†	†		
ISOGENUS	LTL YELLOW STONE	B NEST / LTL YELLOW STONE	10-18	15-31	1-30	1-20	†	†		
CAPNIA	WINTER STONE	P.T. NYMPH / ELK CADDIS	16-20	†						
CADDISFLY										
HYDROPSYCHE	SPOTTED SEDGE	ROCK WORM / ELK CADDIS	12-16	15-31	1-31	1-31	†	†		
RHYACOPHILA	GREEN SEDGE	ROCK WORM / ELK CADDIS	12-18	15-31	1-31	1-31	†	†		
GLOSSOSOMA	SADDLECASE MAKER	BIRD'S NEST / ELK CADDIS	18-20		25-30	1-31	1-15			
HYDROPTILID	MICRO CADDIS	SOFT HACKLE / SFT HACKLE	18-24		25-30	1-31	1-15			
DICOSMOECUS	OCTOBER CADDIS	RED SQUIRREL / BUCK TAIL	6-8					25-30	1-21	
MIDGE										
CHIRONOMUS	MIDGE OR GNAT	MIDGE PUPA / "MOSQUITO"	18-28	!	!	!	!	!	!	!

† Sporadic hatches.   ! Minor hatches occur all year.

TERRESTRIAL INSECTS

In many Sierra waters, up-slope-blow-in (this is a real term!) provides a large portion of a trout's diet. Most alpine and subalpine lakes have such a short food producing season that fish life would be absent if not for up-slope-blow-in. Up-slope-blow-in is caused by the dependable afternoon winds which grace the Sierra. As lowland air warms, it rises and transports with it thousand of pounds of insects. The insects are scattered with the wind and mountain fauna, particularly those above timberline, eagerly ingest the "windfall." Up-slope-blow-in is such a dependable source of trout food that anglers should anticipate insects which are abundant many thousands of feet below.

Some of the finest alpine fishing occurs during and just after ice out. Though appreciable hatches are rare while the ground is still frozen and portions of lakes are choked with ice, up-slope-blow-in will litter the open water with carpenter ants, grasshoppers, jassids, and butterflies. Winter-famished trout inhale the bounty with abandon. Golden trout, sometimes THE most difficult trout to hook in open water, can be caught by the dozens as their frigid tarns break free from the ice.

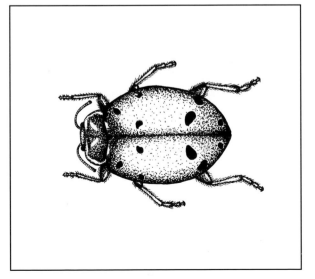

Ladybird beetles (lady bugs) overwinter in deep crevasses and emerge during ice out in great swarms. An incredibly easy imitation to tie (simply pull some orange deer hair or Evazote over the back of a hook) and just as easy to fish, the ladybug can be a sure fire fly during the first few warm days of the season.

Shortly after the ladybugs emerge, carpenter ants and termites appear. Both of these insects live in social colonies deep within dead timber and logs. Termites feed on the rotting wood and provide a valuable service converting relatively inert cellulose into organic debris. Carpenter ants tunnel into the wood but bring in food from the "outside" world to feed the colony. Carpenter ants will catch aphids and caterpillars of Lycaenid butterflies (hairstreaks, metalmarks, and coppers) and take them into their colonies to "milk" them of their secretions.

Early in the season the winged queen and male ants and termites take to the air in search for new territory to begin a fresh colony. Neither of these insects are strong fliers and their wings can be torn off by gusty breezes. Trout gorge on these terrestrials and will often ignore strong mayfly hatches in favor of ants and termites.

Early in the summer tremendous flights of California tortoise shell butterflies descend on the Sierra. In 1989 an entomologist surveying a pass on the Yuba River estimated well over 100,000 tortoise shells per day were funnelling up the river. Mariposa (Spanish for butterfly), a town near Yosemite, is named after the incredible numbers of tortoise shells migrating through the area.

As caterpillars, tortoise shells spend the winter feeding on the chaparral of the coastal hills. Early in June the butterflies leave the coast and migrate to the Sierra where they lay their eggs in the sagebrush and ceonothus. The caterpillars build web tents in the bushes where they spend the summer before turning into butterflies which migrate back to the coast in the early fall.

Lisa Cutter plies this alpine lake with an assortment of terrestrial patterns.

Gusty afternoon winds shower hapless butterflies upon trout waters across the range. This windfall is eagerly awaited by anglers in the know because it is during this time that some of the largest fish of the year are caught on dry flies. Even the trout of Lake Tahoe which uncommonly feed on the surface will freely rise to a number 4 Sofa Pillow.

About the Fourth of July weekend, grasshoppers begin appearing as a trout staple. Hoppers can provide great fishing but their numbers are cyclic and don't provide a dependable "hatch."

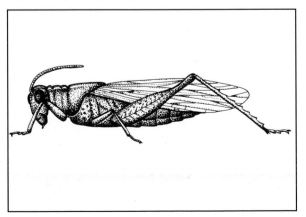

In the fall, grasshoppers oviposit in loose soil where the eggs over winter. When the soil warms, grasshopper nymphs emerge and immediately begin to feed on grasses and other vegetation. These little nymphs are wingless but are strong jumpers. All too often their jumps end up in the water and trout will key in on grasshopper nymphs to the exclusion of other insects. Small tan Elk Hair Caddis plopped into the water during the heat of the day can be surprisingly effective to the angler used to having his offering spurned during midday. As the summer progresses the nymphs transform into the familiar winged hoppers and traditional patterns become effective.

LEPIDOPTERA
Moths and Butterflies
Genus Parargyractis
Common Name: Aquatic moth

Larva size 12-18. In some Sierra waters aquatic moth larvae can exceed forty per square meter. They secrete themselves in shallow depressions on submerged rocks and spin a flat web over their sanctum. Small holes punctuate the edgers of the web so that water flows freely through. Algae often adheres to the web which adds a degree of camouflage. Under the protection of this tent the larvae feed on periphyton. Pale "scars" on boulders exposed by low water often indicate where aquatic caterpillars have been grazing.

A brownish green "rockworm" imitation would mimic the larva but I'm not sure that they are viable trout food. It has been reported that the larvae sometimes exhibit behavioral drift but I've yet to observe this.

Pupation occurs underneath the silk tent where the pupa is protected from predation.

Adult size 12-18. *Paragyractids* superficially resemble caddisflies but can be quickly identified by their coiled mouth siphons. Some forms have elongated, feathery palpi which gives them the common name "snout moths".

Aquatic moths are an often overlooked item in the trout's diet. Unlike mayflies, aquatic moths have well developed mouth parts and can survive for months along stream zones. From late July into early September when most other aquatic insects are poorly represented, the aquatic moths are abundant and available to trout.

The adult moth emerges by crawling along the streambed to shore or swimming to the surface. When egg laying, the moth once again returns to the subsurface domain. During both emergence and ovipositing, the hydrophobic scales ont he wings and body become shethed in glistening bubbles. When aquatic moths are ovipsiting I've often watched trout pluck their shimmering forms from streambed boulders.

Imitation: A cream colored Bird's Nest treated with Fly Magic and drifted or twitched subsurface can be lethal.

AQUATIC INSECTS

Understanding The Basics
Insects are broken into two distinct evolutionary groups: "old" bugs and "new" bugs.

A remote corner of Yosemite National Park.

Old insects go through three stages of development: egg, nymph, and adult. The nymphal stage is where the bug does its growing. Because nymphal skin (exoskeleton) does not grow, it is molted a number of times as the nymph ages. As nymphs mature, the wingpads become increasingly dark and well defined. The mayfly is unique in that the adult form which emerges from the nymph is not sexually mature and must molt one more time. Members of the "old" insects include the stoneflies, mayflies, dragonflies, and damselflies.

New insects undergo four stages of development: egg, larva, pupa and adult. The moth is a familiar insect which is a "new" bug, its larva is the caterpillar and the pupa is the cocoon. The new insects are adapted to a wider variety of habitats than the evolutionarily old insects because the larva is perfectly suited to its niche and the adult is well matched to its environment.

Most species of aquatic insects periodically ride helplessly with the current. This phenomena, called behavioral drift, disseminates the species throughout the river system so that the species is protected should one section of the environment sustain a catastrophic event. Behavioral drift is greatest during early morning and evening hours in most species and provides feeding trout with masses of helpless larva. Unless the angler samples the river with a fine mesh net, he will have little if any clues that a drift is in effect.

Fly fishers should learn insects by their scientific rather than common name. Common names often denote one insect in a certain local and describe another bug in a different region. Scientific names are NOT hard to learn; most anglers have no problem going into their garden and identifying begonias, azaleas, and camellias.

DIPTERA

Flies, Midges, Gnats, Craneflies And Mosquitos

Diptera are two winged (Diptera—two wings) insects that frequent every conceivable habitat in the Sierra. Diptera are common in the highly saline Mono Lake, Carson River hot springs and snow melt ponds on Mt. Whitney. Some Diptera thrive in sewer sludge.

Diptera undergo complete metamorphosis (egg, larva, pupa and adult), and the adult form is always terrestrial. The larva are worm-like and may have a life span of less than a week or more than seven years. Diptera larva can dry completely or be frozen solid and still survive. Some Diptera larva must breath air, some have well developed gills, while others pierce plant stems and steal oxygen from the plant. Still other larva can absorb oxygen directly through their skin.

Some Diptera pupate in cases (tests) built from sand or vegetation. Other Diptera pupa are highly mobile and can flee from predators and migrate to optimal habitat.

Adult Diptera usually do not feed; however, a noticeable few such as the mosquitos and deer flies have specialized biting and sucking mouth parts suitable for extracting blood from their victims. Only the female of these species are blood feeders, the males feed on nectar and pollen.

Mosquitos are of no importance to Sierra trout. Despite the fact that numerous mosquito imitations are commercially available, mosquito larva and pupa inhabit swampy puddles and the adult mosquito rarely comes in contact with trout water.

Sierra trout feed primarily on Diptera of the cranefly (Tipulidae) and midge (Chaoboridae, Deuterophlebiidae, Dixidae, and Chironomidae) families.

The most commonly encountered cranefly in the Sierra resides as a larva on the bottoms and edges of freestone trout streams. Pupation usually takes place under rocks and woody debris along the damp shorelines of these streams and the adults usually emerge mid-May through mid-June.

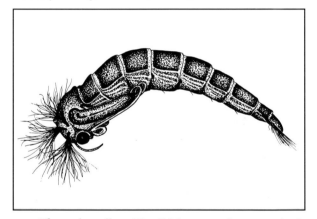

The pale yellow Tipulid larva is about as thick as a three penny finish nail and about 3/4 inch long. I have never seen a Tipulid larva in trout stomach samples, however, an imitation drifted through the riffles can be an early season top producer.

The adult Tipulids oviposit in the evenings or during overcast weather. These insects are readily identified by six legs that are each as long as the body. A size 16 creamy yellow Soft Hackle is a fine imitation.

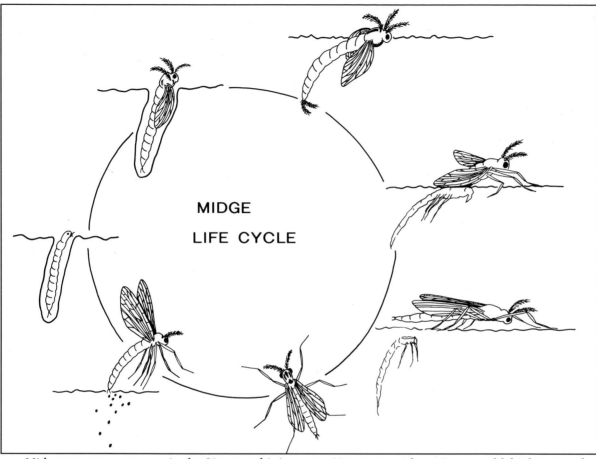

MIDGE
LIFE CYCLE

Dixa and Chironomus are so alike that it is impractical to separate them. Most anglers lump these midges together and call them Chironomids. Chironomids live in every trout water in the world and range in sizes smaller than a tiny hook barb to that of a number twelve hook.

The most noticeable Chironomid is the so called blood midge. Actually there are several midges that fit the category of blood midge because they all share the quality of being bright red. The larva of the blood midge thrives in the oxygen starved muck of lakebeds and sloughs. The larva are filled with hemoglobin (the same stuff that makes our blood red) which has a tremendous affinity for oxygen.

In lakes such as Martis, Davis, and Crowley where baitfish have been introduced, the blood midge has proved a saviour to dry fly fishermen. Baitfish such as perch and sunfish are very efficient at cropping the mayfly nymph population; however, because the blood midge larva lives protected in the mud, their hatches continue in spite of the baitfish.

EPHEMEROPTERA

Mayflies

Nymph: The nymph has gills on the abdomen (last body segment). For ID purposes the nymphs will be broken into *swimmers, clingers, and crawlers* (burrowing mayflies are not important in our area). Swimmers are long, slender and are quite proficient swimmers. Clingers have stout legs, the body is flattened, and the head is narrower than the body. Crawlers are squat and the head is wider than the body.

Nymphs often change hue rapidly and tend to take the general coloration of their surroundings.

Dun: (The sexually immature adult.) Has opaque, often marked wings held high over its back with two or three tails about the length of the body.

Spinner: (The sexually mature adult.) Has crystal clear wings, long forelegs, large eyes, and two or three tails considerably longer than the body length.

Midges are very common in the Sierra and it is safe to say that many of the high altitude lakes would not support fish if it were not for the abundance of midges.

The phantom midges (Chaoboridae) are common in lower elevation alkaline lakes. These midges are unique in that their larva reside in the mud during the day, but as the sun lowers, they escape from the mud and swim toward the surface of the lake. This vertical migration can be mimicked quite efficiently by allowing an imitation to settle on the lake bed then **slowly** (several seconds per foot) swimming it to the surface on a long, light leader.

Mountain midges (Deuterophlebiidae) can be found in every shallow riffle in the Sierra. The larva and pupa encrust exposed surfaces of rocks in colonies that sometimes number in the tens of thousands. I have frequently caught trout that were holding just down current of midge-rich riffles whose stomachs were bulging with Deuterophlebs. Pale cream, olive, and gray imitations size 18-20 dead drifted through a riffle can be amazingly effective. It is best to fish directly downstream and watch for the flash of white that indicates the opening mouth of a trout. Set on the flash of white or the glint of a turning fish because the takes are so subtle that it is nearly impossible to detect a pickup.

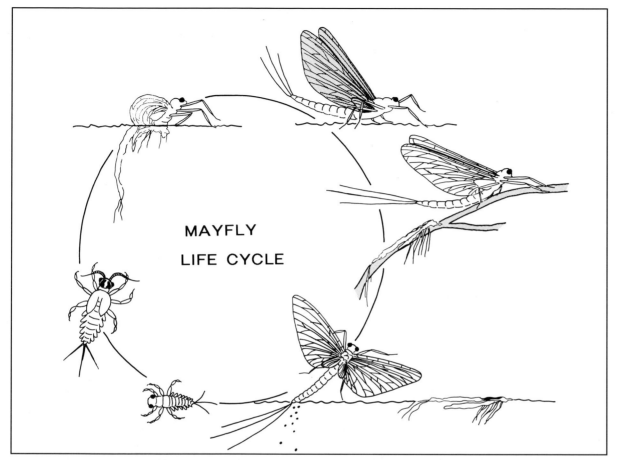

MAYFLY
LIFE CYCLE

Slow and Still Water Mayflies
Callibaetis.

Common name: Speckled dun

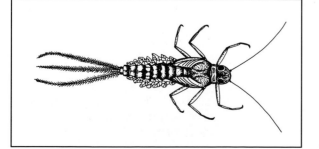

Nymph: Size 12-16. Swimmer. Antennae nearly twice as long as the width of the head. (Think of the two "L's" in Callibaetis as long antennae.) All gills are paired and it has three equal length tails.

Imitation: Hare's Ear, Bird's Nest, and Pheasant Tail.

Dun: Size 12-18. Body can be black, gray, yellowish or olive. Grayish wings with pale veinations. Two tails and dwarfed hind wings.

Imitation: Adams, Gray Quill and Gray Sparkle Dun.

Spinner: Size 12-18. Clear wings with dark blotches on leading edge. Two tails.

Imitation: Rusty Polywing Spinner.

Note: *Callibaetis* will cycle through two or more generations in a season. Each generation, spaced about six weeks apart will result in insects one hook size smaller than the preceding generation. Mid summer duns tend to be pale and early and late season duns can be quite dark (probably to absorb heat). Hatches typically occur late morning and in the evening.

Siphlonurus
Common name: Great gray drake.

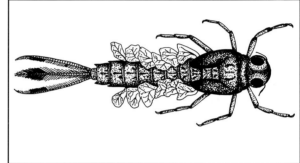

Nymph: Size 8-12. Swimmer with very short antennae (vs long antennae of Callibaetis), gills heavily veined. Three equal tails.

Imitation: Hare's Ear, Bird's Nest, and Pheasant Tail.

Dun: Size 10-14. Gray green body. Tall gray wings, hind wing half the height of the fore wings. Two tails.

Imitation: Adams, Gray Paradrake, and Gray Sparkle Dun.

Spinner: Size 10-12. Rusty body, clear wings with noticeable veination but without blotches. Two tails.

Imitation: Gray polywing spinner.

Note: Common stillwater mayfly which usually hatches a little later in the morning than the Callibaetis. The nymph prefers to crawl out of the water before hatching into an adult but can emerge in open water if prevented from reaching the shore.

Sillwater Mayflies Smaller Than Size 18, See "Tiny Mayflies".

Quick Water Mayflies

Ameletus

Common Name: Brown dun

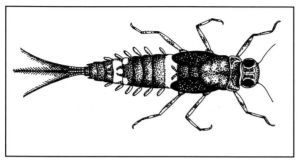

Nymph: Size 12-14. Swimmer. Three equal length tails. Gills are small, single and oval with a dark band on the leading edge. These nymphs are strikingly patterned with shades of cream, black and rust.

Imitation: Hare's Ear, Bird's Nest, and Pheasant Tail.

Dun: Size 12-14. Dark body and wings. Hind wing with pointy projection on leading edge. Two tails.

Imitation: Adams, Gray Paradrake, and Gray Sparkle Dun.

Spinner: Size 12-16. Wings clear with same profile as dun. Two tails.

Imitation: Gray polywing spinner.

Note: The *Ameletus* is in the same family as the *Isonychia and Siphlonurus*. Both crawl out of the water to "hatch". The *Ameletus* hatches mid spring and is often done hatching when the California season opens.

Baetis

Common name: Blue wing olive

Nymph: Size 12-18. Swimmer. Three tails with the middle tail shorter than the outer two. A few species have only two tails.

Imitation: Harc's Ear, Bird's Nest, and Pheasant Tail.

Dun: Size 12-18. Wings slate gray, body green orange. Dwarf hind wing. Two tails.

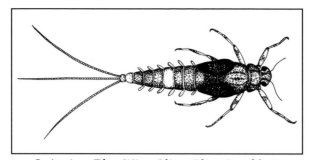

Imitation: Blue Wing Olive, Olive Sparkle Dun, and Olive No Hackle

Spinner: Size 12-18. Dwarfed hind wing. *No* markings on forewing.

Imitation: Dark soft hackle.

Note: The *Baetis* cycle through several generations in a season. This widespread species is often the first and then the last hatch of the year.

Early morning calm on a Sierra Lake.

Ephemerella inermis and infrequens

Common name: Pale morning dun

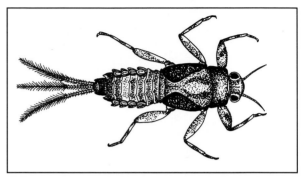

Nymph: Size 14-18. Crawler. Three equal length tails with bushy fringe on last two thirds of tail. Coloration ranges from pale olive to black. Gills ripple in synchrony.

Imitation: Hare's Ear, Bird's Nest, and Pheasant Tail.

Dun: Size 14-20. Three tails, light gray or tan wings over a pale body. Wings exhibit a sharp angle on the leading edge of the hind wing.

Imitation: Tan Sparkle Dun, Tan Paradun, and Adams.

Spinner: Size 14-20. Three tails, wings crystal clear with same profile as dun.

Imitation: Rusty polywing spinner.

Note: Very abundant fastwater manfly. Despite the common name, these mayflies may hatch in the morning, evening, or even midday during cold weather.

Ephemerella tibialis

Common name: Creamy orange

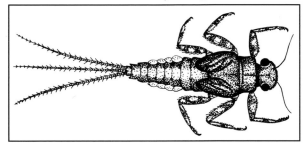

Nymph: Size 14-16. Crawler. Three equal tails fringed with small spines. Almost always has a pale stripe down the thorax. This nymph is often a striking red. Very common.

Imitation: Pheasant Tail, Carrot Nymph, or Red Squirrel

Dun: Size 14-16. Typical *Ephemerella* wing coloration and profile (see *Ephemerella inermis*). Body is often pale orange or red. Three tails.

Imitation: Red Quill

Spinner: Size 14-16. Three tails, Ephemerella wing. Body orange or red.

Imitation: Rusty Polywing Spinner.

Ephemerella grandis and flavilinea

Common name: Green drake

Nymph: Size 8-10. Crawler. Robust nymph with teeth on leading edge of stout forelegs. Three equal

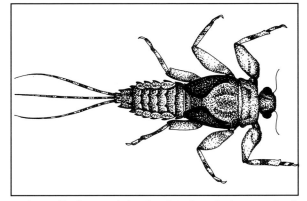

tails. Will often arch back when handled. As with all *Ephemerella* the gills ripple rhythmically.

Imitation: Hare's Ear, Bird's Nest, and Pheasant Tail.

Dun: Size 8-10. Unmarked slate gray wings with typical Ephemerella profile (see *Ephemerella inermis*) and green body. Three tails.

Imitation: Green Paradrake or Green Sparkle Dun.

Spinner: Size 8-10. *Grandis* has mottled brown wings while *flavilinea* is slightly smaller with brownish wings. Size, and three tails should identify spinner without problem (*Hexagenia* are slow water mayflies with clear veined wings).

Spinner: Olive and black soft hackle.

Note: The green drake can coax even the largest trout to the surface. These mayflies can hatch any time during the day but late morning and late evening hatches are heaviest and most dependable.

Paraleptophlebia

Common name: Mahogany dun

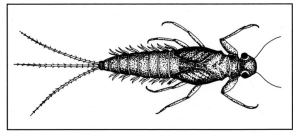

Nymph: Size 12-16. Swimmer. Forked gills. Three equal tails.

Imitation: Hare's Ear, Bird's Nest, and Pheasant Tail.

Dun: Size 12-16. Reddish body and tail narrow gray fore wing. Hind wing is small and oval shaped. Three equal tails.

Imitation: Red Quill.

Spinner: Size 12-18. Male thorax is dark and the abdomen is clear...very distinctive. Three equal tails.

Imitation: Brown Polywing Spinner.

Note: Usually found in smaller creeks though has been quite abundant on the Truckee, Carson, and Kern rivers during the drought of the late '80s. Late afternoon spinner falls can be spectacular.

Looking for clues to fool the trout.

Isonychia

Common name: Western leadwing

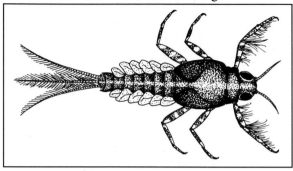

Nymph: Size 8-10. Swimmer. Forelegs fringed with long hairs. Three equal tails.

Imitation: Hare's Ear, Bird's Nest, and Pheasant Tail.

Dun: Size 10-12. Eggplant colored body with gray wings. Well developed hind wing. Forelegs are dark while other legs are light colored.

Imitation: Black Sparkle Dun, Adams, or Black Paradrake.

Spinner: Size 10-12. Size and dark forelegs are a give away identification.

Note: The long hairs on the nymph's forelegs are used to strain food from the current. *Isonychia* are common on alkaline freestone waters such the Feather and East Walker.

Heptageniidae Family

Common name: Clingers

The Heptageniidae are very common in all of the Sierra freestone waters. The nymphs are suited for existing in the most turbulent waters. The bodies are flattened, the legs are strong to help the nymph cling to rocks. All Heptageniidae nymphs have heads which are wider than the bodies.

Prior to emergence, the Heptageniidae nymphs fill with carbon dioxide which inflates the exoskeleton and separates it from the dun within. The trapped gas glows golden under the thin exoskeleton and gives the nymph an unmistakable shimmering effect. The swelling nymph finally becomes buoyant

to the point where it lifts from the rock and ascends toward the surface. As the nymph rises, the pressure of the expanding gas will often split the exoskeleton and the dun will immediately crawl out. It is not uncommon to have fully emerged duns appear at the surface and quickly fly away during a Heptageniidae hatch. This emerging behavior probably evolved to reduce the dun's exposure to trauma in the turbulent waters from which they emerged.

All the duns are easily identified by the characteristically wide, shovel-shaped heads. The spinners are not practical to differentiate in the field.

Rusty Johnson tricks a nice 'bow with a mayfly emerger.

Epeorus

Common name: Sulpher

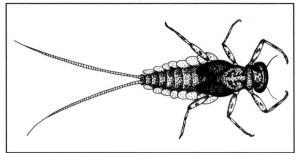

Nymph: Size 12-18. Two tails separate it from all other Heptageniidae. Heart shaped marking on forearm (femur).

Imitation: Zug Bug, LaFontaine Sparkle Pupa, Gold Ribbed Hare's Ear.

Dun: Size 12-18. Two tails. Body gray to cream. Wings gray or yellow. Femur retains the heart shaped marking of the nymph.

Imitation: Light Cahill, Adams, or Light Paradun.

Spinner: Size 12-18. Two tails. Body rusty, wings clear.

Imitation: Rusty Polywing Spinner.

Rhithrogena

Common name: March brown

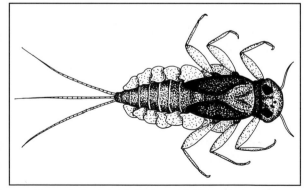

Nymph: Size 12-14. Three tails. Large, overlapping gills on the underside of the abdomen. These gills act as friction plates to help the nymph cling to rocks in the turbulent conditions in which it is found.

Imitation: Zug Bug, LaFontaine Sparkle Pupa, Gold Ribbed Hare's Ear.

Dun: Size 12-14. Two tails. The leading edge of the forewing has a distinctive band of varicose veins. The femur has a dark band (but not heart-shaped like the *Epeorus*).

Imitation: Adams, Red Quill, or Dark Paradrake

Cinygmula

Common Name: Red quill

Nymph: Size 16-18. Three tails. The "cheeks" have distinctive pointed projections.

Imitation: Zug Bug, LaFontaine Sparkle Pupa, Gold Ribbed Hare's Ear.

Dun: Size 16-18. Two tails. Body can be orange, red, or gray and the unmarked, wings range from gray to bright yellow.

Imitation: Red Quill

Note: This "quill" is common in almost every small mountain stream and brook in the high Sierra.

Heptagenia

Common name: Pale evening dun

Nymph: Size 10-18. Three tails, no pointy "cheeks," no overlapping gills.

Imitation: Zug Bug, LaFontaine Sparkle Pupa, Gold Ribbed Hare's Ear.

Dun: Size 10-18. Two tails. Blurry cross veins on wings. Despite the common name, often hatches sporadically throughout the day.

Imitation: Adams, or Green Paradrake.

Tiny Mayflies

Caenis

Common name: Snowflake spinners

Nymph: Size 20-24. Crawler. Square gills lay over back. Three tails.

Imitation: None

Dun: Size 20-24. No hind wing. Three tails. Evening emergers.

Imitation: Brown No Hackle

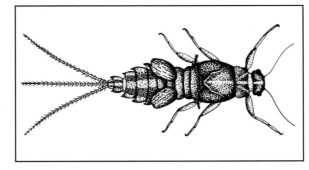

Spinner: Size 20-24. Pale. No hind wing, three tails.

Imitation: Trico Spinner.

Notes: *Caenis* is found in isolated spots in our area but where they occur they can be quite important. *Caenis* has three tails (*Baetis* and *Pseudocloen* have two) and is usually an evening emerger (Trico's usually appear in the early morning).

Tricorythodes

Common name: Trico

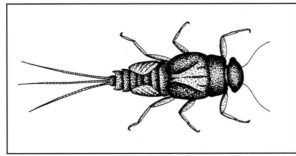

Nymph: Size 20-24. Crawler. Triangular gills lay over back (think TRI for Trico and triangle to differentiate from the square gilled *Caenis*). Three tails (again think TRI for tri-tails to differentiate from *Pseudocloeon*).

Imitation: None.

Dun: Often dark thorax and pale abdomen. No hind wing and three tails. An A.M. emerger.

Imitation: Black No Hackle.

Spinner: Dark abdomen, no hind wing and three tails.

Imitation: Trico Spinner.

Note: Can be found in any habitat but most common in the silty areas of streams and in the stream outflows into lakes. Seems to prefer cooler waters than the *Caenis*. Both the *Caenis* and Trico nymphs have large gills placed atop their abdomens to get the most oxygen from their silty habitat.

Pseudocloeon

Common name: Blue wing olive

Nymph: Size 20-24. Swimmer. Long antennae, two tails.

Imitation: Hare's Ear, Bird's Nest, or Pheasant Tail.

Dun: No hind wing, two tails.

Imitation: Olive No Hackle.

Spinner: No hind wing, two tails.

Imitation: Trico Spinner.

Note: This tiny "blue wing olive" has two tails throughout its life which quickly separates it from the *Caenis* and *Tricorythodes*. The *Pseudocloeon* is most commonly found in riffles with small cobbles. Like other members of the *Baetidae* family this mayfly can have several generations throughout the fishing season.

This eastern Sierra river provides intense caenis and trico hatches.

PLECOPTERA

Stoneflies

Stoneflies are abundant throughout the Sierra. Because of their primitive gill structure, stonefly nymphs require cool, highly oxygenated water. They are most often found in leaf packets or among rocks in freestone streams. Some stoneflies thrive in the rocks along wave washed shores of cold lakes. One species lives at the bottom of deep, high altitude lakes.

Nymphs: Paired wingcases, antennae, and tail. Gills absent on abdomen.

Adult: Paired translucent wings lay flat over the back. In flight they look like lumbering biplanes. Paired tail.

Isogenus, Isoperla, Chloroperla

Common name: Little yellow stone

Nymph: Size 10-18. Yellow or greenish often with black markings.

Imitation: Hare's Ear, Bird's Nest, or Prince Nymph.

Adult: Size 10-18. Yellow or green bodies, often streaked with crimson or orange. Adults spend the day on the undersides of leaves of riparian vegetation. When disturbed they will frequently drop into the depths of the brush rather than take flight. This is an effective survival technique unless the drop ends up in a river rather than on land. Trout feed heavily on little yellow stones throughout late May on into early August...I'm glad that Sierra trout haven't read Leonard Wright's book (see quote at the beginning of the chapter).

Imitation: Perfect Little Yellow Stone, or Yellow Elk Hair Caddis.

Unlike other stoneflies which must emerge on land, the little yellows sometimes emerge from open water in a mayfly like fashion.

Calineuria

Common name: Golden stonefly

Nymph: Size 6-8. Thick bushy gills between legs. Mottled amber and brown coloration. This nymph lives for two to three years before hatching so trout are used to seeing it in all sizes anytime of the year.

Imitation: Simulator, Brooks Stone, or Kaufmann's Stone.

Adult: Size 6-8. Golden orange body. Branched gill remnants along sides of abdomen.

Imitation: Stimulator or Sofa Pillow.

Another "golden" stone, the *Skwala*, is common on Sierra east slope streams and emerges late January on into March.

Pteronarcys

Common name: Salmon fly

Nymph: Size 2-6. Square wing pads. Black with some orange underneath. Like the *Calineuria* this nymph lives for several years before emergence.

Imitation: Simulator, Brooks Stone, or Kaufmann's Stone.

Adult: Size 4-6. Brownish black with an orange collar.

Imitation: Stimulator or Sofa Pillow.

The salmon fly is not widespread throughout the Sierra and only locally important. It is generally found in streams with an abundance of softwoods. The nymph lives in and feeds on rotting leaf packets during part of its development.

Capniidae

Common names: Winter or little brown stones

Nymph: Size 12-18. Black or brown, slender.

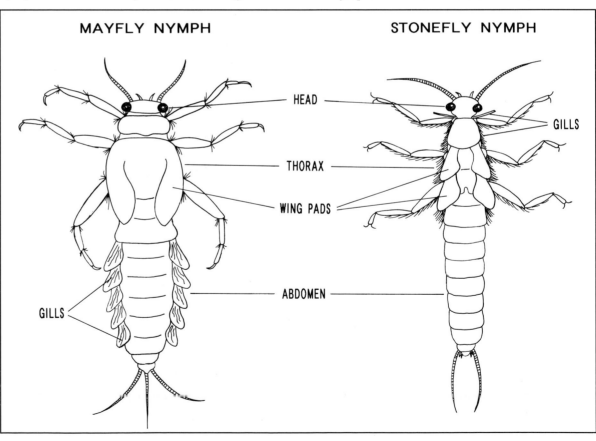

MAYFLY NYMPH — STONEFLY NYMPH

HEAD · GILLS · THORAX · WING PADS · ABDOMEN · GILLS

Imitation: Bird's Nest, Pheasant Tail, or Black AP.

Adult: Size 12-18. Slender dark body. Capniidae has faint pattern on clear wings.

Imitation: Black Elk Hair Caddis.

These stoneflies are very common winter emergers. On warm days riverside snow banks will look like they are covered with soot as the adults clamber about. Important item in the diet of mountain whitefish.

Nemouridae

Common name: Broadback stone

Nymph: Size 14-20. Stout, black or dark brown nymphs covered with coarse hairs and divergent wingpads.

Imitation: Black AP, Pheasant Tail, or Bird's Nest.

Adult: Size 14-20. Dark stonefly with a distinct dusky "X" marking on the wings. Common in the small creeks and brooks. They emerge all year but are most common in May through early July then again in late fall.

Imitation: Black Elk Hair Caddis.

Peltoperlidae

Common name: Roach stone

Nymph: Size 16-18. Black or brown, with overlapping ventral abdominal plates. Unmistakable cockroach-like profile.

Imitation: Black AP, Pheasant Tail, or Bird's Nest.

Adult: Size 16-18. Black or brown and have the same roach-like appearance as the nymph.

Imitation: Black Elk Hair Caddis.

As trout food the Peltoperla is probably not important. To the angler this stonefly is very important as an indicator of springs. When Peltoperlas appear it can be assumed that springs and seeps are feeding the area.

TRICHOPTERA

CADDISFLIES

After midges, the caddisflies are the most im-

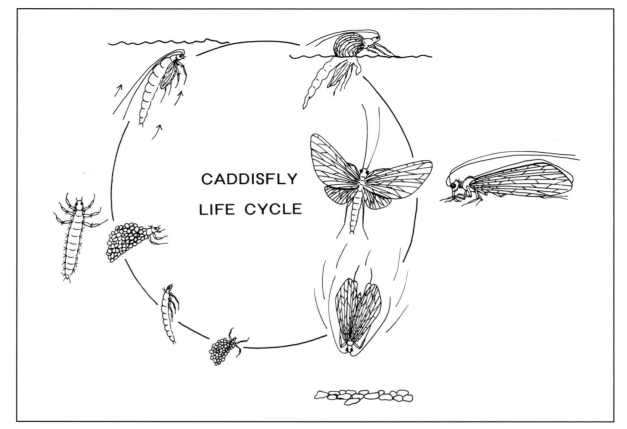

CADDISFLY LIFE CYCLE

portant aquatic insect for Sierra trout. Like midges the caddisfly undergoes a complete metamorphosis (egg, larva, pupa then adult). Many caddisflies build cases (tests) of rock and vegetation while others roam freely without cases. As a rule, caddis from still and slow water environs build light weight shelters of vegetable matter, while caddis from swift water habitats build heavily ballasted cases from sand and gravel. Uncased caddis are common in all stream habitats but are very seldom found in stillwater.

Larva: Worm-like with well developed legs.

Pupa: Caddis larva enter a transitional pupa stage as they evolve into an adult. The caddis pupa, unlike the familiar cocoon pupa of the moth, is very active and swims with great agility. Some pupa spend many hours and even days actively swimming about prior to emergence. Modern nymph fishermen have been drilled with the rules of "drag free drift" and unknowingly render their pupal imitation ineffective. Active "wet fly" retrieves are as effective now as they were in the twenties.

During emergence the pupa will often fill with gas which separates the nymphal exoskeleton from the adult within and buoys the pupa to the surface. As the gas filled pupa ascends, the bubble in some species will expand to the point of bursting the exoskeleton thus freeing the adult before reaching the surface. Other pupa will drift for minutes, even hours, under the film prior to emerging. Still other pupa will crawl along the lake or streambed and drag itself out of the water to emerge.

Adult: The caddis has soft wings which fold over its back in an "A" frame tent profile. Adult caddis are erratic and often quick fliers. Many adult caddis can be identified by their ocelli. Ocelli are small black simple eyes located above and behind the normal eyes.

Adult caddis are most important when they return to the river to lay their eggs. Many females repeatedly throw themselves on the water to break the surface tension as they lay their eggs. Spent caddisflies can be every bit as important as spent spinner mayflies. Many caddisflies swim or crawl underwater to lay their eggs on the streambed. These caddis carry an air bubble sheath over their bodies as they roam about underwater. This glistening sheath is highly attractive to foraging trout.

There are several dozen caddis in the Sierra; only those which are consistently important are listed below.

Brachycentridae

Genus: *Amiocentrus*
Common name: (Western weedy water sedge)

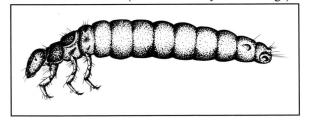

Larva: Size 12-18. Builds a cylindrical tube case usually out of fine grained sand. Lacks humps on the first abdominal segment. Larva with case are frequently found drifting in open water of our slow spring creeks.

Imitation: Peeking Caddis.

Pupa: Size 12-18. This pale green pupa emerges in the evening by swimming to the surface, drifting for a few minutes, then popping quickly out of the water. Emergence occurs all summer but is heaviest mid June through early July.

Imitation: Bird's Nest or LaFontaine Green Sparkle Pupa.

Adult: Size 14-20. Chocolate wings over olive body. The ovipositing females either swim under water to release their eggs or they simply break the surface tension and let the egg clusters drop. The spent females don't attempt to leave the water but simply drift with the flow.

Imitation: Elk Hair Caddis, Soft Hackle, or Bird's Nest during ovipositing.

Genus: *Brachycentrus*
Common Name: Grannom

Larva: Size 10-18. Builds a vegetable tube in a uniquely sharp angled rectangle. Like others of the family the gills are simple or non existent and it lacks any humps on the 1st abdominal segment. The larva rappel from rock to rock by means of a silk thread. In aquariums I've watched *Brachycentrus* larva clutch bubbles from the air pump and hitch a ride to the surface on the ascending bubble. When the bubble bursts at the surface the larva drifts to the bottom, grabs a new bubble and repeats the action. I've also watched them drift exposed under the film of backwater eddies for hours.

Imitation: Peeking Caddis or Pheasant Tail.

Pupa: Size 10-18. Identical to the *Amiocentrus*.

Imitation: Bird's Nest or LaFontaine Green Sparkle Pupa.

Adult: Size 12-18. The adults have mottled brown or gray wings over a green, tan, or brown body. The females return to the river in the evening where they dip the water with their abdomens and release clusters of eggs. Some *Brachycentrus* swim through the water column and affix their eggs directly to the river bed. Ovipositing is usually restricted to areas of high oxygen such as riffles or wave lapped lake shores.

Imitation: Elk Hair Caddis, Soft Hackle, or Bird's Nest during ovipositing.

Note: Often found in the same water with the *Amiocentrus*. *Brachycentrus* concentrate in the quicker water and the *Amiocentrus* is most dense among the weeds of slower stretches.

Lepidostomatidae

Genus: *Lepidostoma*
Common name: Little plain brown sedge.

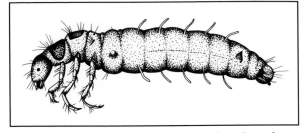

Larvae: size 10-14. Usually found in the calmer sections of small tumbling streams or along the edges of ponds. The cases may be almost identical to the fine grained tubes of the *Amiocentrus* or constructed of square plates of woody debris neatly fitted into a rectangular shaped box. The larvae resemble *Limnephilids* but lack a dorsal hump on the first abdominal segment (well defined lateral humps are present). Very small antenna are located immediately in front of each eye.

The larvae feed on the micro flora which coat rotting cellulose debris. The vegetation is ingested and the micro organisms are selectively digested. Researchers in California and Oregon have noted that *Lepidostatids* can ingest their body weight in pine needles or softwood leaves each day.

Imitation: Peeking caddis or pheasant tail.

Pupae: size 14-18. Actual pupation occurs in the larval case as it remains affixed to the downcurrent side of submerged objects. The dirty brown pupae emerge from their cases an hour or more prior to hatching and drift or weakly swim about along the slower stream edges or backeddies. Emergence into adult occurs in late afternoon and on into the evening hours.

Imitation: Birds Nest or dark La Fontaine sparkle pupae.

Adult: size 14-18. The small brown adults look pretty generic at first glance, however, upon closer inspection many adult *Lepidostomas* will be found to sport leaf shaped legs, paddle shaped mouth parts, and wings with modified pockets. The adults oviposit a day or so after emergence at the same time and place emergence occured. Fish can selectively feed on the ovipositing adults or the ascending pupae. A good tactic is to drift a Bird's Nest (treated with floatant to help trap air bubbles on the nymph) under the film with sporadic twitches. . .this imitates both life stages of the caddis.

Imitation: Birds Nest or Elk Hair Caddis.

Glossosoma
Common name: Saddle case maker

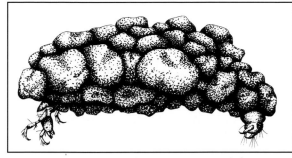

Larva: Size 16-20. Creamy orange, pink, or rust. The *Glossosoma* larva are unique in that they build little igloos of gravel just under the waterline. Colonies of Glossosomatids are often exposed when a river's level abruptly drops.

The larva builds a belly band across the dorsal opening of the case which allows it to carry the case around on its back like a little limpet. When the larva finds a suitable spot on a rock it will glue the edges of the case to the rock and then scrape and consume the periphyton (attached algae) under foot. Because the case is a dome configuration, it cannot be extended as the larva grows so the larva must frequently crawl out from under the case to build a new one.

The larva exit their cases in a synchronous fashion so that entire colonies will be exposed to predation at the same time. The larva rarely rebuild on the same rock but instead choose to drift with the current and build in a new location. Often thousands of Glossosomatids will drift at a time and the trout will feed exclusively on these morsels, often to the frustration of the unknowing angler. The drift occurs early in the morning or after sundown, often as other glossosomatids are emerging as adults.

Pupa: Size 16-18. The rust colored Glossosomatid pupa are exceedingly agile swimmers and when a hatch is in progress (usually coinciding with a drift of larva), the trout will often chase down the pupa and ignore the adults. The angler confronted with a river full of fluttering caddis and splashing trout would be well advised to consider actively twitching a pupa pattern through the water if his adult imitations are failing. Emergence can occur most of the summer but are strongest late May through early July.

Imitation: Bird's Nest or Rusty (rust dubbing over entire hook, ribbed with copper and a head of brown ostrich).

Adult: Size 16-18. The adults have light to dark brown wings over an olive, tan, or brown body. The adult has three ocelli (small simple eyes) and the antennae is slightly shorter than the body.

The females swim through the river to affix their eggs to the streambed. After laying their eggs, these spent caddis will flutter helplessly with the current until they drown or are consumed by a fish. A dark unweighted soft hackle is a perfect imitation. The *Glossosoma* occurs in such tremendous numbers and is so exposed to trout in all of its forms, that I consider this caddisfly to be one of the most important trout foods throughout the Sierra.

Imitation: Elk Hair Caddis or Soft Hackle.

Helicopsychidae
Common Name: Turban case caddis

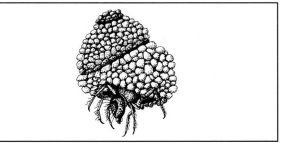

Larva: Size 16-18. The larva of the Helicopsychidae is easily identified by its sand case which is spiracle like that of a snail. When the larva is removed from its case it often remains in a slightly coiled position.

Imitation: Peeking Caddis.

Pupa: Size 16-18. Emergence is in the evening over open water where the pupa swims to the surface and hatches after a brief period of drift.

Imitation: Bird's Nest.

Adult: Size 16-18. The adult is a size 16-18 with a speckled dark brown wing over a creamy body. The female will flutter and twitch on the water's surface while ovipositing. This caddis is abundant in the slower sections of rich, cool, clear streams.

Imitation: Elk hair caddis.

Rhyacophila
Common name: Green sedge

Larva: Size 8-16. Free roaming, does not make a case. Green, gray or brown. Strong anal hook, if abdominal gills are present, they're quite sparse.

The larva is quite vulnerable to predation and stomach samples show that trout eat large quantities of them. The larva have an interesting habit of moving from rock to rock by rappelling from a strand of silk. Though the larva can be quite difficult to see underwater, the glistening silk strand is highly visible to trout, and the angler mimicking the strand by marking his leader with white ink can noticeably increase his success.

Imitation: Rhyacophila or Green Rock Worm.

Pupa: Size 10-18. Green to yellow green. Emerge usually at dusk.

Imitation: Bird's Nest or green and brown LaFontaine Sparkle Pupa.

Adult: Size 10-18. Wings mottled brown and gray and the body can be various shades of green. Three ocelli, antennae shorter than body.

Imitation: Elk Hair Caddis.

The *Rhyacophila* is common in all Sierra freestone environments. Various species are emerging year round with strongest hatches early to mid summer.

Hydropsyche
Common name: Spotted sedge

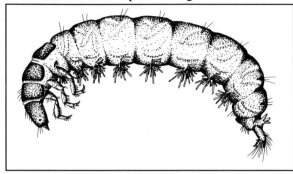

Larva: Size 8-14. The Hydropsychidae larva does not build a case, instead choosing to build a silk lined retreat in a crack between the rocks. Near the retreat they build nets which face into the current and catch bits of drifting seston. The tan, brown, or green larva picks through its net and eats the edible portions and discards the rest. The larva is differentiated from the other common uncased caddis, the *Rhyacophila*, by its bushy gills on the underside of the abdomen and by the thickened plates on the dorsum of its first three segments. The profuse gills are able to extract oxygen from even very sluggish waters and the larva can be found in every water type from fast riffles to slow meadow streams.

Imitation: Rock Worm.

Pupa: Size 8-14. The pupa swims to the surface where it will drift sometimes for hours before it emerges to a quick flying adult. The adults have mottled brown wings with a fawn to olive colored body. This size 10-16 caddis is present through most of the trout season and is commonly encountered by the fly fisher. The adult has no ocelli and the antennae are the same length as the body. Emergence can occur any time of day...I've seen intense hatches during cloudy afternoons on the Truckee.

Imitation: Bird's Nest or Green LaFontaine Sparkle Pupa.

Adult: Size 10-16. Mottled brown wing over brownish body. Ocelli absent, antennae equal to body length. The females oviposit by swimming to the river bottom where she glues her eggs directly to the rocks. After laying her eggs, she drifts with the current and slowly ascends to the surface where she will often flop about. An Elk Hair Caddis or Soft Hackle on a split shot can be deadly.

Imitation: Elk Hair Caddis.

Hydroptilidae
Common name: Micro caddis

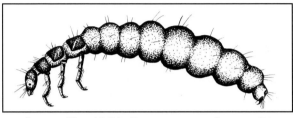

Larva: Size 18-24. Gray, green or brown. Lives in still and slow water environs.

Imitation: Impractical to imitate

Pupa: Size 18-24. Tiny, active swimmers that emerge in tremendous numbers. Small soft hackles twitched in the film will sometimes be taken with abandon.

Imitation: Soft Hackle.

Adult: Size 18-24. Tan to brown with long fine hairs fringing the wings.

Imitation: Soft Hackle.

Leptoceridae
Genus: *Mystacides*
Common name: Black dancer

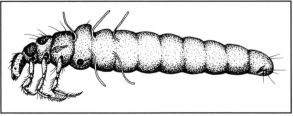

Larva: Size 12-16. Lateral hump on first abdominal segment (usually covered with bristles). *Mystacides* builds a long slender case of sticks, vegetation and pine needles. Usually the case is quite a bit longer than the larva. The larva are quite strong swimmers even while wearing the case.

Imitation: Strawman or Peeking Caddis.

Pupa: Size 14-16. Late in June and well into July these black pupa will swim to the shallows and crawl out onto the shoreline or protruding vegetation. Emergence is usually early in the morning.

Imitation: LaFontaine Black Sparkle Pupa.

Adult: Size 14-16. Black wing over a black body. Like all members of the Leptoceridae family the antennae is several times longer than the body [remember the klepto stealing a TV with very long antenna].

Imitation: Elk Hair Caddis.

The adult swarms throughout the day in shady areas over water. This "dance" is oriented to the height of nearby vegetation. In the evening the females crawl along the bottom of the lake to oviposit.

Limnephilidae

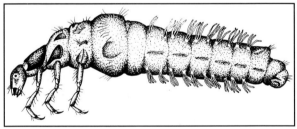

The Limnephilidae family is so large and its member's habits and distinguishing characteristics are so diverse, that the only way to make any angling sense of the family is to break it down to the genus level.

All Limnephilidae larva build tube shaped cases and can be identified by the tiny antennae located halfway between the eye and the mandible. Almost all Limnephilidae larva have bristled lateral and dorsal humps on the first abdominal segment.

Genus: *Hydatophylax*
Common name: Giant sedge
Larva: Size 1-4. The larva is huge, sometimes approaching 35mm in length. Very common on the western slope of the Sierra, the *Hydatophylax* often shares the same water with the *Dicosmoecus* but

prefers the quite pools and backwaters rather than the turbulent areas. As with most slow and still water caddis, the case is vegetative and commonly composed of bits of bark and other woody debris. The larva is a creamy pale color and without its case can be confused with the *Dicosmoecus*.

Imitation: Woolly Worm.

Pupa: Size 1-6. Emergence can occur anytime between late August and October at dusk or dawn. The pupa crawl along the riverbed and emerge at the waterline.

Imitation: LaFontaine Ginger Sparkle Pupa.

Adult: 2-8. The adults are long lived and ovipositing can occur many weeks after emergence. The large moth-like adult is easily imitated with a size 4 or 6 bucktail, but because of the prolonged emergence and ovipositing period, the *Hydatophylax* rarely presents itself in the intense concentrations as the *Dicosmoecus*.

Imitation: Bucktail or Stimulator.

Genus: *Limnephilus*
Common name: Summer flier
Larva: Size 2-8. Tube case of gravel, sticks, or pine needles. Common in sluggish spring creeks and spring fed ponds.

Imitation: Strawman or Peeking Caddis.

Pupa: Size 4-10. Emergence occurs in June during the early morning or evening when the pupa crawls out onto shore.

Imitation: Bird's Nest or ginger LaFontaine Sparkle Caddis.

Adult: Size 4-10. Rusty colored wings over reddish brown body. Upon emergence the adult is unique in that it is sexually immature. The adults hide in riparian growth through the summer until they mature and oviposit in late September and October. The sexually mature female returns to the water where it swims to the lake bottom to lay its eggs. During ovipositing a large burnt orange soft hackle twitched through the water makes an excellent offering to trout keyed on the caddis.

Imitation: Elk Hair Caddis or Bucktail.

Genus: *Apatania*

Common name: Smoky sedge
Larva: Size 12-14. Tapered, tubular stone cases. Common in smaller brooks and creeks of the Truckee area. In six, one foot sections of Sagehen Creek, 1,000 *Apatania* larva were counted...not too bad for a caddis many "authorities" consider uncommon in California!

Imitation: Pheasant Tail or Peeking Caddis.

Pupa: Size 12-14. Soot gray. Emerges during the warmer times of the day in late April through mid May. This is often the first caddis of the season for early Sierra anglers.

Imitation: Bird's Nest or LaFontaine Gray Sparkle Pupa.

Adult: Size 14. Gray wing over a light gray body.
Imitation: Elk Hair Caddis.

Genus: *Hesperophylax*
Common name: Silver stripe sedge
Larva: Size 1/0-6. The larva of the *Hesperophylax* is found in the cool swift streams of the Sierra. The cases are stout tubes constructed of stones heavy enough to ballast the larva in turbulent waters.

Imitation: Woolly Worm.

Pupa: Size 1/0-6. The pupa emerge at night mid summer through mid fall depending on latitude and elevation. The adults apparently have a long life span and are commonly encountered in the early mornings and evenings when they come to the creek banks to drink.

Imitation: LaFontaine Ginger Sparkle Pupa.

Adult: Size 1/0-6. These caddis are instantly recognized by their size (size 1/0 to 6) and by the characteristic longitudinal silver stripe running over a cream and pale brown forewing. Though I've never encountered *Hesperophylax* adults in fishable numbers in the Sierra, a large light brown over pale orange bucktail would be a close imitation.

Imitation: Bucktail or Stimulator.
Genus: *Psychoglypha*
Common name: Snow sedge
Larva: Size 2-8. The *Psychoglypha* is found in almost any trout habitat and the larva often form a significant portion of the winter drift. The larva

builds a tubular case of gravel and/or vegetation and will join in a synchronous drift about midday in the winter months. Though I've never found trout selectively keying on the drifting larva, whitefish will frequently be packed with them.

Imitation: Peeking Caddis.

Pupa: Size 4-8. The pupa is active from late fall into mid- winter when it moves into the relatively warm shallows to emerge.

Imitation: Bird's Nest.

Adult: Size 4-8. The adult resembles the *Hesperophylax* in that it sports a silver stripe through the forewing. The wing base coloration is a dull rust and the body is brown. The adult *Psychoglypha* will commonly rest on the snow where the dark coloration absorbs warmth from the sun and melts the insect into the bank. This caddis can be important to winter anglers in Nevada and on all season California waters such as the Kings River.

Imitation: Bucktail or Stimulator.

Lahontan cutthroat taken on a generic leech pattern.

Genus: *Ecclisomyia*
Common name: Western mottled sedge
Larva: Size 4-8. Slender gravel case often mixed with bits of vegetation. *Ecclisomyia* is active in small fast streams throughout the winter. It is THE large caddis available to trout in the early spring.

Imitation: Bird's Nest, Peeking Caddis, or Pheasant Tail.

Pupa: Size 6-10. Pupation begins in late winter

and emergence takes place mid April through mid May. I've never encountered a fishable hatch, but the large pupa crawling about in the shallows when most other food forms are wanting can trigger selective feeding.

Imitation: Bird's Nest or Casual Dress.

Adult: Size 8-12. Dark mottled brown wing over deep green body.

Imitation: Elk Hair Caddis.

Tiger lily.

Genus: *Neophylax*

Common name: Mottled sedge

Larva: Size 8-14. Builds a gravel case with pieces of rock affixed to the lateral aspects to act as ballast in the swift riffles they inhabit. The larva affix their cases to the undersides of rocks in well oxygenated riffles then, like the *Dicosmoecus*, enter a state of dormancy for a few weeks before actually pupating.

Imitation: Bird's Nest or Peeking Caddis.

Pupa: Size 8-14. These golden colored pupa emerge from their stone cases from mid-September through early October. They actively swim to the surface and emerge from the riffles or in the slack immediately downstream of the fast water.

Imitation: Bird's Nest or LaFontaine Gold Sparkle Pupa.

Adult: Size 10-14. Mottled brown wings with ragged rear edges. Body tan often with a dark spot on the abdomen. The adults reportedly lay their eggs under overhanging banks and into the water while perched on objects protruding from the water. I've only seen *Neophylax* ovipositing by gliding to the water, breaking the surface tension, then releasing eggs under the surface in typical Limnephilidae fashion.

Imitation: Elk Hair Caddis.

Genus: *Dicosmoecus*

Common name: October caddis

Larva: Size 2-8. Pale orange/yellow with a tubular case built of coarse gravel. Commonly found under rocks in riffles. The larva vacate their cases several times in late July through early September and drift helplessly with the current. This is probably a method to disseminate the population should a section of river dry up or suffer some other catastrophe. The trigger for these drifts is unknown, but due to their synchronous nature (many larva drift at a time), trout quickly key on the larva and the angler is pretty helpless unless he understands this phenomena.

Imitation: Tangerine Dream or Red Squirrel.

Pupa: Size 2-8. Pupation occurs in September and continues into early October when the pupa chews free from its cobbled shelter and swims and crawls to the shallows where it emerges. Emergence can occur at any time but is most intense in the late afternoon and evening.

Imitation: Tangerine Dream, Red Squirrel, or LaFontaine Orange Sparkle Pupa.

Adult: Size 4-8. Orange body with brown wings. Unlikely to be confused with anything except a large moth. Flight is quick and very erratic. The females oviposit by gliding to the water and smacking it with their abdomen to break the surface tension and release eggs. As egg laying commences the females will flop about on the water and create an irresistible meal for a trout.

Imitation: Bucktail, Stimulator, or Elk Hair Caddis.

Phryganeidae

Genus: *Phryganea*

Common name: Travelling sedge

Larva: Size 4-8. The larva builds a vegetable case in a spiracle fashion somewhat resembling a barber pole. I have had *Phryganea* in an aquarium which jettisoned their cases and wandered about for almost a week before rebuilding. It has been reported that some caddis will drop their cases when being pursued and I wouldn't be surprised if *Phryganea* do this.

Imitation: Strawman or Peeking Caddis.

Pupa: Size 4-8. The pupa emerge by crawling out onto the vegetation of the shorelines of the lakes and marshes in which they live.

Imitation: Bird's Nest, or Elk Hair Caddis on a split shot.

Adult: Size 6-10. Patterned wings of tan and gray over a tan or rusty body. The females oviposit in late evening and on into the night by gliding into the water with enough momentum to break the surface film. Some will continue through the water and swim to the bottom to affix their eggs to the stems of vegetation while other are content to spill their eggs on the water's surface.

After laying their eggs the females run and gyrate about on the water's surface in a "motor boat" fashion that chums trout to the surface. Some of my most memorable nights have been in a warm sleeping bag on a chilly Sierra night listening to the splashing of large trout chasing travelling sedges.

Imitation: Goddard Caddis or heavily hackled Elk Hair Caddis.

Polycentropididae

Common name: Net spinner caddis

Larva: Size 14-18. This amber colored larva builds a tube retreat. This feisty little larva is easily differentiated from the other uncased caddis because it lacks gills. When captured it will regurgitate its stomach contents and viciously bite (the bite is painless).

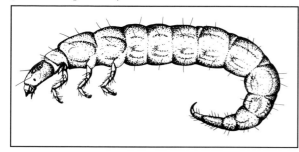

Imitation: Tan Rockworm.

Pupa: Size 14-18. Emergence occurs from early summer into the fall. I've seen strong hatches from smaller creeks in June and from lakes in late July.

Imitation: Bird's Nest or LaFontaine Yellow Sparkle Pupa.

Adult: Size 14-20. The females crawl from shore or dive through the water to oviposit on the lake or streambed.

Imitation: Soft Hackle or Bird's Nest.

ODONATA

Damselflies and Dragonflies

Odonates of the Sierra are typically found in ponds and sluggish, weedy streams. The nymphs have specialized mouthparts (labium) that extend and capture prey. These "prehensile labium" differentiate them from any other aquatic nymph in the Sierra.

Damsel and dragonflies are primitive insects whose nymphs live for one to four years before emergence into adults. The adults live anywhere from a few weeks to several months.

Zygoptera
Common name: Damselflies

Nymph: Size 8-14. Damselfly nymphs are able to change hue rapidly. Tan, brown, and green are the most common colors. The nymphs have three paddle-like gills (lamellae) which extend from the abdomen. The abdomen and lamellae propel the nymph with a sculling action that is nearly impossible to imitate with a fly. Damselfly nymphs can be exceedingly important trout fare late in June through July when they're preparing to hatch. Damselfly nymphs crawl onto weeds, logs, float tubes, and other objects to hatch.

Imitation: Kaufmann's Damsel Nymph.

Adult: Size 6-10. The newly emerged (teneral) adults are a pale brown or green. The tenerals are weak fliers and frequently end up in the water. The adults are typically bright blue or brown and hold their wings folded high over their backs. Ovipositing adults can be important trout food. When adults are swarming low over the water and fish are rising explosively tie on a damsel. Don't get tunnel vision on the small splashy fish, often the largest trout will be right at the edge of the shoreline gently sucking in spent adults.

Imitation: Parachute Damsel.

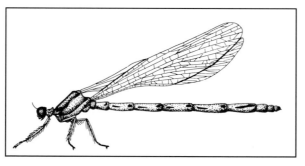

Anisoptera
Common name: Dragon flies

Nymph: Size 1/0-10. Dragon fly nymphs have highly developed biting mouthparts which can easily break the skin. The nymphs swim by squirting water out their anus. As the nymph fills with water it swells, then elongates as the water is expelled. A smooth stop and go retrieve does a good job imitating the dragonfly nymph's behavior.

Imitation: Woolly Worm or Carey Special.

Adult: Size 1-6. The adults hold their paired wings flat out to the sides when at rest. Trout will take the occasional adult opportunistically however, dragonflies are fast and strong fliers and seldom make themselves available.

Imitation: Parachute dragonfly.

A golden trout aggressively works a caddisfly hatch.

CRUSTACEANS

Crayfish and Scuds
Decapoda

Common name: Crayfish

Crayfish are abundant in most Sierra waters. On mid- elevation lakes and rivers they can be a very important food for medium to very large trout. During the drought of the late eighties the crayfish population exploded on the Truckee River. The trout of the Truckee became highly selective and fed almost exclusively on the crayfish. Anglers used to catching the fish on nymphs and other standard imitations walked away from the river convinced the trout had disappeared!

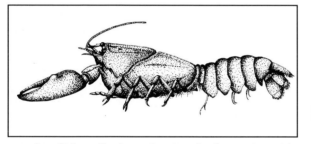

Crayfish walk along the river bed or swim with rapid bursts in a fashion nearly impossible to mimic with a fly. The best method for taking trout on a crayfish imitation is to fish it *dead drift* through the riffles then let it drop into eddies and pools.

Like all crustaceans, crayfish periodically molt and it is said that fish prefer their crayfish while the shell is still soft from the molt. I can't say whether this is true or not, but it sounds good so I normally fish gray green patterns which imitate the soft shelled stage. Woolly Buggers make as good an imitation as any.

I don't know of any size that consistently out fishes another, so carry an assortment and using a dropper, fish two different sized crayfish at a time until the fish start to hit.

Mooching a crayfish pattern along a lake bed can be very productive. Retrieve the fly by lifting the rod tip and rapidly taking in several long strips.

Lower the rod tip, keeping in contact with the fly, until the crayfish hits bottom. Repeat this until the fly is at the shore. This mooching action causes bursts of silt every time the fly hits bottom and presents a nearly irresistible meal for a trout (or bass).

Imitation: Woolly bugger or Whitlock Crayfish.

Gammarus

Common name: Scud

Gammarus are shrimp-like creatures that dwell in rich weedy waters. *Gammarus* are not only prime trout fare, but are in themselves good indicators of productive waters. Almost all Sierra "big fish" waters are crawling with scuds.

Scuds are photophobic, which means they like to hide during bright days. On cloudy days or when the sun is low, scuds will leave the protection of the weeds and venture into open water.

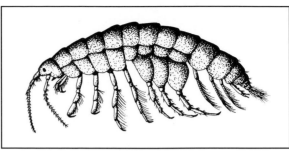

There are many scud patterns on the market, including some with plastic backs and others with eyes and feelers. The best scud imitation is a plain old Bird's Nest. Underwater the Bird's Nest gives the impression of depth and movement that the traditional scud imitations lack.

When a scud is swimming it lays almost straight out rather than partially curled up like many of the scud imitations.

This obese brook trout came from a scud rich lake.

Even a fast moving scud doesn't cover much over an inch a second. The best way to imitate their movement is to make a slow three or four inch strip then pause several seconds then slowly strip again.

VERTEBRATES

Tadpoles

Trout love tadpoles and effectively hunt them. In many Sierra lakes where trout have been introduced the mountain yellow legged frog has disappeared. The typical yellow legged frog tadpole matures over two years and reaches almost three inches when legs develope.

Tadpoles are dark brown on top and a highly reflective gold and silver on the belly. An easy tadpole imitation to make is to tie a rabbit fur strip over a hook wrapped with crystal chenille or mylar piping. A Woolly Bugger is about as good as you'll find commercially available.

BAITFISH

A "baitfish" is any fish a trout can eat. Bait fish don't necessarily need to be small...many large browns are taken as they lurk around boat ramps waiting for the hatchery truck to dump its load of ten-inch trout. I've had three inch trout that would eat full grown guppies.

Perch and sunfish are locally important in some mid- elevation lakes, but the most important bait fish throughout the Sierra is the sculpin.

Sculpins can reach densities as great as six fish per square meter of streambed. As bottom dwellers that feed on insects, carrion, and fish eggs, sculpins have little need for speed. Sculpins are poor swimmers, but make up for their lack of mobility by having excellent camouflage.

Sculpins have oversized pectoral fins which many sculpin-specific patterns copy in great detail. In truth, the pectoral fins are pressed against the sides of the sculpin as it swims, and the "realistic" sculpin patterns look quite fake when swimming.

The best sculpin pattern is something that can be fished slowly, close to the bottom, and has a lot of built in action. Woolly Buggers in shades of brown and green are perfect.

The sculpin is a favored big trout food all over the Sierra range.

ROE

Salmon eggs are sold as bait, so it should come as no surprise that trout feast on eggs when available. During spawning, both in the spring and fall, fish will sometimes key in on spilled roe and reject all other foods.

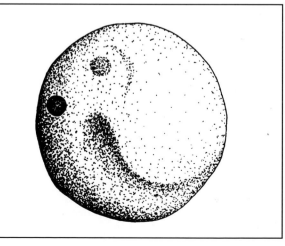

Roe is typically translucent pale orange when its fresh but turns a milky white after a day or two. Roe is only slightly heavier than water so weighted imitations should be avoided. The best roe patterns can be made by spearing 3mm pom poms on a size 18 hook. Pom poms can be purchased at most large variety and craft store for about a penny each.

A problem with roe flies is that they tend to be taken deeply. ONLY use roe flies when fishing to visible trout so that the hook can be set as soon as the fly is taken.

It goes without saying that actively spawning fish should not be harassed. Most spawning fish won't take the fly anyway.

The author took this nice Truckee River brown on a sculpin imitation.

DISTRIBUTION CHARTS

The following distribution charts of the Sierra trout delineate every trout bearing lake in the Sierra (nearly 2,000). The charts also show every stream longer than five miles in the Sierra.

The stream charts list one topo map for each stream. This is the map used by California Department of Water Resources as a bench mark for that stream. Since some streams cross a dozen or more maps, it would be impractical to list all topos. The trout species for the streams do not necessarily all live in the stream section that crosses the listed map. Stream trout are very mobile and entire species populations will migrate in and out of a stream section. Brook, golden and cutthroat will tend to be in the upper reaches of a stream while browns are usually found in the lower stretches. Rainbows can be found anywhere.

For our purposes the scope of the Sierra Nevada Mountains fall between the following borders: South to the southern boundary of the Kern County Line (about Kernville/Lake Isabella), north to the northern boundaries of Butte and Plumas county lines, west to the 3,500 foot level of the Sierra foothills, and east to where the foot of the range meets the Great Basin.

Though Sierra trout fisheries are relatively stable, population shifts are bound to occur. The record winters of the early '80s followed by the record drought of the late '80s have left their marks in the Sierra. Natural phenomena such as avalanches, rock slides, and infiltration of fish species can dramatically alter a fishery structure.

Lakes not mentioned in the charts have been deleted for one of three reasons: 1) The lake doesn't contain trout 2) The existing trout population is ex-pected to disappear soon. 3) Some Sierra lakes contain fragile or experimental populations of trout and in the best interest of the fisheries they have not been mentioned.

HOW TO USE THE CHARTS

The charts are arranged by county. Most readers will be using them in conjunction with U.S. Forest Service maps or U.S.G.S. topographical maps. Both types of maps clearly describe county boundaries.

LAKE or STREAM: The name used is that described on the U.S.G.S. topo maps. If the water is not named on the map, the most popular name is used. Many waters are named only on Department of Fish and Game aerial fish planting photos. Sometimes the U.S.G.S. name is different than the popular alias.

U.S.G.S. TOPO MAP: The standard reference to place names and geological features in the Sierra Nevada.

L: Lahontan

RB: Rainbow (G# Kern River Rainbow).

BK: Brook trout.

BN: Brown trout.

GN: Golden trout (W# Little Kern Golden)

CT: Cutthroat trout (P# Paiute Cutthroat)

LK: Lake Trout

X: Denotes the trout species in the described water.

?: Denotes a trout species that has been in the water but present or future status is in question. Waters which lack spawning areas, planned biological "treatment," or encroachment of non compatible species will be given the "?".

An August snowstorm typifies the complex weather conditions of the High Sierra.

ALPINE COUNTY RIVERS

RIVER/STREAM	TRIBUTARY TO	TOPO MAP	RB	BK	BN	GN	CT
ARNOT CREEK	STANISLAUS, CLARK FORK	DARDANELLE CONE	X	X			X
CARSON RIVER, WF	CARSON RVR	FREEL PEAK	X	X	X		X
CARSON RIVER, EF	CARSON RVR	MT. SIEGEL	X		X		X
CHARITY VALLEY CREEK	HOT SPRINGS CREEK	MARKLEEVILLE		X			X
DISASTER CREEK	STANISLAUS, CLARK FORK	SONORA PASS	X			X	
GROUSE CREEK	MOKELUMNE RVR, NF	MARKLEEVILLE	X	X			
HAWKINS PEAK CREEK	CARSON RVR, WF	MARKLEEVILLE		X			
HIGHLAND LAKE CREEK	SPICER MEADOWS RES.	DARDANELLE CONE	X	X			
HOT SPRINGS CREEK	CARSON RVR, EF	MARKLEEVILLE	X	X			X
INDIAN CREEK	CARSON RVR, EF	MARKLEEVILLE	X		X		X
MOKELUMNE RVR, NF	SALT SPRINGS RES.	MARKLEEVILLE	X	X	X		
MOUNTAINEER CREEK	BRYANT CREEK	TOPAZ LAKE					X
NOBEL CREEK	SILVER CREEK	MARKLEEVILLE	X	X			X
PACIFIC CREEK	MOKELUMNE, NF	MARKLEEVILLE	X	X			
PLEASANT VALLEY CREEK	HOT SPRINGS CREEK	MARKLEEVILLE	X	X			X
RED LAKE CREEK	CARSON RVR, WF	MARKLEEVILLE	X	X			
SILVER CREEK	STANISLAUS, NF	BIG MEADOW	X	X			
SILVER CREEK	CARSON RVR, EF	TOPAZ LAKE	X	X			X
SILVER KING CREEK	LLEWELLYN FALLS	SONORA PASS					P
SILVER KING CREEK	CARSON RVR, EF	TOPAZ LAKE	X	X	X		X
SPRATT CREEK	HOT SPRINGS CREEK	MARKLEEVILLE	X				X
STANISLAUS RVR, CLARK F.	STANISLAUS, MF	DARDANELLE CONE	X	X	X		
SUMMIT CITY CREEK	MOKELUMNE, NF	SILVER LAKE	X	X			X
UPPER TRUCKEE RIVER	LAKE TAHOE	SILVER LAKE	X	X	X		X
WALKER RVR, WF	TOPAZ LAKE	SONORA PASS	X	X	X		X
WILDERNESS CREEK	SPICER MEADOWS CREEK	DARDANELLE CONE	X	X			
WOLF CREEK	CARSON RVR, EF	TOPAZ LAKE	X	X	X		

AMADOR COUNTY RIVERS

RIVER/STREAM	TRIBUTARY TO	TOPO MAP	RB	BK	BN	GN	CT
BEAR RIVER	MOKELUMNE RVR	SILVER LAKE	X	X	X		
BEAVER CREEK	BEAR RVR	BLUE MOUNTAIN	X	X	X		
COLE CREEK	MOKELUMNE, NF	BIG MEADOW	X	X	X		
MILL CREEK	TIGER CREEK	BLUE MOUNTAIN	X	X	X		
MOKELUMNE RIVER, NF	SALT SPRINGS RES.	BIG MEADOW	X	X	X		X
PANTHER CREEK, EF	PANTHER CREEK	BLUE MOUNTAIN	X		X		
PANTHER CREEK, WF	PANTHER CREEK	BLUE MOUNTAIN	X		X		
TANGLEFOOT CANYON CREEK	MOKELUMNE RVR, NF	BIG MEADOW	X	X	X		
TIGER CREEK	MOKELUMNE RVR, NF	BIG MEADOW	X	X	X		
TRAGEDY CREEK	BEAR RVR	SILVER LAKE	X				

EL DORADO COUNTY RIVERS

RIVER/STREAM	TRIBUTARY TO	TOPO MAP	RB	BK	BN	GN	CT
ALDER CREEK	AMERICAN RVR	LEEK SPRING HILL	X		X		
AMERICAN RVR, SILVER FK	AMERICAN RVR, SF	ROBBS PEAK	X	X	X		
AMERICAN RVR, SOUTH FK	SLAB CREEK RES.	SADDLE MT	X	X			
ANDERSON CANYON CREEK	COSUMNES RVR, MF	LEEK SPRING HILL	X	X	X		
BARRETT LAKE CREEK	BASSI FORK	LOON LAKE	X	X	X		
BIG SILVER CREEK	UNION VALLEY RES.	LOON LAKE	X	X	X		
CAMP CREEK	COSUMNES RVR, NF	CAMINO	X	X	X		
CAPLES CREEK	AMERICAN, SILVER FK	SILVER LAKE	X	X	X		
CASCADE CREEK	LAKE TAHOE	TAHOE	X	X	X		
CAT CREEK	COSUMNES RVR, MF	LEEK SPRING HILL	X	X	X		
CODY CREEK	STRAWBERRY CREEK	PYRAMID CREEK	X	X	X		
COLD CREEK	TROUT CREEK	FREEL PEAK	X	X	X		
COSUMNES RIVER, MF	COSUMNES RVR	CAMINO	X	X	X		
COSUMNES RVR, NF	COSUMNES RVR	CAMINO	X	X	X		
COSUMNES RVR. SF	COSUMNES RVR	CAMINO	X		X		
DOGTOWN CREEK	COSUMNES RVR, MF	CAMINO	X		X		
MIDDLE DRY CREEK	DOGTOWN CREEK	LEEK SPRING HILL	X				
GENERAL CREEK	LAKE TAHOE	TAHOE	X	X	X		
GERLE CREEK	RUBICON RVR, SF	ROBBS PEAK	X	X	X		
LITTLE SILVER CREEK	SILVER CREEK	ROBBS PEAK	X		X		

RIVER/STREAM	TRIBUTARY TO	TOPO MAP	ELEV.	RB	BK	BN	GN	CT	LK
LONG CANYON CREEK	AMERICAN, SILVER FK	SILVER LAKE			X		X		
LYONS CREEK	SILVER CREEK	ROBBS PEAK			X		X		
McKINNEY CREEK	DOGTOWN CREEK	LEEK SPRING HILL			X				
MEEKS CREEK	LAKE TAHOE	LAKE TAHOE			X	X	X		
ONION CREEK	SILVER CREEK	POLLOCK PINE			X		X		
PILOT CREEK	STUMPY MEADOWS RES.	SADDLE MT					X		
PLUM CREEK	AMERICAN RVR, SF	ROBBS PEAK			X				
PYRAMID CREEK	AMERICAN RVR, SF	FALLEN LEAF LAKE			X	X			
RUBICON RIVER	RUBICON RESERVOIR	FALLEN LEAF LAKE			X	X	X		
RUBICON RIVER, SF	HELL HOLE RESERVOIR	TAHOE			X	X	X		
SAXON CREEK	UPPER TRUCKEE RVR	FREEL PEAK			X	X			
SAYLES CANYON CREEK	AMERICAN RVR, SF	FALLEN LEAF LAKE			X	X			
SILVER CREEK	AMERICAN RVR, SF	SADDLE MT			X	X	X		X
SILVER CREEK, BASSI FK	BIG SILVER CREEK	LOON LAKE			X	X	X		
SILVER CREEK, JONES FK	UNION VALLEY RES.	ROBBS PEAK			X	X	X		
SILVER CREEK, NF BASSIN	SILVER CREEK	LOON LAKE			X	X			
SILVER CREEK, SF BASSIN	SILVER CREEK	LOON LAKE			X	X			
SILVER CREEK, SF	UNION VALLEY RES.	ROBBS PEAK			X		X		
SLAB CREEK	AMERICAN RVR, SF	SADDLE MT			X	X	X		
SLY PARK CREEK	JENKINS LAKE	CAMINO			X		X		
SOPIAGO CREEK	COSUMNES RVR, MF	CAMINO			X		X		
STRAWBERRY CREEK	AMERICAN RVR, SF	FALLEN LEAF LAKE			X				
TALLAC CREEK	LAKE TAHOE	TAHOE				X			
TELLS CREEK	UNION VALLEY RES.	ROBBS PEAK			X	X	X		
TROUT CREEK	LAKE TAHOE	FREEL PEAK			X	X			X
UPPER TRUCKEE RIVER	LAKE TAHOE	FREEL PEAK			X	X	X		X

FRESNO COUNTY RIVERS

RIVER/STREAM	TRIBUTARY TO	TOPO MAP	RB	BK	BN	GN	CT
ABBOTT CREEK	KINGS RVR	PATTERSON MT	X	X			
ARKANSAS CREEK	DINKEY CREEK	HUNTINGTON LAKE		X			
BEAR CREEK	DINKEY CREEK	HUNTINGTON LAKE	X	X	X		
BEAR CREEK	SAN JOAQUIN RVR, SF	MT. ABBOTT	X		X	X	
BIG CREEK	SAN JOAQUIN RVR, SF	SHAVER LAKE	X	X			
BIG CREEK	HUNTINGTON LAKE	HUNTINGTON LAKE	X	X	X		
BIG CREEK, SF	BIG CREEK	HUNTINGTON LAKE	X	X			
BLUE CANYON CREEK	KINGS RVR, MF	MARION PEAK	X				
BOULDER CREEK	KINGS RVR, SF	TEHIPITE DOME	X	X	X		
BUBBS CREEK	KINGS RVR, SF	MARION PEAK	X			X	
BURNT CORRAL CREEK	POST CORRAL CREEK	BLACKCAP MT	X	X			
CARTRIDGE CREEK	KINGS RVR, MF	MARION PEAK	X	?			
COLD CREEK	LAKE EDISON	KAISER PEAK	X	?			
CONVERSE CREEK	KINGS RVR	TEHIPITE DOME	X				
CROWN CREEK	KINGS RVR	TEHIPITE DOME	X	X	X		
DEER CREEK	DINKEY CREEK	HUNTINGTON LAKE	X		X		
DINKEY CREEK	KINGS RVR, NF	PATTERSON MT	X	X	X		
FISH CREEK	MADERA COUNTY LINE	DEVILS POSTPILE	X	X	X		
FLEMING CREEK	KINGS RVR, NF	BLACKCAP MT	X	X			
FOUR FORKS CREEK	SAN JOAQUIN RVR, SF	KAISER PEAK	X	X			
GODDARD CREEK	KINGS RVR, MF	MARION PEAK	X			X	
GRANITE CREEK	KINGS RVR, SF	MARION PEAK	X				
HILGARD CREEK	BEAR CREEK	MT. ABBOTT				X	
HELMS CREEK	COURTRIGHT RES.	BLACKCAP MT	X	X			
HOOPER CREEK	FLORENCE LAKE	MT. ABBOTT				X	
JOSE CREEK	SAN JOAQUIN RVR	SHAVER LAKE	X			X	
KAISER CREEK	SAN JOAQUIN RVR	SHUTEYE PEAK	X	X	X		
KINGS RVR, MF	KINGS RVR	TEHIPITE DOME	X	X	X		
KINGS RVR, NF	WISHON RESERVOIR	BLACKCAP MT	X	X	X		
KINGS RVR, NF	KINGS RVR	PATTERSON MT	X			X	
KINGS RVR, SF	KINGS RVR	TEHIPITE DOME	X	X	X	X	
LEWIS CREEK	KINGS RVR, SF	MARION PEAK	X	X	X		
MILL CREEK	KINGS RVR, SF	PINE FLAT DAM					
MILL FLAT CREEK	KINGS RVR	PATTERSON MT	X				
MONO CREEK	SAN JOAQUIN RVR	KAISER PEAK	X				
MONO CREEK	LAKE EDISON	MT. ABBOTT	X	X	X	X	

RIVER/STREAM	TRIBUTARY TO	TOPO MAP	ELEV.	RB	BK	BN	GN	CT	LK
PALISADE CREEK	KINGS RVR, MF	MT GODDARD						X	
PIUTE CREEK	SAN JOAQUIN RVR,SF	BLACKCAP MT			X			X	
POST CORRAL CREEK	KINGS RVR, NF	BLACKCAP MT			X	X			
RANCHERIA CREEK	HUNTINGTON RES.	KAISER PEAK			X	X	X		
RANCHERIA CREEK	KINGS RVR, NF	PATTERSON MT			X		X		
ROCK CREEK	FOUR FORKS CREEK	KAISER PEAK			X		X		
RUSH CREEK	BIG CREEK	PATTERSON MT			X		X		
SAN JOAQUIN RVR, SF	MADERA COUNTY LINE	BLACKCAP MT			X	X	X	X	
SCEPTER CREEK	CROWN CREEK	TEHIPITE DOME			X		X		
SHORTHAIR CREEK	WISHON RESERVOIR	BLACKCAP MT			X		X		
SILVER CREEK	FISH CREEK	DEVILS POSTPILE			X	X			
TAMARACK CREEK	PITMAN CREEK	HUNTINGTON LAKE			X	X	X		
WARM CREEK	SAN JOAQUIN RVR,SF	KAISER PEAK			X				
KAISER CREEK, WF	KAISER CREEK	KAISER PEAK			X	X			
WOODCHUCK CREEK	WISHON RESERVOIR	BLACKCAP MT			X				

INYO COUNTY RIVERS

RIVER/STREAM	TRIBUTARY TO	TOPO MAP	RB	BK	BN	GN	CT
ASH CREEK	LA AQUADUCT	OLANCHA	X	X	X		
ASH CREEK, SF	ASH CREEK	OLANCHA	X		X		
BAIRS CREEK	LA AQUADUCT	LONE PINE	X		X		
BAIRS CREEK, NF	LA AQUADUCT	LONE PINE	X	X	X		
BAKER CREEK	BIG PINE CANAL	BIG PINE	X	X	X		
BIG PINE CREEK	OWENS RVR	BIG PINE	X	X	X		
BIG PINE CREEK, NF	BIG PINE CREEK	BIG PINE	X	X			
BIRCH CREEK	OWENS RVR	MT. TOM	X				
BIRCH CREEK	TINEMAHA CREEK	BIG PINE	X	X	X		
BISHOP CREEK	OWENS	BISHOP	X		X		
BISHOP CREEK, MF	BISHOP CREEK	MT. TOM	X	X			
BISHOP CREEK, NF OF MF	BISHOP CREEK, MF	MT. GODDARD	X	X	X		
BISHOP CREEK, NF	OWENS RVR	BISHOP	X	X			
BISHOP CREEK, SF	SOUTH LAKE	BISHOP	X	X	X		
BISHOP CREEK, SF OF NF	BISHOP CREEK CANAL	BISHOP	X		X		
BRALEY CREEK	LA AQUADUCT	OLANCHA		X	X		
CARTAGO CREEK	LA AQUADUCT	OLANCHA		X	X	X	
COTTONWOOD CREEK	LA AQUADUCT	OLANCHA	X		X	X	
COYOTE CREEK	BISHOP CREEK	MT. TOM	X	X			
COYOTE CREEK, EF	COYOTE CREEK	BISHOP	X	X			
COYOTE CREEK, WF	COYOTE CREEK	BISHOP	X	X			
GEORGE CREEK	LA AQUADUCT	LONE PINE	X		X		
GOODALE CREEK	LA AQUADUCT	MT. PINCHOT	X		X		
HOGBACK CREEK	OWENS RVR	LONE PINE	X		X		
HORSESHOE MDW CREEK	COTTONWOOD CREEK	OLANCHA				X	
HORTON CREEK	OWENS RVR	BISHOP	X	X	X		
INDEPENDENCE CREEK	LA AQUADUCT	INDEPENDENCE	X		X		
LITTLE PINE CREEK	BIG PINE CREEK	BIG PINE	X		X		
LONE PINE CREEK	LA AQUADUCT	LONE PINE	X	X	X		
McGEE CREEK	HORTON CREEK	BISHOP	X		X		
OAK CREEK, NF	OAK CREEK	MT. PINCHOT	X		X		
OAK CREEK, SF	OAK CREEK	MT. PINCHOT	X	X	X		
OLANCHA CREEK	LA AQUADUCT	OLANCHA	X	X	X	X	
OWENS RIVER	OWENS LAKE	CASA DIABLO	X		X		
PINE CREEK	ROCK CREEK	MT. TOM	X	X	X		
PINYON CREEK	INDEPENDENCE CREEK	MT. PINCHOT	X	X	X		
RAWSON CANAL	OWENS RVR	BISHOP			X		
RED MOUNTAIN CREEK	TINEMAHA CREEK	BIG PINE	X		X	X	
SAWMILL CREEK	LA AQUADUCT	MT. PINCHOT	X		X		
SHEPHERD CREEK	OWENS RVR	LONE PINE	X	X	X		
SILVER CANYON CREEK	OWENS RVR	BISHOP		X	X		
SYMMES CREEK	OWENS RVR	INDEPENDENCE	X	X	X		
TABOOSE CREEK	OWENS RVR	WAUCOBA MT	X		X		
THIBAUT CREEK	LA AQUADUCT	MT. PINCHOT		X			
TINEMAHA CREEK	TINEMAHA RESERVOIR	WAUCOBA MT	X	X	X	X	
TUTTLE CREEK	LA AQUADUCT	LONE PINE	X	X			

MARIPOSA COUNTY RIVERS

RIVER/STREAM	TRIBUTARY TO	TOPO MAP	RB	BK	BN	GN	CT
ALDER CREEK	SF MERCED RVR	YOSEMITE	X				
BIG CREEK	SF MERCED RVR	YOSEMITE	X		X		
BRIDALVEIL CREEK	MERCED RVR	YOSEMITE	X	X			
BUENA VISTA CREEK	ILLILOUETTE CREEK	YOSEMITE	X	X			
CASCADE CREEK	TAMARACK CREEK	YOSEMITE	X	X			
CHILNUALNA CREEK	SF MERCED RVR	YOSEMITE		X			
CRANE CREEK	MERCED RVR	EL PORTAL	X	X	X		
ECHO CREEK	MERCED RVR	MERCED PEAK	X	X			
FLETCHER CREEK	LEWIS CREEK	MERCED PEAK	X		X		
FRESNO RVR, LEWIS FK	MADERA COUNTY LINE	BASS LAKE	X		X		
GROUSE CREEK	MERCED RVR	YOSEMITE	X		X		
ILLILOUETTE CREEK	MERCED RVR	YOSEMITE	X	X			
INDIAN CREEK	MERCED RVR	EL PORTAL	X				
LEWIS CREEK	MERCED RVR	MERCED PEAK		X			
MERCED RIVER	LAKE McCLURE	COULTERVILLE	X	X	X		
MERCED RIVER, S. FORK	MERCED RVR	EL PORTAL	X		X		
MOSS CREEK	MERCED RVR	EL PORTAL	X	X	X		
NEDS GULCH	MERCED RVR	EL PORTAL	X		X		
OLIVER CREEK	CHOWCHILLA RVR	EL PORTAL	X		X		
PORCUPINE CREEK	SNOW CREEK	HETCH HETCH	X				
SNOW CREEK	TENAYA CREEK	HETCH HETCH	X	X			
SUNRISE CREEK	MERCED RVR	YOSEMITE	X				
TAMARACK CREEK	MERCED RVR	YOSEMITE	X	X	X		
TENAYA CREEK	MERCED RVR	YOSEMITE	X	X			
YOSEMITE CREEK	MERCED RVR	YOSEMITE	X			?	

MONO COUNTY RIVERS

RIVER/STREAM	TRIBUTARY TO	TOPO MAP	RB	BK	BN	GN	CT
BUCKEYE CREEK	BRIDGEPORT RES	FALES HT SPRNG	X	X	X		
BYDAY CREEK	BRIDGEPORT RES	FALES HT SPRNG					X
CLEAR WATER CREEK	VIRGINIA CREEK	BODIE	X		X		
CONVICT CREEK	CROWLEY LAKE	MT. MORRISON	X	X			
DEADMAN CREEK	OWENS RVR	MT. MORRISON	X	X	X		
DEEP CREEK	WALKER RVR, WF	FALES HT SPRNG	X	X			
DOG CREEK	VIRGINIA CREEK	BODIE	X				
EAGLE CREEK	BUCKEYE CREEK	MATTERHORN	X	X			
EAST SLOUGH	WALKER RVR, WF	TOPAZ LAKE	X		X		
FRYING PAN CANYON CREEK	WALKER RVR, EF	BRIDGEPORT	X	X			
GLASS CREEK	DEADMAN CREEK	MT. MORRISON	X	X			
GREEN CREEK	WALKER RVR, EF	MATTERHORN	X	X	X		
HILTON CREEK	CROWLEY LAKE	CASA DIABLO MT	X		X		
HOT CREEK	OWENS RVR	MT. MORRISON	X		X		
LAUREL CREEK	MAMMOTH CREEK	MT. MORRISON		X	X		
LEAVITT CREEK	WALKER RVR, WF	SONORA PASS	X	X			
LEE VINING CREEK	MONO LAKE	MONO CRATERS	?		X		
LITTLE WALKER RIVER	WALKER RVR, WF	FALES HT SPRNG		X			
LONG VALLEY CREEK	SWAUGER CREEK	FALES HT SPRNG	X	X			
LOST CANNON CREEK	MILL CREEK	FALES HT SPRNG	X	X			
MAMMOTH CREEK	HOT CREEK	MT. MORRISON	X	X	X		
MAMMOTH CREEK	OLD MAMMOTH LAKE	MT. MORRISON	X	X	X		
McGEE CREEK	CONVICT CREEK	MT. MORRISON	X	X	X		
MILL CREEK	MONO LAKE	BODIE	X	X	X		
MOLYBDENITE CREEK	LITTLE WALKER RVR	FALES HT SPRNG	X	X			
MURPHY CREEK	WALKER RVR, EF	BRIDGEPORT		X	X		
OWENS RIVER	CROWLEY LAKE	MT. MORRISON	X		X		
PARKER CREEK	RUSH CREEK	MONO CRATERS		X			
ROBINSON CREEK	BRIDGEPORT RES.	FALES HT SPRNG	X		X		
ROBINSON CREEK	TWIN LAKES	MATTERHORN PK	X	X	X		
ROCK CREEK	OWENS RVR	MT. TOM	X				
RUSH CREEK	GRANT LAKE	MONO CRATERS	X	X	X		
RUSH CREEK	MONO LAKE	MONO CRATERS	X		X		
SLINKARD CREEK	TOPAZ LAKE	TOPAZ	X	X	X		
SUMMERS CREEK	GREEN CREEK	MATTERHORN		X	X		
SWAUGER CREEK	BUCKEYE CREEK	FALES HT SPRNG	X		X		
VIRGINIA CREEK	WALKER RVR, EF	BODIE	X	X	X		
WALKER CREEK	RUSH CREEK	MONO CRATERS		X			

RIVER/STREAM	TRIBUTARY TO	TOPO MAP	RB	BK	BN	GN	CT
WALKER RIVER, EF	WALKER LAKE	BRIDGEPORT	X		X		
WALKER RIVER, EF	BRIDGEPORT RES	BRIDGEPORT	X	X	X		
WALKER RIVER, WF	TOPAZ LAKE	TOPAZ	X	X	X		
WILSON CREEK	MONO LAKE	BODIE	X	X	X		
WOLF CREEK	WALKER RVR, WF	SONORA PASS	X	X			

NEVADA COUNTY RIVERS

RIVER/STREAM	TRIBUTARY TO	TOPO MAP	RB	BK	BN	GN	CT
ALDER CREEK	PROSSER CREEK RES.	TRUCKEE	X	X	X		
BEAR RIVER	ROLLINS RESERVOIR	COLFAX	X		X		
BLOODY RUN CREEK	YUBA RVR, MF	ALLEGHANY	X	X	X		
CANYON CREEK	YUBA RVR, SF	EMIGRANT GAP	X	X	X		
CANYON CREEK	BOWMAN LAKE	EMIGRANT GAP	X	X	X		
DEER CREEK, NF	DEER CREEK	N. BLOOMFIELD	X	X			
DEER CREEK, SF	DEER CREEK	N. BLOOMFIELD	X	X			
DIAMOND CREEK	YUBA RVR, SF	EMIGRANT GAP	X				
DONNER CREEK	TRUCKEE RVR	TRUCKEE	X	X	X		
DRY CREEK	BOCA RESERVOIR	TRUCKEE	X				
EAST FORK CREEK	YUBA, MF	EMIGRANT GAP	?	X	L		
FALL CREEK	YUBA, SF	EMIGRANT GAP	X	X			
FORDYCE CREEK	LAKE SPAULDING	EMIGRANT GAP	X	X	X		
FORDYCE CREEK	FORDYCE LAKE	DONNER PASS	X	X			
GRANITE CREEK	FORDYCE CREEK	EMIGRANT GAP	X	X			
HUMBUG CREEK	YUBA RVR, SF	N. BLOOMFIELD	X				
JUNIPER CREEK	TRUCKEE RVR	TRUCKEE	X	X	X		
MACKLIN CREEK	LOWER CASTLE CREEK	SIERRA CITY	L				
MARTIS CREEK	MARTIS CREEK RES.	TRUCKEE	X	X	X	L	
NORTH CREEK	FORDYCE LAKE	DONNER PASS	X	X			
POORMAN CREEK	YUBA RVR, SF	ALLEGHANY	X	X	X		
POORMAN CREEK, SF	POORMAN CREEK	ALLEGHANY	X	X			
PROSSER CREEK	TRUCKEE RVR	TRUCKEE	X	X	X		
PROSSER CREEK, NF	PROSSER CREEK	TRUCKEE	X	X	X		
PROSSER CREEK, SF	PROSSER CREEK	TRUCKEE	X	X	X		
SAGEHEN CREEK	STAMPEDE RESERVOIR	TRUCKEE	X	X	X		
STEEPHOLLOW CREEK	BEAR RVR	COLFAX	X	X			
STEEPHOLLOW CREEK	STEEPHOLLOW CREEK	ALLEGHANY	X				
TEXAS CREEK	CANYON CREEK	EMIGRANT GAP	X	X	X		
THOMPSON CREEK	FORDYCE CREEK	DONNER PASS	X				
TROUT CREEK	TRUCKEE RVR	TRUCKEE	X	X	X		
TRUCKEE RIVER	PYRAMID LAKE	TRUCKEE	X	X	X	L	
YUBA RIVER, NF	4,000'	SIERRA CITY	X	X	X		
YUBA RIVER, SF	LAKE SPAULDING	EMIGRANT GAP	X	X	X	X	
YUBA RIVER, SF	4,000'	EMIGRANT GAP	X	X	X		

PLACER COUNTY RIVERS

RIVER/STREAM	TRIBUTARY TO	TOPO MAP	RB	BK	BN	GN	CT
AMERICAN RVR, EF OF NF	AMERICAN RVR, NF OF NF	DUNCAN PEAK	X		X		
AMERICAN RVR, MF	FRENCH MDW RESERVOIR	GRANITE CHIEF	X	X	X		
AMERICAN RVR, NF	AMERICAN RVR	GRANITE CHIEF	X	X	X		
AMERICAN RVR, NF OF NF	AMERICAN RVR, NF	COLFAX	X		X		
BARKER CREEK	RUBICON RVR	GRANITE CHIEF	X	X	X		
BEAR RIVER	ROLLINS RESERVOIR	COLFAX	X		X		
BIG GRANITE CREEK	AMERICAN RVR, NF	DUNCAN PEAK	X		X		
BIG GRIZZLY CYN CREEK	RUBICON RVR	GRANITE CHIEF			X		
BIG MOSQUITO CREEK	AMERICAN RVR, MF	DUNCAN PEAK	X				
BLACKWOOD CREEK	LAKE TAHOE	TAHOE	X	X	X		
BLUE CANYON CREEK	AMERICAN RVR, NF OF NF	DUNCAN PEAK	X		X		
BURNETT CANYON CREEK	AMERICAN RVR, EF OF NF	DUNCAN PEAK	X				
CEDAR CREEK	AMERICAN RVR, NF	DONNER PASS		X			
DEEP CANYON CREEK	AMERICAN RVR, WFOF MF	DUNCAN PEAK		X			
DUNCAN CANYON CREEK	AMERICAN RVR, MF	DUNCAN PEAK	X	X	X		
EL DORADO CYN CREEK	EL DORADO CANYON	DUNCAN PEAK	X		X		
EL DORADO CYN CREEK	EL DORADO CANYON	DUNCAN PEAK	X		X		
FIVE LAKES CREEK	HELL HOLE RESERVOIR	GRANITE CHIEF	X	X	X		
FULDA CREEK	AMERCIAN RVR, NF OF NF	DUNCAN PEAK	X		X		
GRAYHORSE CREEK	HELL HOLE RESERVOIR	GRANITE CHIEF	X	X			
GROUSE CREEK	AMERICAN RVR, NF OF MF	DUNCAN PEAK	X		X		

RIVER/STREAM	TRIBUTARY TO	TOPO MAP	RB	BK	BN	GN	CT
HUMBUG CANYON CR	AMERICAN RVR, NF	DUNCAN PEAK	X	X	X		
LONG CYN CREEK, NF	LONG CANYON CREEK	DUNCAN PEAK	X				
LONG CYN CREEK, SF	LONG CANYON CREEK	DUNCAN PEAK	X				
MARTIS CREEK	TRUCKEE RVR	TRUCKEE	X	X	X		L
ONION CREEK	AMERICAN RVR, NF	DONNER PASS	X	X	X		
PALISADE CREEK	AMERICAN RVR, NF	GRANITE CHIEF	X	X	X		
PEAVINE CREEK	AMERICAN RVR, NF OF MF	DUNCAN PEAK	X				
PICAYUNE VALLEY CR	AMERICAN RVR, MF	GRANITE CHIEF	X	X			
SAILOR CANYON CRE	AMERICAN RVR, NF	GRANITE CHIEF		X			
SCREW AUGER CYN CREEK	AMERICAN RVR,NF OF MF	DUNCAN PEAK	X		X		
SECRET CANYON CREEK	AMERICAN RVR,NF OF MF	DUNCAN PEAK	X		X		
SQUAW VALLEY CREEK	TRUCKEE RVR	TAHOE CITY	X	X	X		
WABENA CREEK	AMERICAN RVR, NF	GRANITE CHIEF	X	X	X		
WARD CREEK	LAKE TAHOE	TAHOE	X		X		
WILDCAT CANYON CREEK	AMERICAN RVR, NF	GRANITE CHIEF	X				
YUBA RIVER, SF	LAKE SPAULDING	EMIGRANT GAP	X	X	X		

PLUMAS COUNTY RIVERS

RIVER/STREAM	TRIBUTARY TO	TOPO MAP	RB	BK	BN	GN	CT
BEAR CREEK	FEATHER RVR, MF	BUCKS LAKE	X				
BIG GRIZZLY CREEK	LAKE DAVIS	BLAIRSDEN	X		X		
CHIPS CREEK	FEATHER RVR, NF	JONESVILLE	X				
DIXIE CREEK	RED CLOVER CREEK	PORTLOA	X		X		
DIXON CREEK	NELSON CREEK	QUINCY	X				
ESTRAY CREEK	GREENHORN CREEK	QUINCY	X	X			
FEATHER RVR, MF	PLUMAS COUNTY LINE	MOOREVILLE RDG	X		X		
FEATHER RVR, NF	FEATHER RVR	PORTOLA	X		X		
FEATHER RVR, NF OF MF	FEATHER RVR, NF	PORTOLA	X		X		
FEATHER RVR, SF	LITTLE GRASS RES.	DOWNIEVILLE	X				
FREEMAN CREEK	LITTLE LAST CHANCE	CHILCOOT	X				
GRAYEAGLE CREEK	FEATHER RVR, MF	BLAIRSDEN	X		X		
GREENHORN CREEK	SPANISH CREEK	QUINCY	X		X		
HOPKINS CREEK	NELSON CREEK	QUINCY	X				
JAMISON CREEK	FEATHER RVR, MF	BLAIRSDEN	X		X		
LITTLE GRIZZLY CREEK	YELLOW CREEK	JONESVILLE	X	X	X		
LITTLE LAST CHANCE	SIERRA VALLEY CHANNELS	PORTOLA	X		X		
LONG VALLEY CREEK	FEATHER RVR, MF	BLAIRSDEN	X		X		
MILL CREEK	BUCKS LAKE	BUCKS LAKE	X		X		
NELSON CREEK	FEATHER RVR, MF	QUINCY	X		X		
ONION VALLEY CREEK	FEATHER RVR, MF	BUCKS LAKE	X				
POPLAR CREEK	FEATHER RVR, MF	BLAIRSDEN	X		X		
RABBIT CREEK	SLATE CREEK	DOWNIEVILLE	X				
RED CLOVER CREEK	LAST CHANCE CREEK	PORTOLA	X		X		
ROCK CREEK	FEATHER RVR, NF	PORTOLA	X	X	X		
ROCK CREEK, EAST BRANCH	ROCK CREEK	BUCKS LAKE	X				
SILVER CREEK	SPANISH CREEK	BUCKS LAKE	X	X			
SMITH CREEK	FEATHER RVR, MF	BLAIRSDEN			X		
SODA CREEK	YELLOW CREEK	BLAIRSDEN	X	X			
SOLDIER CREEK	BUTT CREEK	BLAIRSDEN	X	X			
TAYLOR CREEK	GREENHORN CREEK	QUINCY	X				
WILLOW CREEK	FEATHER RVR, MF	SIERRA CITY	X		X		

SIERRA COUNTY RIVERS

RIVER/STREAM	TRIBUTARY TO	TOPO MAP	RB	BK	BN	GN	CT
BADENOUGH CANYON CREEK	SMITHNECK CREEK	LOYALTON	X	X	X		
BALLS CREEK	LONG VALLEY CREEK	LOYALTON			X		
BEAR VALLEY CREEK	SMITHNECK CREEK	LOYALTON	X	X	X		
BERRY CREEK	HAMLIN CREEK	SIERRAVILLE	X	X	X		
BLACKJACK RAVINE CREEK	JIM CROW CREEK	DOWNIEVILLE	X				
BONITA CREEK	COLD STREAM	SIERRAVILLE	X	X	X		
CHEROKEE CREEK	YUBA RVR, NF	STRAWBERRY VLY	X	X			
CHURCH CREEK	SALMON CREEK	SIERRA CITY	X	X			
COLD STREAM	SIERRA VALLEY CHANNELS	SIERRAVILLE	X	X	X		
COTTONWOOD CREEK	COLD STREAM	SIERRAVILLE	X	X	X		
DARK CANYON CREEK	SIERRA VALLEY CHANNELS	SIERRAVILLE			X		
DAVIES CREEK	STAMPEDE RESERVOIR	TRUCKEE	X	X	X		

RIVER/STREAM	TRIBUTARY TO	TOPO MAP	RB	BK	BN	GN	CT
DEER CREEK	YUBA RVR, NF	SIERRA CITY	X		X		
DOG CREEK	TRUCKEE RVR	LOYALTON		X			
DOWNIE RIVER	YUBA RVR, NF	DOWNIEVILLE	X		X		
DOWNIE RIVER, WF	DOWNIE RIVER	DOWNIEVILLE	X		X		
EMPIRE CREEK	LAVEZZOLA CREEK	DOWNIEVILLE	X	X			
FIDDLE CREEK	YUBA RVR, NF	GOODYEARS BAR	X	X	X		
GOODYEARS CREEK	YUBA RVR, NF	GOODYEARS BAR	X	X	X		
HAMLIN CREEK	SIERRA VALLEY CHANNELS	SIERRAVILLE		X			
HAYPRESS CREEK	YUBA RVR, NF	SIERRA CITY	X	X	X		
HOWARD CREEK	YUBA RVR, NF	SIERRA CITY	X	X			
HUMBUG CREEK	YUBA RVR, NF	GOODYEARS BAR	X				
INDEPENDENCE CREEK	LITTLE TRUCKEE RVR	DONNER PASS	X	X	X		X
LAVEZZOLA CREEK	DOWNIE RIVER	DOWNIEVILLE	X	X	X		
LITTLE CANYON CREEK	CANYON CREEK	GOODYEARS BAR	X		X		
LITTLE FIDDLE CREEK	FIDDLE CREEK	GOODYEARS BAR	X		X		
LITTLE TRUCKEE RIVER	BOCA RESERVOIR	TRUCKEE	X	X	X		
LONG VALLEY CREEK	HAYPRESS CREEK	SIERRA CITY	X		X		
MERRILL CREEK	DAVIES CREEK	LOYALTON	X	X	X		
OREGON CREEK	YUBA RVR, MF	CAMPTONVILLE	X		X		
PASS CREEK	YUBA RVR, MF	SIERRA CITY	X	X			
PAULEY CREEK	DOWNIE RVR	DOWNIEVILLE	X	X	X		
ROCK CREEK	YUBA RVR, NF	GOODYEARS BAR	X	X	X		
SALMON CREEK	YUBA RVR, NF	SIERRA CITY	X	X	X		
SLATE CREEK	YUBA RVR, NF	AMERICAN HOUSE	X		X		
SMITHNECK CREEK	SIERRA VALLEY CHANNELS	SIERRAVILLE	X	X	X		
SULPHER CREEK	FEATHER RVR, MF	SIERRA CITY	X	X	X		
TURNER CANYON CREEK	SIERRA VALLEY CHANNELS	SIERRAVILLE	X	X	X		
YUBA RIVER, MF	MILTON RESERVOIR	SIERRA CITY	X	X			
YUBA RIVER, MF	YUBA COUNTY LINE	CAMPTONVILLE	X		X		
YUBA RIVER, NF	NEW BULLARDS BAR RES	STRAWBERRY VLY	X	X			

TULARE COUNTY RIVERS

RIVER/STREAM	TRIBUTARY TO	TOPO MAP	RB	BK	BN	GN	CT
BEAR CREEK	TULE RVR	SPRINGVILLE	X				
BIG ARROYO CREEK	KERN RVR	KERN PEAK	G	X			
BIG MEADOWS CREEK	KINGS RVR	GIANT FOREST	X	X			
BRUSH CREEK	KERN RVR	KERNVILLE	X	X			
BUCK CREEK	KAWEAH RVR, M	TRIPLE DIVIDE PEAK	X				
CANNELL CREEK	KERN RVR	KERNVILLE	X	X			
CAPINERO CREEK	DEER CREEK	CA HOT SPRING	X	X			
CHAGOOPA CREEK	KERN RVR	KERN PEAK	G	X			
CLICKS CREEK	KERN RVR	HOCKETT PEAK	W				
COLD CREEK	KERN RVR	HOCKETT PEAK	X				
DEER CREEK	MORTON FLAT	WHITE RIVER	X	X			
DORST CREEK	KAWEAH RVR, N	GIANT FOREST	X	X			
DRY MEADOW CREEK	KERN RVR	KERNVILLE	X	X			
DURRWOOD CREEK	KERN RVR	HOCKETT PEAK	X	X			
ESHOM CREEK	KAWEAH RVR, N	GIANT FOREST	X				
FISH CREEK	KERN RVR, SF	KERNVILLE	X				
FISH CREEK	LITTLE KERN RVR	HOCKETT PEAK	W				
FREEMAN CREEK	KERN RVR	HOCKETT PEAK	X	X			
GOLDEN TROUT CREEK	KERN RVR	KERN PEAK	X				
GROUSE CREEK	KAWEAH RVR, SF	KAWEAH	X				
KAWEAH RVR, EF	KAWEAH RVR, M	KAWEAH	X	X	X		
KAWEAH RVR, MARBLE FK	KAWEAH RVR, M	GIANT FOREST	X	X	X		
KAWEAH RVR, MF	LAKE KAWEAH	KAWEAH	X	X			
KAWEAH RVR, NF	KAWEAH RVR, M	KAWEAH	X	X			
KAWEAH RVR, SF	LAKE KAWEAH	KAWEAH	X	X	X		
KERN RVR	KERN COUNTY LINE	KERNVILLE	X	X			
KERN RVR, SF	KERN COUNTY LINE	KERNVILLE	X	X	X		
KESSING CREEK	TULE RVR, SF	CAMP NELSON	X	X			
LITTLE KERN RIVER	KERN RVR	HOCKETT PEAK	G	?	?	W	
MANTER CREEK	KERN RVR, SF	KERNVILLE	X	X	X		
MOUNTAINEER CREEK	ALPINE CREEK	CAMP NELSON	X	X			
MULKEY CREEK	KERN RVR, SF	OLANCHA		X	X		
BIGGER RUBE CREEK	DEER CREEK	CA HOT SPRING	X	X			
NINE MILE CREEK	COLD CREEK	HOCKETT PEAK	X	X			
NOBE YOUNG CREEK	DRY MEADOW CR	CAMP NELSON	X	X			
APARKER MEADOW CREEK	SOUTH CREEK	CA HOT SPRING	X	X			
PEPPERMINT CREEK	KERN RVR	HOCKETT PEAK	X	X	X		
RATTLESNAKE CREEK	KERN RVR	KERN PEAK	X	X			
RATTLESNAKE CREEK	KERN RVR	HOCKETT PEAK	X	X			
REDWOOD CREEK	KAWEAH RVR, N	GIANT FOREST	X				
ROARING RIVER	FRESNO COUNTY	TRIPLE DIVIDE PEAK	X				
ROCK CREEK	KERN RVR	KERN PEAK	X				
SALMON CREEK	KERN RVR	KERNVILLE	X	X	X		
SODA CREEK	BIG ARROYO CREEK	KERN PEAK	X				
SODA CREEK	KERN RVR	HOCKETT PEAK	X				
SODA SPRING CREEK	LITTLE KERN RVR	MINERAL KING	W				
SODA SPRING CREEK	SODA SPRING CR	MINERAL KING	W				
SOUTH CREEK	KERN RVR	KERNVILLE	X				
TOBIAS CREEK	KERN RVR	KERNVILLE	X				
TROUT CREEK	KERN RVR, SF	KERNVILLE	X	X	X		
TULE RIVER, NF	TULE RVR	SPRINGVILLE	X	X			
TULE RIVER, NF OF MF	TULE RVR, MF	CAMP NELSON	X	X			
TULE RIVER, SF	LAKE SUCCESS	SPRINGVILLE	X	X	X		
TULE RIVER, SF OF MF	TULE RIVER, MF	CAMP NELSON	X	X			
TYLER CREEK	DEER CREEK	CA HOT SPRING	X	X			
TYNDAL CREEK	KERN RVR	MT. WHITNEY	X	?	X		
WALLACE CREEK	KERN RVR	MT. WHITNEY	X				
WHITMAN CREEK	HORSE CREEK	MINERAL KING	X				
WHITNEY CREEK	KERN RVR	MT. WHITNEY	X				

TUOLUMNE COUNTY RIVERS

RIVER/STREAM	TRIBUTARY TO	TOPO MAP	RB	BK	BN	GN	CT
ACKERSON CREEK	TUOLUMNE RVR	LAKE ELEANOR	X		X		
ALKALI CREEK	TUOLUMNE RVR	TUOLUMNE MDW	X	X			
BIG RATTLESNAKE CR	STANISLAUS, NF	BIG MEADOW	X	X	X		
BOURLAND CREEK	LOONEY CREEK	LONG BARN	X				
BREEZE CREEK	TUOLUMNE RVR	HETCH HETCH	X				
CATHEDRAL CREEK	TUOLUMNE RVR	HETCH HETCHY		X			
CATHEDRAL CREEK, SF	CATHEDRAL CREEK	TUOLUMNE MDW		X			
CHERRY CREEK	CHERRY LAKE	PINECREST		X			
CHERRY CREEK	TUOLUMNE RVR	LAKE ELEANOR	X		X		
CHERRY CREEK, EF	CHERRY CREEK	PINECREST	X	X			
CHERRY CREEK, EF	HUCKLEBERRY LAKE	TOWER PEAK	X	X			
CHERRY CREEK, NF	CHERRY CREEK	PINECREST	X				
CHERRY CREEK, NF	EMIGRANT LAKE	PINECREST	X				
CHERRY CREEK, NF	EMIGRANT LAKE	TOWER PEAK	X	X			
CHERRY CREEK, WF	CHERRY CREEK	PINECREST	X	X			
CLAVEY RIVER	TUOLUMNE RVR	JAWBONE RIDGE	X		X		
COMPOODLE CREEK	SMOOTHWIRE CREEK	BIG MEADOW	X	X			
CONNESS CREEK	TUOLUMNE RVR	TUOLUMNE MDW	X	X			
COTTONWOOD CREEK	CLAVEY RVR	DUCKWALL MT	X				
COTTONWOOD CREEK	CHERRY LAKE	LAKE ELEANOR	X				
COTTONWOOD CREEK	TUOLUMNE RVR, MF	LAKE ELEANOR	X		X		
COW CREEK	BEARDSLEY LAKE	LONG BARN	X				
DEADMAN CREEK	STANISLAUS RVR, MF	SONORA PASS	X	X			
DELANEY CREEK	TUOLUMNE RVR	TUOLUMNE MDW		X			X
DOUGLAS CREEK	STANISLAUS, MF	DARDANELLE	X	X			
DRY MEADOW CREEK	STANISLAUS, MF	LONG BARN	X	X			
EAGLE CREEK	ROSE CREEK	COLUMBIA	X				
ELEANOR CREEK	LAKE ELEANOR	LAKE ELEANOR	X				
ELEANOR CREEK	CHERRY CREEK	LAKE ELEANOR	X	X			
FALLS CREEK	HETCH HETCHY	LAKE ELEANOR	X				
FISCHER CREEK	SKULL CREEK	LONG BARN	X				
FROG CREEK	LAKE ELEANOR	LAKE ELEANOR	X				
HERRING CREEK	STANISLAUS RVR, SF	PINECREST	X	X			
HIGHLAND CREEK	STANISLAUS RVR, SF	BIG MEADOW	X	X	X		
HULL CREEK	CLAVEY RVR	LONG BARN	X				
JAWBONE CREEK	TUOLUMNE RVR, LYE	LAKE ELEANOR	X				
KENDRICK CREEK	ELEANOR CREEK	PINECREST	X				
KENNEDY CREEK	STANISLAUS RVR, MF	SONORA PASS	X	X	X		
KIBBIE CREEK	LAKE ELEANOR	LAKE ELEANOR	X				
ALOONEY CREEK	REED CREEK	LONG BARN	X				
AMATTERHORN CANYON CREEK	RETURN CREEK	TUOLUMNE MDW	X	X			
MILL CREEK	STANISLAUS RVR	BIG MEADOW	X				
MORRISON CREEK	TUOLUMNE RVR	HETCH HETCH	X				
NIAGRA CREEK	STANISLAUS, MF	DARDANELLE CONE	X				
PARKER PASS CREEK	TUOLUMNE MDW	TUOLUMNE MDW	X	X	X		
PIUTE CREEK	TUOLUMNE RVR	HETCH HECTHY	X	X			
RANCHERIA CREEK	HETCH HETCHY RES.	HETCH HECTHY	X				
REED CREEK	CLAVEY RVR	DUCKWALL MT	X		X		
REGISTER CREEK	TUOLUMNE RVR	HETCH HETCH	X	X			
RETURN CREEK	TUOLUMNE RVR	TUOLUMNE MDW	X	X			
REYNOLDS CREEK	REED CREEK	LONG BARN	X				
ROCK CREEK	CLAVEY RVR	LONG BARN	X				
SHOOFLY CREEK	STANISLAUS RVR, MF	BIG MEADOW	X		X		
SKULL CREEK	GRISWOLD CREEK	LONG BARN	X				
SOAP CREEK	GRISWOLD CREEK	COLUMBIA	X				
SPILLER CREEK	RETURN CREEK	TUOLUMNE MDW	X				
STANISLAUS RVR, SF	PINECREST LAKE	PINECREST	X				
STANISLAUS RVR, SF	LYON'S RESERVOIR	LONG BARN	X				
SUGARPINE CREEK	TUOLUMNE RVR, NF	LONG BARN	X		X		
STANISLAUS, CLARK FK	STANISLAUS RVR, MF	DARDANELLE	X	X	X		
STANISLAUS RVR, MF	BEARDSLEY LAKE	LONG BARN	X	X	X		
STANISLAUS RVR, NF	STANISLAUS	COLUMBIA	X	X	X		
SUMMIT CREEK	RELIEF RESERVOIR	SONORA PASS	X	X			
SILDEN CREEK	FALLS CREEK	TOWER PEAK	X				
TILDEN CANYON CREEK	RANCHERIA	TOWER PEAK	X				
TILTILL CREEK	HETCH HETCHY RES.	HETCH HETCHY	X				
TOMPSON CANYON CREEK	RANCHERIA	TOWER PEAK	X				
TROUT CREEK	CLAVEY RVR	LONG BARN	X				
TUOLUMNE RIVER	HETCH HETCHY RES.	HETCH HETCHY	X	X	X		
TUOLUMNE RVR, DANA FK	TUOLUMNE RVR	TUOLUMNE MDW	X	X			
TUOLUMNE RVR, LYELL FK	TUOLUMNE RVR	TUOLUMNE MDW	X	X			
TUOLUMNE RVR, MF	TUOLUMNE RVR, SF	JAWBONE RIDGE	X	X			
TUOLUMNE RVR, NF	TUOLUMNE RVR	LONG BARN	X	X			
TUOLUMNE RVR, SF	TUOLUMNE RVR	JAWBONE RIDGE	X	X			
TWO MILE CREEK	CLAVEY RVR	LONG BARN	X				
WRIGHTS CREEK	TUOLUMNE RVR, NF	LONG BARN					

ALPINE COUNTY LAKES

LAKE	TRIBUTARY TO	TOPO MAP	ELEV.	RB	BK	BN	GN	CT	LK
ALPINE	WOLF CREEK	DARDANELLES CONE	7300	X	X				
ASA	WOLF CREEK	MARKLEEVILLE	9000		X				
BEEBE, LOWER	SUMMIT CITY CREEK	SILVER LAKE	8500		?				
BEEBE, UPPER	LOWER BEEBE LAKE	SILVER LAKE	8600		X				
BLUE, LOWER	BLUE CREEK	SILVER LAKE	8055	X	?			L	
BLUE, UPPER	LOWER BLUE LAKE	SILVER LAKE	8131	X				L	
BOULDER	BOULDER CREEK	SONORA PASS	8240		X				
BULL	WOLF CREEK	MARKLEEVILLE	8400					P	
BULL RUN	NF STANISLAUS RVR	DARDANELLES CONE	8500		X				
BURNSIDE	CHERRY VALLEY CREEK	MARKLEEVILLE	8800	X	X				
CAPLES	CAPLES CREEK	SILVER LAKE	7800	X	X				X
CRATER LAKE	RED LAKE CREEK	MARKLEEVILLE	8500		X				
DOROTHY	KINNEY RESERVOIR	MARKLEEVILLE	8700				X	L	
ELEPHANT ROCK	NF STANISLAUS RVR	DARDANELLES CONE	7100	X	X				
EMIGRANT	NF STANISLAUS RVR	SILVER LAKE	9000		X				
EVERGREEN	MEADOWS LAKE	MARKLEEVILLE	8500					L	
FOURTH OF JULY	SUMMIT CITY CREEK	SILVER LAKE	8600	X	X				
FROG	NF MOKELUMNE RVR	MARKLEVILLE	9000		X				
FROG	NO OUTLET	MARKLEEVILLE	8050	X	X				
GRANITE	UPPER BLUE LAKE	MARKLEEVILLE	8800					L	
GROUSE	SUMMIT CITY CREEK	SILVER LAKE	8400	X				L	
HEENAN	MONITOR CREEK	TOPAZ LAKE	7084					L	
HEISER	NF STANISLAUS RVR	DARDANELLES CONE	8500		X				
HELL HOLE	PLEASANT VALLEY CREEK	MARKLEVILLE	8000				X		
HIDDEN	NO OUTLET	SONORA PASS	8000	X					
HIGHLAND, LOWER	NF MOKELUMNE RVR	DARDANELLES CONE	8600		X				
HIGHLAND, UPPER	HIGHLAND CREEK	DARDANELLES CONE	8600		X				
INDIAN CREEK	CARSON RIVER	MARKLEEVILLE	5560	X					
KINNEY MEADOWS	SILVER CREEK	MARKLEEVILLE	8316	X	X				
KINNEY, LOWER	SILVER CREEK	MARKLEEVILLE	8743					L	
KINNEY, UPPER	SILVER CREEK	MARKLEEVILLE	8800					L	
LILY PAD	PLEASANT VALLEY CREEK	MARKLEEVILLE	8000		X				
LOST, LOWER	WF CARSON RVR	MARKLEEVILLE	8750		X				
LOST, UPPER	WF CARSON RVR	MARKLEEVILLE	8700		X				
MEADOW	NF MOKELUMNE RVR	MARKLEEVILLE	7769					L	
MEISS	UPPER TRUCKEE RVR	SILVER LAKE	8350		?			L	
MOSQUITO, LOWER	STANISLAUS RVR	MARKLEEVILLE	8400	X	?				
MOSQUITO, UPPER	STANISLAUS RVR	MARKLEEVILLE	8400	X	?				
NOBLE	NOBLE CREEK	MARKLEVILLE	8200		X				
POISON	POISON CREEK	SONORA PASS	9000		X		X		
PRARIE (SUMMIT)	NO OUTLET	MARKLEEVILLE	6200		X				
PRIDE	SPICER MEADOW RESERVOIR	DARDANELLES CONE	7000	X	X				
RAYMOND	PLEASANT VALLEY CREEK	MARKLEEVILLE	9157				X		
RED	RED LAKE CREEK	MARKLEEVILLE	7875		X				
ROCK	WILDERNESS CREEK	SILVER LAKE	7300	X					
ROUND TOP	WOODS LAKE	SILVER LAKE	9400				X		
SCOTTS	WF CARSON RVR	MARKLEEVILLE	8202	X	X				
SCOUT CARSON	SILVER LAKE	SILVER LAKE	9100		X		X		
SPICER MEADOW	HIGHLAND CREEK	DARDANELLES CONE	6421	X	X				
SUMMIT	DEER CREEK	MARKLEEVILLE	8000					L	
SUMMIT MEADOW	SILVER LAKE	SILVER LAKE	8500		X				
SUNSET, LOWER	PLEASANT VALLEY CREEK	MARKLEEVILLE	8038		X				
SUNSET, UPPER	LOWER SUNSET LAKE	MARKLEEVILLE	8067		X				
SWORD	HIGHLAND CREEK	DARDANELLES CONE	6850		X				
TAMARACK	SILVER KING CREEK	SONORA PASS	8000					P	
TAMARACK	PLEASANT VALLEY CREEK	MARKLEEVILLE	8000					L	
THREE QUARTERS	NF STANISLAUS RVR	DARDANELLES CONE	7200		X				
TWIN	MEADOW LAKE	DARDANELLES CONE	8172		X			L	
UNION	NF STANISLAUS RVR	DARDANELLES CONE	6880	X					
UTICA	NF STANISLAUS RVR	DARDANELLES CONE	6775	X					
VIRGINIA, LOWER	PLEASANT VALLEY CREEK	MARKLEEVILLE	8000					L	
VIRGINIA, UPPER	PLEASANT VALLEY CREEK	MARKLEEVILLE	8000		X				
WHEELER	JACKASS CANYON CREEK	MARKLEEVILLE	7850		X				
WHITECLIFF	SILVER KING CREEK	SONORA PASS	9709				?	?	
WINNAMUCCA	WOOD LAKE	MARKLEEVILLE	8642	X					
WOODS	TWIN LAKES RESERVOIR	SILVER LAKE	8390	X	X				

AMADOR COUNTY LAKES

LAKE	TRIBUTARY TO	TOPO MAP	ELEV.	RB	BK	BN	GN	CT	LK
BEAR RIVER, LOWER	BEAR RIVER	SILVER LAKE	5820	X		X			X
BEAR RIVER, UPPER	BEAR RIVER	LEEK SPRING HILL	5880	X					X
BLACK ROCK	NF MOKELUMNE RVR	SILVER LAKE	7900		X				
COLE CREEK, NORTH	COLE CREEK	SILVER LAKE	8120		X				
COLE CREEK, SOUTH	COLE CREEK	SILVER LAKE	8100		X				
DEVIL'S	TRAGEDY CREEK	SILVER LAKE	7000		X				
DEVIL'S HOLE	SILVER LAKE	SILVER LAKE	8300		X				
GRANITE	SILVER LAKE	SILVER LAKE	7800		X				
SHRINER	TANGLEFOOT CANYON	SILVER LAKE	6850	X					
SILVER	SILVERFORK OF THE AMERICA	SILVER LAKE	7260	X	X	X			X

EL DORADO COUNTY LAKES

LAKE	TRIBUTARY TO	TOPO MAP	ELEV.	RB	BK	BN	GN	CT	LK
ALOHA	PYRAMID CREEK	FALLEN LEAF LAKE	8115		X				
ALTA MORRIS	SUSIE LAKE	FALLEN LEAF LAKE	8100		X		X		
AMERICAN	PYRAMID CREEK	FALLEN LEAF LAKE	8100		X				
ANGORA, LOWER	ANGORA CREEK	FALLEN LEAF LAKE	7500					L	
ANGORA, UPPER	LOWER ANGORA LAKE	FALLEN LEAF LAKE	7500					L	
AUDRIAN	SF AMERICAN RVR	FALLEN LEAF LAKE	7200	X	?				
AVALANCHE	PYRAMID CREEK	FALLEN LEAF LAKE	7500	X	X				
AZURE	CASCADE LAKE	FALLEN LEAF LAKE	7625	X	X				
BARRETT	SILVER CREEK	FALLEN LEAF LAKE	7800	X	X				
BERTS	ROCKY BASIN CREEK	ROBBS PEAK	6750	X	X				
BISBEE	LOON LAKE	ROBBS PEAK	6352		X				
BOOMERANG	TWIN LAKE	FALLEN LEAF LAKE	8050		X				
BUCK ISLAND	RUBICON RIVER	GRANITE CHIEF	6346	X	X	X			
BUGLE	NO OUTLET	GRANITE CHIEF	6800		X				
CAGWIN	TAMARACK LAKE	FALLEN LEAF LAKE	7800	X					
CASCADE	LAKE TAHOE	FALLEN LEAF LAKE	6464	X		X		L	X
CATHEDRAL	FALLEN LEAF LAKE	FALLEN LEAF LAKE	7500				X		
CHANNEL	PYRAMID CREEK	FALLEN LEAF LAKE	8100		X				
CLIFF	STONEY RIDGE LAKE	FALLEN LEAF LAKE	8380		X				
CLYDE	RUBICON RVR	FALLEN LEAF LAKE	8200				X		
CODY	CODY CREEK	FALLEN LEAF LAKE	7000		X				
CRAG	MEEKS CREEK	FALLEN LEAF LAKE	7400	X	X	X			
CUP	SF AMERICAN RVR	FALLEN LEAF LAKE	8700				X		
DARDANELLES	UPPER TRUCKEE RVR	FALLEN LEAF LAKE	7750		X				
DARK	SILVER CREEK	FALLEN LEAF LAKE	7770	X		X			
DESOLATION	ROPI LAKE	FALLEN LEAF LAKE	8000		X				
DICKS	EAGLE CREEK	FALLEN LEAF LAKE	8420	X					
DIPPER	MEEKS CREEK	FALLEN LEAF LAKE	7900		X				
EAGLE	EAGLE CREEK	FALLEN LEAF LAKE	7200	X					
ECHO, LOWER	ECHO CREEK	FALLEN LEAF LAKE	7414	X	X			L	
ECHO, UPPER	LOWER ECHO LAKE	FALLEN LEAF LAKE	7415	X					
EDSON	PILOT CREEK	SADDLE MOUNTAIN	4270	X					
ELBERT	UPPER TRUCKEE RVR	FALLEN LEAF LAKE	7550	X	X				
ELLIOT	UNNAMED LAKE 2	ROBBS PEAK	8700				X		
FALLEN LEAF	TAYLOR CREEK	FALLEN LEAF LAKE	6375	X		X			X
FRANCIS	ROCKY BASIN CREEK	ROBBS PEAK	6250	X					
FRATA	PYRAMID CREEK	FALLEN LEAF LAKE	8200		X				
FAWN	RUBICON RVR	TAHOE	6400	X					
FLOATING ISLAND	LAKE TAHOE	FALLEN LEAF LAKE	7200		X				
FONTANILLIS	EAGLE CREEK	FALLEN LEAF LAKE	8400		X				
FORNI	SILVER CREEK	ROBBS PEAK	7650				X		
FORNI	FORNI CREEK	FALLEN LEAF LAKE	7800		X				
FOUR LAKES, LOWER	UPPER TRUCKEE RVR	SILVER LAKE	8300				?		
FOUR LAKES, MIDDLE	UPPER TRUCKEE RVR	SILVER LAKE	8300				?		
FOUR LAKES, UPPER	UPPER TRUCKEE RVR	SILVER LAKE	8300				?		
FOX	RUBICON RVR	FALLEN LEAF LAKE	6700		X				
GEFO	TOTEM LAKE	FALLEN LEAF LAKE	8300		X				
GEM	SILVER CREEK	FALLEN LEAF LAKE	7900		X				
GENEVIEVE	MEEKS CREEK	FALLEN LEAF LAKE	7350		X	X			
GERLE	SF RUBICON RVR	ROBBS PEAK	5231	X		X			
GERTRUDE	SILVER CREEK	FALLEN LEAF LAKE	7800				X		
GILMORE	GLEN ALPINE CREEK	FALLEN LEAF LAKE	8300	X					X

LAKE	TRIBUTARY TO	TOPO MAP	ELEV.	RB	BK	BN	GN	CT	LK
GRANITE	LAKE TAHOE	FALLEN LEAF LAKE	7700		X				
GRASS	GLEN ALPINE CREEK	FALLEN LEAF LAKE	7200	X					
GRASS	GRASS LAKE CREEK	FREEL PEAK	7706		X				
GROUSE	WRIGHTS LAKE	FALLEN LEAF LAKE	7700	X					
GROUSE, LOWER	EAGLE CREEK	FALLEN LEAF LAKE	7820		X				
GROUSE, UPPER	EAGLE CREEK	FALLEN LEAF LAKE	8300		X				
HALFMOON	SUSIE LAKE	FALLEN LEAF LAKE	8150	X	X				
HEATHER	GLEN ALPINE CREEK	FALLEN LEAF LAKE	7900	X		X			
HEMLOCK	GROUSE LAKE	FALLEN LEAF LAKE	8100		X				
HIDDEN	CRAG LAKE	FALLEN LEAF LAKE	7300	X	X			L	
HIGHLAND	RUBICON RVR	FALLEN LEAF LAKE	7820	X					
HORSESHOE	RUBICON RVR	FALLEN LEAF LAKE	7550		X				
HUTH	NO OUTLET	ROBBS PEAK	7560					L	
ICE HOUSE	AMERICAN RVR	ROBBS PEAK	5437	X		X			
ISLAND	TWIN LAKES	FALLEN LEAF LAKE	8160				X		
ISLAND, LOWER	WRIGHTS LAKE	FALLEN LEAF LAKE	7900					?	
JABU	NO OUTLET	FALLEN LEAF LAKE	8450				X		
JUNCTION	SILVER CREEK	ROBBS PEAK	4450	X	X				
KALMIA	AZURE LAKE	FALLEN LEAF LAKE	8450				X		
KIRKWOOD	CAPLES CREEK	SILVER LAKE	7700	X	X				
LAKE OF THE WOOD	ROPI LAKE	FALLEN LEAF LAKE	8060		X				
LAWRENCE	SILVER CREEK	FALLEN LEAF LAKE	7900	X	X	?			
LE CONTE	HEATHER LAKE	FALLEN LEAF LAKE	8300		X				
LELAND, LOWER	McCONNELL LAKE	FALLEN LEAF LAKE	8150				X		
LELAND, UPPER	McCONNELL LAKE	FALLEN LEAF LAKE	8180				X		
LOIS	RUBICON RIVER	FALLEN LEAF LAKE	8400		X				
LOON	GERLE CREEK	ROBBS PEAK	6410	X					
LOST	GENERAL CREEK	TAHOE	7780	X	X				
LOST	GLEN ALPINE CREEK	FALLEN LEAF LAKE	8200				X		
LOST	BASSI FORK	FALLEN LEAF LAKE	7700	X			X		
LUCILLE	GLEN ALPINE CREEK	FALLEN LEAF LAKE	8200		X				
LYONS	LYONS CREEK	FALLEN LEAF LAKE	8500		X				
MARGARET	CAPLES CREEK	SILVER LAKE	7500		X				
MARGERY	LAKE LUCILLE	FALLEN LEAF LAKE	6500		X				
MARY'S LAKE	LOON LAKE	ROBBS PEAK	6360		X				
MAUD	SILVER CREEK	FALLEN LEAF LAKE	7900	X	X				
McCONNELL	LELAND LAKE	FALLEN LEAF LAKE	7750				X		
NUMBER 3	SILVER CREEK	FALLEN LEAF LAKE	9000				X		
NUMBER 4	SILVER CREEK	FALLEN LEAF LAKE	8500		X		X		
NUMBER 5	SILVER CREEK	FALLEN LEAF LAKE	8000		X				
OSMA	NO OUTLET	FALLEN LEAF LAKE	7650		X				
PEARL	BIG SILVER LAKE	ROBBS PEAK	7500	X					
PHIPPS	RUBICON RIVER	FALLEN LEAF LAKE	8500		X		X		
PITT	PYRAMID LAKE	FALLEN LEAF LAKE	7700		X				
PYRAMID	PYRAMID CREEK	FALLEN LEAF LAKE	8300		X				
Q LAKE, LOWER	RUBICON RVR	FALLEN LEAF LAKE	7525		X				
Q LAKE, MIDDLE	LOWER Q LAKE	FALLEN LEAF LAKE	7575		X				
Q LAKE, UPPER	MIDDLE Q LAKE	FALLEN LEAF LAKE	7800		X				
RALSTON	CAGWIN LAKE	FALLEN LEAF LAKE	7800		X				
RICHARDSON	MILLER CREEK	TAHOE	7500		?				
ROCKBOUND	BUCK ISLAND LAKE	TAHOE	6529	X	X	X			
RODDIE	PLEASANT LAKE	GRANITE CHIEF	6900		X				
ROPI	PYRAMID CREEK	FALLEN LEAF LAKE	7800	?	X				
ROUND	UPPER TRUCKEE RVR	FALLEN LEAF LAKE	8200					L	
RUBICON	STONEY RIDGE LAKE	FALLEN LEAF LAKE	8500	X	X				
RUBICON DIVERSION	RUBICON RIVER	FALLEN LEAF LAKE	6548	X					
SAUCER	ECHO LAKE	FALLEN LEAF LAKE	8580				X		
SCHMIDELL	RUBICON RVR	FALLEN LEAF LAKE	7880		X				
SCHULER	PLEASANT LAKE	ROBBS PEAK	7600		X				
SECRET	SILVER CREEK	FALLEN LEAF LAKE	8300		X				
SHADOW	SF RUBICON RVR	ROBBS PEAK	7250	X					
SHADOW	CRAG LAKE	FALLEN LEAF LAKE	7650		X				
SHEALOR	N TRAGEDY CREEK	SILVER LAKE	7000		X				
SHOWERS	UPPER TRUCKEE RVR	SILVER LAKE	8600		X				
SIXTEEN SHOT	SF RUBICON RVR	ROBBS PEAK	6500		X				
SMITH	GROUSE LAKES	FALLEN LEAF LAKE	8400		X				
SNOW	CASCADE CREEK	FALLEN LEAF LAKE	7350		X				
SPIDER	RUBICON RVR	GRANITE CHIEF	6500	X	?				
STAR	COLD CREEK	FREEL PEAK	9200		X				

LAKE	TRIBUTARY TO	TOPO MAP	ELEV.	RB	BK	BN	GN	CT	LK
STONEY RIDGE	MEEKS CREEK	FALLEN LEAF LAKE	7820	X	X	X			X
SUSIE	GLEN ALPINE CREEK	FALLEN LEAF LAKE	7800	X	X				
SYLVIA	LYONS CREEK	FALLEN LEAF LAKE	8300		X				
TALLAC	SNOW CREEK	FALLEN LEAF LAKE	7900				X		
TAMARACK	TAMARACK CREEK	FALLEN LEAF LAKE	7820		X				
TOEM	PYRAMID LAKE	FALLEN LEAF LAKE	7800	X	?				
TOP	LAWRENCE LAKE	FALLEN LEAF LAKE	8800				X		
TRIANGLE	GLEN ALPINE CREEK	FALLEN LEAF LAKE	8020	X					
TWIN, LOWER	TWIN LAKE CREEK	FALLEN LEAF LAKE	7950	X					
TWIN, UPPER	TWIN LAKE RESERVOIR	FALLEN LEAF LAKE	7952	X					
TYLER	SILVER CREEK	FALLEN LEAF LAKE	8000		X				
UNION VALLEY	SILVER CREEK	ROBBS PEAK	4870	X		X			X
VELMA	EAGLE CREEK	FALLEN LEAF LAKE	7800	X	X				
4-Q, MIDDLE	PHIPPS CREEK	FALLEN LEAF LAKE	7300		X				
VELMA, LOWER	EAGLE CREEK	FALLEN LEAF LAKE	7760	X					
VELMA, MIDDLE	VELMA, LOWER	FALLEN LEAF LAKE	7800	X					
VELMA, UPPER	VELMA, MIDDLE	FALLEN LEAF LAKE	7840	X					
WACA	PYRAMID CREEK	FALLEN LEAF LAKE	8240		X				
WINIFRED	SPIDER LAKE	GRANITE CHIEF	6800		X				
WRIGHTS	SF SILVER CREEK	FALLEN LEAF LAKE	6941	X		X			
ZITELLA	RUBICON RVR	FALLEN LEAF LAKE	7660		X				

FRESNO COUNTY LAKES

LAKE	TRIBUTARY TO	TOPO MAP	ELEV.	RB	BK	BN	GN	CT	LK
"L"	FRENCH CANYON CREEK	MT. TOM	11050				X		
ALSACE	SF FRENCH CANYON	MT. TOM	11060				X		
AMBITION	NF KINGS RVR	MT. GODDARD	10800	X	X				
AMPHITHEATRE	MF KINGS RVR	MT. GODDARD	10706	X			X		
AMY	FISH CREEK	MT. ABBOTT	9950		X				
APOLLO	UPPER BEAR LAKE	MT. ABBOTT	10400				X		
ARCTIC	HORSESHOE LAKE	BLACKCAP MT.	11000				X		
ARROWHEAD	COLD CREEK	MT. ABBOTT	9800	X					
AVALANCHE	KAISER CREEK	KAISER PEAK	9000		X				
AWEETASAL	COUNCIL LAKE	MT. ABBOTT	11400				X		
BABY	SILVER CREEK	KAISER PEAK	9840	X	X				
BARRETT 1	PALISADE BASIN	MT. GODDARD	11500	X			X		
BARRETT 2	PALISADE BASIN	MT. GODDARD	11420	X					
BARRETT 3	PALISADE BASIN	MT. GODDARD	11500	X					
BATHTUB	RAINBOW LAKE	KAISER PEAK	9960		X				
BATTALION	REGIMENT LAKE	MT. GODDARD	11000	X					
BEAR CREEK RES.	BEAR CREEK	MT. ABBOTT	7350	X		X			
BEARPAW	URSA LAKE	MT. ABBOTT	11500				X		
BEARTRAP	HILGARD CREEK	MT. ABBOTT	11100				X		
BEARTWIN, EAST	BEAR CREEK	MT. ABBOTT	9600		X				
BEARTWIN, WEST	BEAR CREEK	MT. ABBOTT	9600		X				
BEETLEBUG	BEETLEBUG CANYON CREEK	KAISER PEAK	9680		X				
BENCH	SF KINGS RVR	MT. PINCHOT	10495	X		X			
BERYL	PITMAN CREEK	HUNTINGTON LAKE	8790		X				
BIG BEAR	LITTLE BEAR LAKE	MT. ABBOTT	11450				X		
BIG CHIEF	PINNACLES CREEK	MT. ABBOTT	10875				X		
BIGHORN	NF KINGS RVR	BLACKCAP MT.	10700	X					
BIG PINE	SF BIG PINE CREEK	BIG PINE	11600	X					
BIG HORN	NF MONO CREEK	MT. GODDARD	10525				X		
BILL	KAISER CREEK	KAISER PEAK	9600		X				
BLACK BEAR	BIG BEAR LAKE	MT. ABBOTT	11650				X		
BLACKROCK	FLEMING CREEK	BLACKCAP MT.	10500	X					
BLACKROCK RES.	NF KINGS RVR	PATTERSON MT.	4066	X		X			
BLUE CANYON 1	BLUE CANYON CREEK	MT. GODDARD	9600	X					
BLUE CANYON 2	BLUE CANYON CREEK	MT. GODDARD	9800	X					
BLUE CANYON 3	BLUE CANYON CREEK	MT. GODDARD	10020	?					
BLUE CANYON 4	BLUE CANYON CREEK	MT. GODDARD	10040	X					
BLUE CANYON 5	BLUE CANYON CREEK	MT. GODDARD	10360	?					
BLUE CANYON 6	BLUE CANYON CREEK	MT. GODDARD	10364	X					
BLUE CANYON 7	BLUE CANYON CREEK	MT. GODDARD	10700	?					
BLUE JAY 1	NF MONO CREEK	MT. ABBOTT	10200	X					
BLUE JAY 2	NF MONO CREEK	MT. ABBOTT	10200	X					
BOBBY	KAISER CREEK	KAISER PEAK	9700		X				
BONITA	SF SAN JOAQUIN	KAISER PEAK	10500				X		
BONNIE	KAISER CREEK	KAISER PEAK	9560	X					
BRAVE	FISH CREEK	MT. ABBOTT	9920		X				
BREWER	TAMARACK CREEK	HUNTINGTON LAKE	8750	X	X				
BROWN BEAR	TEDDY BEAR LAKE	MT. ABBOTT	11100				X		
BULLET	HOLSTER LAKE	BLACKCAP MT.	10800	X					
BULLFROG	HELMS CREEK	HUNTINGTON LAKE	9300	X	X				
BULLFROG	BUBBS CREEK	MT. PINCHOT	10660	X	X				
CAMP SIXTYONE	WF CAMP SIXTYONE CREEK	KAISER PEAK	8700		X				
CAMPFIRE	KAISER CREEK	KAISER PEAK	9700		X				
CARDINAL	UPPER BASIN	MT. PINCHOT	11444	?					
CATHEDRAL	MIDWAY LAKE	MT. GODDARD	10700	X					
CECIL	FISH CREEK	MT. MORRISON	11050	X					
CHAGRIN	SF FLEMING CREEK	MT. GODDARD	10350	X					
CHAIN, LOWER	NF KINGS	TEHIPITE DOME	9300		X				
CHAIN, UPPER	NF KINGS	TEHIPITE DOME	9400		X				
CHAMBERLAIN	HOOPER CREEK	MT. ABBOTT	10000				X		
CHAPEL	NF KINGS	MT. GODDARD	10700				X		
CHEVAUX	FRENCH CANYON CREEK	MT. ABBOTT	11000				X		
CHIEF	FISH CREEK	MT. ABBOTT	10000	X	X				
CHIMNEY	WOODCHUCK CREEK	BLACKCAP MT.	9500	X					
CIRQUE	BEAR CREEK	MT. ABBOTT	10400	X					
CLAW	VEE LAKE	MT. ABBOTT	11150				X		
CLIFF	HELMS CREEK	HUNTINGTON LAKE	9400	X	X				
COLLEGE	KAISER CREEK	KAISER PEAK	9500		X				
COLT	HORSEHEAD LAKE	BLACKCAP MT.	10300		X				
COMPLEAT	IZAAK WALTON LAKE	MT. ABBOTT	10600				X		
CONY	PIUTE CREEK	MT. TOM	11300		X		X		
CORBETT	BOLSILLO CREEK	KAISER PEAK	9000	?	X				
CORONET	EF BEAR CREEK	MT. ABBOTT	11700				X		
COTTON	FISH CREEK	MT. ABBOTT	10600				X		
COURTRIGHT RES.	HELMS CREEK	BLACKCAP MT.	8170	X	X	X			
COYOTE	BIG CREEK	KAISER PEAK	9000	X	X				
COYOTE	SILVER CREEK	KAISER PEAK	9600	X	X				
CRABTREE	FALL CREEK	BLACKCAP MT.	10500	X					
CRATER	HELL HOLE CREEK	KAISER PEAK	9300		X				
CRAZY	HOOPER CREEK	MT. ABBOTT	11200				?		
CROWN	SCEPTER CREEK	BLACKCAP MT.	9750	X					
CROWN BASIN, LOWER	CROWN CREEK	BLACKCAP MT.	9850				X		
CROWN BASIN, UPPER	CROWN CREEK	BLACKCAP MT.	10125				X		
CUB	BEAR CREEK	MT. ABBOTT	11000				X		
CUNNINGHAM	CAMP SIXTYONE CREEK	KAISER PEAK	9400		X				
DALE	FLEMING CREEK	BLACKCAP MT.	10200	X	X				
DARWIN 1	EVOLUTION CREEK	MT. GODDARD	11600				X		
DARWIN 2	EVOLUTION CREEK	MT. GODDARD	11680				X		
DARWIN 3	EVOLUTION CREEK	MT. GODDARD	11680				X		
DAVIS	FLEMING CREEK	BLACKCAP MT.	10500	X					
DEDE (LOST KEYS)	FISH CREEK	DEVILS POSTPILE	9950		X				
DEER	RANCHERIA CREEK	KAISER PEAK	9300	X	X				
DEER 1	DEER CREEK	MT. MORRISON	10600	X					
DEER 2	DEER CREEK	MT. MORRISON	10640	X					
DEER 3	DEER CREEK	MT. MORRISON	10840	X					
DEN	CLAW LAKE	MT. ABBOTT	11600				X		
DESOLATION, BIG	PIUTE CREEK	MT. TOM	11381				X		
DESOLATION, LITTLE	PIUTE CREEK	MT. TOM	11150				X		
DEVIL'S BATHTUB	COLD CREEK	MT. ABBOTT	9127	X	X				
DEVIL'S PUNCHBOWL	FLEMING CREEK	BLACKCAP MT.	10098	X	X				
DIAMOND X	FLEMING CREEK	BLACKCAP MT.	10830	X					
DINKEY 1	DINKEY CREEK	HUNTINGTON LAKE	9150	X	X	X			
DINKEY 2	DINKEY CREEK	HUNTINGTON LAKE	9650		X				
DISAPPOINTMENT	FLEMING CREEK	BLACKCAP MT.	10300	?	X				
DIVISION	NF KINGS RVR	BLACKCAP MT.	10700	X					
DORIS	MONO CREEK	KAISER PEAK	7000	X					
DORIS, LITTLE	SWAMP CREEK	KAISER PEAK	10000		X				
DOUBLE ELEVEN-O	SAN JOAQUIN RVR	MT. GODDARD	11106	X			X		
DRAGON	WOODS CREEK	MT. PINCHOT	11000		X				
DUCK	FISH CREEK	MT. MORRISON	10427	X	X				
DUCK	NF RANCHERIA	TEHIPITE DOME	9300	X	X				
DUMBELL 1	MF KINGS RVR	MT. GODDARD	11100	X					
DUMBELL 2	MF KINGS RVR	MT. GODDARD	10800	X					
DUMBELL 3	MF KINGS RVR	MT. GODDARD	10900	X					
DUMBELL 4	MF KINGS RVR	MT. GODDARD	11120	X			?		
DUSY BASIN 1	MF KINGS RVR	MT. GODDARD	10715	X					
DUSY BASIN 2	MF KINGS RVR	MT. GODDARD	10734	X					
DUSY BASIN 3	MF KINGS RVR	MT. GODDARD	10745	X			?		
DUSY BASIN 4	MF KINGS RVR	MT. GODDARD	11200	X			X		
DUSY BASIN 5	MF KINGS RVR	MT. GODDARD	11360	X			X		
DUSY BASIN 6	MF KINGS RVR	MT. GODDARD	11400	X			X		
DUSY BASIN 7	MF KINGS RVR	MT. GODDARD	11393	X					
DUTCH	FLORENCE LAKE	MT. ABBOTT	9100		X				
EASTERN BROOK	DINKEY CREEK	HUNTINGTON LAKE	9300		X				
EDISON, THOMAS	MONO CREEK	KAISER PEAK	7642	X	X	X			
ELBA	FRENCH CANYON	MT. TOM	10900				X		
ELEVEN 110	SF SAN JOAQUIN RVR	BLACKCAP MT.	11110	X					
ERSHIM	SF BIG CREEK	HUNTINGTON LAKE	7000	?	X				
EVOLUTION	EVOLUTION VALLEY CREEK	MT. GODDARD	10850				X		
EWE	FISH CREEK	MT. ABBOTT	10600				X		
EWE	RAM LAKE	MT. GODDARD	11100				X		
FEATHER	COLD CREEK	MT. ABBOTT	10400		X				
FERN	COYOTE LAKE	KAISER PEAK	9980	X	X				
FILLEY	HORSEHEAD LAKE	BLACKCAP MT.	10400		X				
FINGERBOWL	DINKEY CREEK	HUNTINGTON LAKE	9500	?	X				
FISCHER	BIG CREEK	HUNTINGTON LAKE	8600	X			?		
FLAT NOTE	MEDLEY	MT. ABBOTT	10600				X		
FLEMING	FLEMING CREEK	BLACKCAP MT.	9800		X				
FLOE	F LAKE	BLACKCAP MT.	11040				X		
FLORENCE	SF SAN JOAQUIN RVR	MT. ABBOTT	7327	X					
FOOLISH	HOOPER CREEK	MT. ABBOTT	11200				X		
FORSAKEN	PIUTE CREEK	MT. TOM	11500				X		
FOURTH RECESS	MONO CREEK	MT. ABBOTT	10125	X					
FRANKLIN 1	FISH CREEK	MT. MORRISON	10800				X		
FRANKLIN 2	FISH CREEK	MT. MORRISON	10900				X		
FRANKLIN 3	FISH CREEK	MT. MORRISON	11100				X		
FRENCH, BIG	FRENCH CANYON	MT. TOM	11240				X		
FRENCH, LITTLE	FRENCH CANYON	MT. TOM	11350				X		
FROG	SILVER CREEK	KAISER PEAK	9750	X	X				
FROG	MONO CREEK	MT. ABBOTT	10400	X					
FUNERAL	COLD CREEK	MT. ABBOTT	10000		X				
GEORGE	SAN JOAQUIN RVR	KAISER PEAK	9100		X				
GERALDINE, LOWER	RODGERS CREEK	TEHIPITE DOME	8700		X				
GERALDINE, UPPER	RODGERS CREEK	TEHIPITE DOME	9200	X	X				
GHOST	UPPER GRAVEYARD	MT. GODDARD	10500	X					
GLACIER 1	GLACIER CREEK	MT. GODDARD	10429				X		
GLACIER 2	GLACIER CREEK	MT. GODDARD	10540				?		
GLEN	PURPLE CREEK	MT. MORRISON	10700	X			X		
GLENETTE	GLEN LAKE	MT. MORRISON	10700				X		
GOETHE, LOWER	MURIEL LAKE	MT. GODDARD	11528				X		
GOETHE, UPPER	LOWER LOST LAKE	MT. GODDARD	11530				X		
GOLDEN	MONO CREEK	MT. ABBOTT	10950				X		
GOLDEN TROUT, LOWER	PIUTE CREEK	MT. GODDARD	10764				X		
GOLDEN TROUT, UPPER	PIUTE CREEK	MT. GODDARD	10790				X		
GORDON	HOOPER CREEK	MT. ABBOTT	9900				X		
GRANITE	GRANITE BASIN	MARION PEAK	10456		X				
GRASSY	MINNOW CREEK	MT. ABBOTT	9480	X	X		X		
GRAVEYARD, LOWER	GRAVEYARD CREEK	MT. ABBOTT	10000		X				
GRAVEYARD, UPPER	GRAVEYARD CREEK	MT. ABBOTT	10400	X					
GRINNEL	LAUREL CREEK	MT. ABBOTT	10810		X				
GROUSE	SF DINKEY CREEK	HUNTINGTON LAKE	9150		X				
GROUSE	SF KINGS RVR	MARION PEAK	10473	?					
GUEST	McGUIRE LAKE	BLACKCAP MT.	10200	?	X				
HALFMOON	NF KINGS RIVER	BLACKCAP MT.	9422	X	X				
HARVEY	HOOPER CREEK	MT. ABBOTT	10100				X		
HATCH	RUBY CREEK	HUNTINGTON LAKE	8900		X				
HEADSTONE	PUMICE LAKE	MT. GODDARD	10500		X				
HEART	SALLY KEYES LAKE	MT. ABBOTT	10490				X		
HELEN	MF KINGS RVR	MT. GODDARD	11612				X		
HELL-FOR-SURE	FLEMING CREEK	BLACKCAP MT.	10803		X				
HEMLOCK	NO OUTLET	DEVILS POSTPILE	10500	X					
HIDDEN	FLORENCE LAKE	BLACKCAP MT.	9100		X				

LAKE	TRIBUTARY TO	TOPO MAP	ELEV.	RB	BK	BN	GN	CT	LK
HIDDEN	WEST FALL	KAISER PEAK	8340		X				
HILGARD	NF HILGARD CREEK	MT. ABBOTT	11400		X				
HOBLER	BURNT CORRAL CREEK	BLACKCAP MT.	9000		X				
HOLSTER	WAH-HOO LAKE	BLACKCAP MT.	10700	X	X				
HONEYMOON, LOWER	PIUTE CREEK	MT. ABBOTT	9900				X		
HONEYMOON, UPPER	PIUTE CREEK	MT. ABBOTT	9100				X		
HOOF	FISH CREEK	MT. MORRISON	10700				X		
HOOPER	HOOPER CREEK	MT. ABBOTT	10500				X		
HOPKINS, LOWER	HOPKINS CREEK	MT. ABBOTT	10400	X	X				
HOPKINS, UPPER	HOPKINS CREEK	MT. ABBOTT	11060				?		
HORN	FISH CREEK	MT. MORRISON	10650				?		
HORSEHEAD	FALL CREEK	BLACKCAP MT.	10300	X	X				
HORSESHOE	FLEMING CREEK	BLACKCAP MT.	10700	X	X				
HORSESHOE 1	MF KINGS RVR	MARION PEAK	10560	X					
HORSESHOE 2	MF KINGS RVR	MARION PEAK	10500	?					
HORSESHOE 3	MF KINGS RVR	MARION PEAK	10500	?					
HORTENSE, LOWER	FISH CREEK	MT. ABBOTT	10499		X				
HORTENSE, UPPER	FISH CREEK	MT. ABBOTT	10500		X				
HUME	TEN MILE CREEK	TEHIPITE DOME	5200	X	X				
HUMMINGBIRD	CROWN CREEK	BLACKCAP MT.	10825		X				
HUMPHREYS, LOWER	PIUTE CREEK	MT. TOM	11800		X				
HUMPHREYS, MIDDLE	PIUTE CREEK	MT. TOM	11827		X				
HUMPHREYS, UPPER	PIUTE CREEK	MT. TOM	12003		X				
HUNTINGTON	BIG CREEK	HUNTINGTON LAKE	6950	X	X				
IDAHO	KAISER CREEK	KAISER PEAK	8800		X				
INDIAN, LOWER	FLEMING CREEK	BLACKCAP MT.	10070		X				
NDIAN, UPPER	FLEMING CREEK	BLACKCAP MT.	10500		X		?		
ISLAND	DINKEY CREEK	HUNTINGTON LAKE	9800				X		
ITALY	HILGARD CREEK	MT. ABBOTT	11130			X			
IZAAK WALTON	FISH CREEK	MT. ABBOTT	10350			X			
JAWBONE	COUNCIL LAKE	MT. ABBOTT	11500				X		
JEWEL	KAISER CREEK	KAISER PEAK	9900		X				
JIGGER, SHORT	FLEMING CREEK	BLACKCAP MT.	9850		X				
JIGGER, TALL	FLEMING CREEK	BLACKCAP MT.	9800		X				
JUMBLE	LAKE ITALY	MT. ABBOTT	11600				X		
KEARSARGE 1	BULLFROG CREEK	MT. PINCHOT	11040	X					
KEARSARGE 2	BULLFROG CREEK	MT. PINCHOT	10960	X					
KEARSARGE 3	BULLFROG CREEK	MT. PINCHOT	10800	X					
KID 1	SF KINGS RVR	MARION PEAK	10550	X					
KID 2	SF KINGS RVR	MARION PEAK	10570	X					
KID 3	SF KINGS RVR	MARION PEAK	10500	?					
KNOB	PIUTE CREEK	MT. TOM	10000				X		
LA SALLE	FRENCH CANYON CREEK	MT. TOM	11700				X		
LA TETE	FRENCH CANYON CREEK	MT. TOM	11500				X		
LADDER	MF KINGS RVR	MT. GODDARD	10491	X					
LAKE CAMP	EF BIG CREEK	KAISER PEAK	9730	X					
LAUREL	LAUREL CREEK	MT. ABBOTT	10270		X				
LEE	FISH CREEK	MT. ABBOTT	10980	X					
LINE CREEK	LINE CREEK	KAISER PEAK	9800		X				
LITTLE	HELMS CREEK	HUNTINGTON LAKE	9250	?	X				
LITTLE BEAR	EF BEAR CREEK	MT. ABBOTT	11300				X		
LITTLE CHIEF	SPEARPOINT CREEK	MT. ABBOTT	10800				X		
LITTLE JO	COLT	BLACKCAP MT.	10900		X		X		
LITTLE LOU	COLT LAKE	BLACKCAP MT.	10880				X		
LOBE, LOWER	PIUTE CREEK	BLACKCAP MT.	10500	X			X		
LOBE, UPPER	PIUTE CREEK	BLACKCAP MT.	10850				X		
LONE DOE	FALL CREEK	BLACKCAP MT.	10200		X				
LONE INDIAN	FISH CREEK	MT. ABBOTT	10300		X				
LONG	KAISER CREEK	MT. ABBOTT	10300	X	X		X		
LONG	KAISER CREEK	KAISER PEAK	9000		X				
LORRAINE	FRENCH CREEK	MT. TOM	11225				X		
LOST	BOULDER CREEK	BLACKCAP MT.	9500		X				
LOST 1	PIUTE CREEK	MT. GODDARD	11800				X		
LOST 2	PIUTE CREEK	MT. GODDARD	11890				X		
LOST 3	PIUTE CREEK	MT. GODDARD	11900				?		
LOST 4	PIUTE CREEK	MT. GODDARD	11902				?		
LOST KEYS, EAST	BENCH CREEK	DEVILS POSTPILE	9500	X					
LOST KEYS, MIDDLE	BENCH CREEK	DEVILS POSTPILE	9380	X					
LOST KEYS, WEST	BENCH CREEK	DEVILS POSTPILE	9280	X					

LAKE	TRIBUTARY TO	TOPO MAP	ELEV.	RB	BK	BN	GN	CT	LK
LOU BEVERLY	SF BEAR CREEK	MT. GODDARD	10000		X		X		
MALLARD	EF BIG CREEK	KAISER PEAK	9400	X					
MARCELLA	CIRQUE CREEK	MT. ABBOTT	9760	X	X				
MARGARET, BIG	BATHTUB LAKE	KAISER PEAK	10000	X	X				
MARGARET, COYOTE	FISH CREEK	KAISER PEAK	9520	X	X				
MARGARET, FERN	FISH CREEK	KAISER PEAK	10000	X	X				
MARGARET, FROG	FISH CREEK	KAISER PEAK	9300	X	X				
MARGARET, SEDGE	FISH CREEK	KAISER PEAK	10500	X					
MARIE	WF BEAR CREEK	MT. ABBOTT	10576				X		
MARILYN	MINNOW CREEK	MT. ABBOTT	9900	X	X				
MARILYN, EAST	MARILYN LAKE OUTLET	KAISER PEAK	10100	X					
MARION PEAK 1	MF KINGS RVR	MARION PEAK	10350	X					
MARION PEAK 3	MF KINGS RVR	MARION PEAK	10640	X					
MARION PEAK 4	MF KINGS RVR	MARION PEAK	10640	?					
MARMOT	PIUTE CREEK	MT. TOM	11740		X		X		
MARSH	WOODCHUCK	BLACKCAP MT.	9500	X	X				
MARSHALL	WF BEAR CREEK	MT. ABBOTT	10400		X				
MARTHA	SF SAN JOAQUIN RVR	MT. GODDARD	11007	X			X		
MAXON	NF KINGS RVR	BLACKCAP MT.	9950		X				
McGEE 1	SAN JOAQUIN RVR	MT. GODDARD	10850				X		
McGEE 2	SAN JOAQUIN RVR	MT. GODDARD	10890				X		
McGEE 3	SAN JOAQUIN RVR	MT. GODDARD	10900				X		
McGEE 4	SAN JOAQUIN RVR	MT. GODDARD	10970				X		
McGUIRE	FALL CREEK	MT. GODDARD	10000		X				
MEDLEY	SANDPIPER LAKE	MT. ABBOTT	10500				X		
MERMAID	SAN JOAQUIN RVR	MT. ABBOTT	7700				X		
MERRIAM	FRENCH CREEK	MT. ABBOTT	10950				X		
MESA (TOMAHAWK)	PIUTE CREEK	MT. TOM	11300				X		
MIDGE	BETTLEBUG CREEK	KAISER PEAK	10400		X				
MIDWAY	PORTAL LAKE	BLACKCAP MT.	10600	X					
MILLS CREEK, LOWER	MILLS CREEK	MT. ABBOTT	10845				?		
MILLS CREEK, UPPER	MILLS CREEK	MT. ABBOTT	11200				?		
MINNIE	MARILYN LAKE	MT. ABBOTT	10184	X					
MIRROR	STRAWBERRY CREEK	HUNTINGTON LAKE	8840		X				
MOCCASIN, BIG	PINNACLES CREEK	MT. ABBOTT	11150				X		
MOON	FRENCH CREEK	MT. TOM	10998				X		
MOSQUITO	SF SAN JOAQUIN RVR	MT. GODDARD	10100		X				
MOTT	NF MONO CREEK	MT. ABBOTT	10025	X					
MT. GODDARD	NF KINGS RVR	MT. GODDARD	10212	X					
MT. PINCHOT 2	SF KINGS RVR	MT. PINCHOT	11320		X				
MT. SHINN	BOULDER CREEK	BLACKCAP MT.	9900		X				
MURDER	COLD CREEK	MT. ABBOTT	10100	X	X				
MURIEL	PIUTE CREEK	MT. GODDARD	11328		X		X		
MYSTERY	DINKEY CREEK	HUNTINGTON LAKE	8850		X				
NEEDLE	FOURTH RECESS CREEK	MT. ABBOTT	11250				X		
NEGIT	EAST PINNACLES CREEK	MT. ABBOTT	11100				X		
NEIL	HOOPER	MT. GODDARD	10600				X		
NELLIE	HOME CAMP CREEK	KAISER PEAK	8800	X					
NELSON, LOWER	NELSON CREEK	HUNTINGTON LAKE	8900				X		
NELSON, UPPER	NELSON CREEK	HUNTINGTON LAKE	8900				X		
OLD BOOT	BULLET	MT. GODDARD	10910	X					
OLD PIPE	NICHOLS CANYON	MT. GODDARD	9200		X				
OLD SQUAW	BIG CHIEF LAKE	MT. ABBOTT	11050				X		
OLIVE	MINNOW LAKE	MT. ABBOTT	9720	X					
ORCHID	BEAR CREEK	MT. ABBOTT	10500				X		
PACKSADDLE	PIUTE CREEK	MT. GODDARD	10653				X		
PAINE	PIUTE CREEK	MT. GODDARD	11209				?		
PALISADE 1	PALISADE CREEK	BIG PINE	10920	X			X		
PALISADE 2	PALISADE CREEK	BIG PINE	10900	X			X		
PAPOOSE	LAKE OF THE LONE INDIAN	MT. ABBOTT	10040		X				
PARIS	FRENCH CANYON CREEK	MT. TOM	11160				X		
PEARL	NF KINGS RVR	MT. GODDARD	10600	X					
PEMMICAN	PINNACLES CREEK	MT. ABBOTT	10750				X		
PETITE, LOWER	FRENCH CANYON CREEK	MT. TOM	11460				X		
PETITE, UPPER	FRENCH CANYON CREEK	MT. TOM	11480				X		
PHANTOM	MURDER LAKE	MT. ABBOTT	10400	X					
PIKA	FISH CREEK	MT. MORRISON	10500	X					
PIONEER 1	PIONEER CREEK	MT. ABBOTT	10345	X	X				
PIONEER 1A	PIONEER CREEK	MT. ABBOTT	10300		X				

LAKE	TRIBUTARY TO	TOPO MAP	ELEV.	RB	BK	BN	GN	CT	LK
PIONEER 2	PIONEER CREEK	MT. ABBOTT	10850		X		?		
PIONEER 2A	PIONEER CREEK	MT. ABBOTT	10900		X		?		
PIONEER 3	PIONEER CREEK	MT. ABBOTT	10875		X		X		
PIONEER 4	PIONEER CREEK	MT. ABBOTT	11065		X				
PIONEER 5	PIONEER CREEK	MT. ABBOTT	11000				X		
PIONEER 6	PIONEER CREEK	MT. ABBOTT	11500				X		
PORTAL	NF KINGS RVR	BLACKCAP MT.	10300		X				
PORTAL FOREBAY	SF SAN JOAQUIN RVR	KAISER PEAK	7200	X					
POST CORRAL	POST CORRAL CREEK	BLACKCAP MT.	10000		X				
PRIOR	KAISER CREEK	KAISER PEAK	9040				X		
PUMICE	PHANTOM LAKE	MT. GODDARD	10500	X					
PUPPET	FRENCH CANYON CREEK	MT. TOM	11220				X		
PURPLE	FISH CREEK	MT. MORRISON	9862	X					
RAE	FLEMING CREEK	BLACKCAP MT.	10000	?	X				
RAINBOW	DINKEY CREEK	HUNTINGTON LAKE	9300	X					
RAINBOW	MARGARET LAKE	KAISER PEAK	9700	X	X				
RAINBOW 1	MF KINGS RVR	MT. GODDARD	10500		X				
RAINBOW 2	MF KINGS RVR	MT. GODDARD	10600		X				
RAM	KINGS	BLACKCAP MT.	11100				X		
RAM	FISH CREEK	MT. MORRISON	10600				X		
RAMONA	PIUTE CREEK	BLACKCAP MT.	10720				X		
RANCHERIA	NF RANCHERIA CREEK	TEHIPITE DOME	9200		X				
RECESS, UPPER	FIRST RECESS CREEK	MT. ABBOTT	11170		?				
RED	PITMAN CREEK	HUNTINGTON LAKE	9000	X					
RED AND WHITE MT	FISH CREEK	MT. ABBOTT	11100	X					
REGIMENT	DIVISION LAKE	MT. GODDARD	10900	X					
ROCK	HELMS CREEK	HUNTINGTON LAKE	9600		X				
ROCK CREEK	ROCK CREEK	HUNTINGTON LAKE	9350		X				
ROMAN 4	HORSEHEAD LAKE	BLACKCAP MT.	10300		X				
ROSE	BEAR CREEK	MT. ABBOTT	10627	X			X		
ROSEBUD	ROSE LAKE	MT. ABBOTT	11000				X		
ROSYFINCH	NF MONO CREEK	MT. ABBOTT	10800	X					
ROYCE 1	FRENCH CANYON CREEK	MT. ABBOTT	11320				X		
ROYCE 2	FRENCH CANYON CREEK	MT. ABBOTT	11620				X		
ROYCE 3	FRENCH CANYON CREEK	MT. ABBOTT	11725				X		
ROYCE 4	FRENCH CANYON CREEK	MT. ABBOTT	11725				X		
ROYCE 5	FRENCH CANYON CREEK	MT. ABBOTT	11770				X		
RUST	FRENCH CANYON CREEK	MT. ABBOTT	11570				X		
SALLY KEYES, LOWER	HEART CREEK	MT. ABBOTT	10200		?		x		
SALLY KEYES, UPPER	HEART CREEK	MT. ABBOTT	10200				X		
SANDPIPER	SF BEAR CREEK	MT. ABBOTT	10450				X		
SCARAB	BEETLE BUG CREEK	KAISER PEAK	10550		X				
SCEPTOR	SCEPTOR CREEK	BLACKCAP MT.	9625	X					
SCHOOLMARM	CRABTREE	BLACKCAP MT.	10780	X					
SCOOP	FISH CREEK	MT. MORRISON	8900		X				
SEDGE	MARGARET	KAISER PEAK	10460	X					
SEQUOIA	MILL FLAT CREEK	GIANT FOREST	5300	X					
SEVEN GABLES	EF BEAR CREEK	MT. ABBOTT	10700				X		
SHARPNOTE	THREE ISLAND LAKE	MT. ABBOTT	10800				X		
SHAVER	STEVENSON CREEK	KAISER PEAK	5370	X	X	X			
SHELF	COLD CREEK	MT. ABBOTT	9500		X				
SHINER	MARILYN LAKE	MT. ABBOTT	10340				X		
SHORTY	RAINBOW LAKE	KAISER PEAK	10380		X				
SHOT, BIG	DEVIL'S PUNCHBOWL	BLACKCAP MT.	10300		X				
SHOT, LITTLE	DEVIL'S PUNCHBOWL	BLACKCAP MT.	10200		X				
SIDE POCKET,	NO OUTLET	KAISER PEAK	9800	X					
SILVER PASS	NO OUTLET	MT. ABBOTT	10360				X		
SIX SHOOTER	SCHOOLMARM LAKE	BLACKCAP MT.	10800	X	X				
SIXTY 1	SF KINGS RVR	MT. PINCHOT	9980	X					
SIXTY 12	SF KINGS RVR	MT. PINCHOT	11040	?					
SIXTY 2	SF KINGS RVR	MT. PINCHOT	10630				X		
SIXTY 3	SF KINGS RVR	MT. PINCHOT	10640	X			X		
SIXTY 8	SF KINGS RVR	MT. PINCHOT	10980	X			X		
SLIDE 2	MF KINGS RVR	MARION PEAK	9900				?		
SLIDE 3	MF KINGS RVR	MARION PEAK	10240				?		
SLIDE 4	MF KINGS RVR	MARION PEAK	10800				?		
SNOW, LOWER	FOURTH RECESS CREEK	MT. ABBOTT	11200				X		
SNOW, UPPER	FOURTH RECESS CREEK	MT. ABBOTT	11250				X		
SOUTH	DINKEY CREEK	KAISER PEAK	9250		X				

LAKE	TRIBUTARY TO	TOPO MAP	ELEV.	RB	BK	BN	GN	CT	LK
SPANISH, BIG	STATUM CREEK	TEHIPITE DOME	8500	X					
SPANISH, LITTLE	STATUM CREEK	TEHIPITE DOME	8600	X					
SPEARPOINT	WEST PINNACLES CREEK	MT. ABBOTT	10625				X		
SPIRE	TOE LAKE	MT. ABBOTT	11800				X		
SPLIT MOUNTAIN	SF KINGS RVR	BIG PINE	1200	?					
SPOOK	GHOST LAKE	MT. ABBOTT	10500	X	X				
SPORTSMAN	SF DINKEY CREEK	HUNTINGTON LAKE	9200		X				
SQUARE	PIUTE CREEK	MT. TOM	11350				X		
SQUAW	FISH CREEK	MT. ABBOTT	10300	X	X				
SQUIRT	FLEMING CREEK	BLACKCAP MT.	10500				?		
STAR	FRENCH CANYON CREEK	MT. TOM	11400				X		
STATE 1	MF KINGS RVR	MARION PEAK	10300	X			X		
STATE 2	MF KINGS RVR	MARION PEAK	10300				?		
STEELHEAD	FRENCH CANYON CREEK	MT. TOM	11330				x		
STRAWBERRY	STRAWBERRY CREEK	HUNTINGTON LAKE	8850		X				
SUMMIT	BOULDER CREEK	BLACKCAP MT.	9500				X		
SUMMIT	GOLDEN CREEK	MT. ABBOTT	12000				X		
SUMMIT	PIUTE CREEK	MT. GODDARD	11300				X		
SWAMP	SWAMP CREEK	HUNTINGTON LAKE	9100	X	X				
SWEDE	DINKEY CREEK	HUNTINGTON LAKE	9100	X					
THIRD RECESS	THIRD RECESS CREEK	MT. ABBOTT	10550	X			X		
THOMAS EDISON	SAN JOAQUIN RVR	MT. ABBOTT	7643	X	X	X			
THOMSON	BOULDER CREEK	BLACKCAP MT.	9500		X				
THREE ISLAND	MEDLEY LAKE	MT. ABBOTT	10575				X		
TOCHER	PITMAN CREEK	HUNTINGTON LAKE	8760	X					
TOE	LAKE ITALY	MT. ABBOTT	11180				X		
TOMAHAWK	PIUTE CREEK	MT. TOM	11150		X		X		
TOOTH	CLAW LAKE	MT. ABBOTT	11160				X		
TRAIL	FOURTH RECESS CREEK	MT. ABBOTT	11200		X				
TULE	MONO CREEK	KAISER PEAK	7000	X	X				
TULE	SF SAN JOAQUIN RVR		6500	X					
TULLY	FISH CREEK	MT. ABBOTT	10300		X		X		
TUNEMAH	MF KINGS RVR	MT. GODDARD	11150	?					
TURF, LOWER	FLEMING CREEK	BLACKCAP MT.	10700				X		
TURF, UPPER	FLEMING CREEK	BLACKCAP MT.	10700				X		
TURRET, LOWER	TURRET CREEK	MT. ABBOTT	10742				X		
TWIN	KAISER CREEK	KAISER PEAK	8557		X				
TWIN	KAISER CREEK	KAISER PEAK	8550	X	X				
TWIN	WOODS CREEK	MT. PINCHOT	10566			X			
TWIN BUCK, EAST	FALL CREEK	BLACKCAP MT.	10700	X					
TWIN BUCK, WEST	FALL CREEK	BLACKCAP MT.	10700	X					
TWIN, LONG	BIG SPANISH LAKE	TEHIPITE DOME	8800		X				
TWIN, ROUND	BIG SPANISH CREEK	TEHIPITE DOME	8900		X				
URSA	BEAR CREEK	MT. ABBOTT	11500				X		
VALOR	AMBITION LAKE	MT. GODDARD	11000	X					
VEE	SEVEN GABLES	MT. ABBOTT	11050				X		
VENGEANCE	GRAVEYARD LAKE	MT. ABBOTT	10100	X					
VERMILLION	NF MONO CREEK	MT. ABBOTT	10500	X					
VEXED	DISAPPOINTMENT LAKE	BLACKCAP MT.	10350		X				
VIRGINIA	SF DINKEY CREEK	HUNTINGTON LAKE	8600				X		
VIRGINIA	FISH CREEK	MT. MORRISON	10319				X		
VOLCANIC 1	MF KINGS RVR	MARION PEAK	10250	X			X		
VOLCANIC 10	MF KINGS RVR	MARION PEAK	10390	?					
VOLCANIC 2	MF KINGS RVR	MARION PEAK	9580	X					
VOLCANIC 3E	MF KINGS RVR	MARION PEAK	9400	X					
VOLCANIC 3W	MF KINGS RVR	MARION PEAK	9500	X			X		
VOLCANIC 4	MF KINGS RVR	MARION PEAK	9820	X					
VOLCANIC 5	MF KINGS RVR	MARION PEAK	9720	X					
VOLCANIC 7E	MF KINGS RVR	MARION PEAK	10300	X					
VOLCANIC 7W	MF KINGS RVR	MARION PEAK	10238	X					
WAH-HOO	SIX SHOOTER LAKE	BLACKCAP MT.	10820	X			X		
WAHOO 1	PIUTE CREEK	MT. GODDARD	11173		X				
WAHOO 2	PIUTE CREEK	MT. GODDARD	11300		X				
WALLING	KAISER CREEK	KAISER PEAK	9300		X				
WAMPUM	OLD SQUAW LAKE	MT. ABBOTT	11500				X		
WARD	NO OUTLET	MT. ABBOTT	7300	X	X				
WARD MOUNTAIN	BOULDER CREEK	BLACKCAP MT.	9900	X	X				
WARRIOR	SQUAW LAKE	MT. ABBOTT	10750		X				
WEDGE	PIUTE CREEK	BLACKCAP MT.	10886		?				
WEST	PITMAN CREEK	HUNTINGTON LAKE	8800		X				
WHITE BEAR	BIG BEAR LAKE	MT. ABBOTT	11950				X		
WILBUR MAY	GRASSY LAKE	MT. ABBOTT	9730	X					
WISHON RESERVOIR	NF KINGS RVR	BLACKCAP MT.	6550	X		X			
WOODCHUCK	WOODCHUCK CREEK	BLACKCAP MT.	9900				X		
WOODS	SF KINGS RVR	MT. PINCHOT	10720		X				

INYO COUNTY LAKES

LAKE	TRIBUTARY TO	TOPO MAP	ELEV.	RB	BK	BN	GN	CT	LK
BABOON, LOWER	BISHOP CREEK	MT. GODDARD	10500	X					
BABOON, MIDDLE	BISHOP CREEK	MT. GODDARD	11000	X	X				
BABOON, UPPER	BISHOP CREEK	MT. GODDARD	11100	X	X				
BAKER	BAKER CREEK	BIG PINE	10500		X				
BEAR	MORGAN CREEK	MT. TOM	10000	X					
BENCH	INDEPENDENCE CREEK	MT. PINCHOT	10950	X					
BIG FISH	ROCK CREEK	MT. ABBOTT	11100	X					
BIG PINE	BIG PINE CREEK	BIG PINE	9975	X	X	X			
BIG PINE 2	BIG PINE CREEK	BIG PINE	10050	X	X	X			
BIG PINE 3	BIG PINE CREEK	BIG PINE	10250	X	X				
BIG PINE 4	BIG PINE CREEK	MT. GODDARD	10750	X	X				
BIG PINE 5	BIG PINE CREEK	MT. GODDARD	10850	X	X				
BIG PINE 6	BIG PINE CREEK	MT. GODDARD	11050	X	X				
BIG PINE 7	BIG PINE CREEK	MT. GODDARD	11150		X				
BIG PINE 8	BIG PINE CREEK	MT. GODDARD	11100				X		
BIRCH	BIRCH CREEK	BIG PINE	10950					L	
BISHOP	BISHOP CREEK	MT. GODDARD	11200	X	X				
BLACK	BIG PINE CREEK	BIG PINE	10690	X	X				
BLUE	BISHOP CREEK	MT. GODDARD	10200	X	X				
BLUE HEAVEN	BISHOP CREEK	MT. GODDARD	12000		X				
BOTTLENECK	BISHOP CREEK	MT. GODDARD	11500		X				
BOX	ROCK CREEK	MT. ABBOTT	10590		X	X			
BOY SCOUT	LONE PINE CREEK	MT. WHITNEY	11280					L	
BRAINARD	BIG PINE CREEK	BIG PINE	10500		X				
BROWN	BISHOP CREEK	MT. GODDARD	10850	X					
BUCK	EF ROCK CREEK	MT. TOM	11600		X				
BULL	BISHOP CREEK	MT. GODDARD	10800		X				
CHALFANT, LOWER	PINE CREEK	MT. ABBOTT	11450	X				?	
CHALFANT, UPPER	PINE CREEK	MT. ABBOTT	11450	X					
CHIKENFOOT	ROCK CREEK	MT. ABBOTT	10761	X	X				
CHOCOLATE 1	BISHOP CREEK	MT. GODDARD	11050		X				
CHOCOLATE 2	BISHOP CREEK	MT. GODDARD	11090		X				
CHOCOLATE 3	BISHOP CREEK	MT. GODDARD	11150		X				
CIRQUE	COTTONWOOD CREEK	OLANCHA	11060				X		
CONSULTATION	LONE PINE CREEK	MT. WHITNEY	11780	X					
COTTONWOOD	COTTONWOOD CREEK	OLANCHA	11000				X		
COTTONWOOD 2	COTTONWOOD CREEK	OLANCHA	11030				X		
COTTONWOOD 3	COTTONWOOD CREEK	OLANCHA	11045				X		
COTTONWOOD 4	COTTONWOOD CREEK	OLANCHA	11151				X		
COTTONWOOD 5	COTTONWOOD CREEK	LONE PINE	11160				X		
COTTONWOOD 6	COTTONWOOD CREEK	LONE PINE	11600				X		
COYOTE	BISHOP CREEK	MT. GODDARD	10640		?				
DADE	ROCK CREEK	MT. ABBOTT	11600				X		
DINGLEBERRY	MF BISHOP CREEK	MT. GODDARD	10560		X				
DOG LEG	ROCK CREEK	MT. TOM	10600	?					
DONKEY	MF BISHOP CREEK	MT. GODDARD	10640		X				
DOROTHY	ROCK CREEK	MT. TOM	10300	?					
EASTERN BROOK	ROCK CREEK	MT. TOM	10350		X				
EASTERN BROOK 2	ROCK CREEK	MT. TOM	10350		X				
ECHO	BISHOP CREEK	MT. GODDARD	11500	?					
ELINORE (GLACIER)	BIG PINE CREEK	BIG PINE	11450		X				
EMERALD 1	MF BISHOP CREEK	MT. GODDARD	10500	X					
EMERALD 2	MF BISHOP CREEK	MT. GODDARD	10400	X	X				
EMERALD 3	MF BISHOP CREEK	MT. GODDARD	10400	X	X				
EMERALD 4	MF BISHOP CREEK	MT. GODDARD	10400	X	X				
EMERSON	NF BISHOP CREEK	MT. GODDARD	11200		X				
FINCH	MORGAN CREEK	MT. TOM	10650		X				
FINGER	BIG PINE CREEK	BIG PINE	11500		X		?		
FISH GUT	BISHOP CREEK	MT. GODDARD	11400		X				
FISH GUT 2	BISHOP CREEK	MT. GODDARD	11450		X				
FISH GUT 3	BISHOP CREEK	MT. GODDARD	11450		X				
FLOWER	INDEPENDENCE CREEK	MT. PINCHOT	10550		X				
FRANCIS	ROCK CREEK	MT. TOM	10840	?	?				
FROG POND	COTTONWOOD CREEK	OLANCHA	11090				X		
FUNNEL	COYOTE CREEK	MT. GODDARD	10450	?					
GABBRO	GREEN CREEK	MT. TOM	10500		X				
GABLE 1	GABLE CREEK	MT. TOM	10500		X				
GABLE 2	GABLE CREEK	MT. TOM	10700		X				
GABLE 3	GABLE CREEK	MT. TOM	10800		X				
GABLE 4	PINE CREEK	MT. TOM	10900		X				
GABLE 5	PINE CREEK	MT. TOM	11100		X				
GEM, LOWER	ROCK CREEK	MT. ABBOTT	11000		X				
GEM, MIDDLE	ROCK CREEK	MT. ABBOTT	11010	?	X				
GEM, UPPER	ROCK CREEK	MT. ABBOTT	11050		X				
GEORGE	BISHOP CREEK	MT. GODDARD	10700	X	X				
GEORGE CREEK	GEORGE CREEK	MT. WHITNEY	11200	X	X				
GEORGE, LITTLE	BISHOP CREEK	MT. GODDARD	10160		?				
GILBERT	INDEPENDENCE CREEK	MT. PINCHOT	10450		X	X			
GOLDEN	PINE CREEK	MT. TOM	10800				X		
GOLDEN TROUT 1	INDEPENDENCE CREEK	MT. PINCHOT	11400				X		
GOLDEN TROUT 2	INDEPENDENCE CREEK	MT. PINCHOT	11200		X		X		
GOLDEN TROUT 3	INDEPENDENCE CREEK	MT. PINCHOT	11150				?		
GOLDEN TROUT 4	INDEPENDENCE CREEK	MT. PINCHOT	11350		X		X		
GOLDEN, LITTLE	PINE CREEK	MT. TOM	11200				X		
GRANITE	MF BISHOP CREEK	MT. GODDARD	11200	X	X				
GRANITE PARK 1	PINE CREEK	MT. ABBOTT	11650				?		
GRANITE PARK 2	PINE CREEK	MT. ABBOTT	11800				?		
GRANITE PARK 3	PINE CREEK	MT. ABBOTT	12000				?		
GRASS	NF BISHOP CREEK	MT. GODDARD	9800		X				
GREEN	SF BISHOP CREEK	MT. GODDARD	11050	X					
HALF MOON TARNS	ROCK CREEK	MT. TOM	10800		X				
HEART	ROCK CREEK	MT. ABBOTT	10500		X	X			
HEART	INDEPENDENCE CREEK	MT. PINCHOT	10850	X	X				
HELL DIVER 1	BISHOP CREEK	MT. GODDARD	11400		X				
HELL DIVER 2	BISHOP CREEK	MT. GODDARD	11600		X				
HELL DIVER 3	BISHOP CREEK	MT. GODDARD	11800		X				
HIDDEN	BAKER CREEK	BIG PINE	10700				X		
HIDDEN	MORGAN CREEK	MT. TOM	10750	X					
HIDDEN	COTTONWOOD CREEK	OLANCHA	10870				?		
HIGGENS	OLANCHA CREEK	OLANCHA	9918				X		
HIGH	COTTONWOOD CREEK	OLANCHA	11500				X		
HONEYMOON	PINE CREEK	MT. TOM	10500		X		X		
HORTON 1	HORTON CREEK	MT. TOM	9550		X				
HORTON 2	HORTON CREEK	MT. TOM	9750		?				
HORTON 3	HORTON CREEK	MT. TOM	11000				X		
HORTON 4	HORTON CREEK	MT. TOM	11400				X		
HUNGRY PACKER	BISHOP CREEK	MT. GODDARD	11300	X					
HURD	BISHOP CREEK	MT. GODDARD	10350	X					
INCONSOLABLE	SF BISHOP CREEK	MT. GODDARD	10850		X				
INSPIRATION	PINE CREEK	MT. TOM	11600				?		
INTAKE 2 POND	BISHOP CREEK	MT. GODDARD	8107	X		X			
KENNETH	ROCK CREEK	MT. TOM	10400		X				
LAMARCK, LOWER	LAMARCK CREEK	MT. GODDARD	10200	X	X				
LAMARCK, UPPER	LAMARCK CREEK	MT. GODDARD	11,00	X	X				
LITTLE FISH	ROCK CREEK	MT. ABBOTT	11000		X				
LOCH LEVEN	BISHOP CREEK	MT. GODDARD	10700	X	X				
LONE PINE	LONE PINE CREEK	LONE PINE	9925	X	X				
LONG	ROCK CREEK	MT. ABBOTT	10543	X	X	X			
LONG	BISHOP CREEK	MT. GODDARD	10751	X	X	X			
LONG	COTTONWOOD CREEK	OLANCHA	11135				X		
LOST	ROCK CREEK	MT. ABBOTT	10700		X				
MACK	ROCK CREEK	MT. TOM	10470		X	X			
MARGARET	BISHOP CREEK	MT. GODDARD	10970		X				
MARSH	ROCK CREEK	MT. ABBOTT	10480		X	X			
MARY LOUISE, LOWER	SF BISHOP CREEK	MT. GODDARD	10550		X				
MARY LOUISE, UPPER	SF BISHOP CREEK	MT. GODDARD	10550		X				
MATLOCK	OWENS RVR	MT. PINCHOT	10575		X				
McGEE	McGEE CREEK	MT. TOM	10780		X				

LAKE	TRIBUTARY TO	TOPO MAP	ELEV.	RB	BK	BN	GN	CT	LK
MEYSAN, LOWER	MEYSAN CREEK	LONE PINE	10300		X				
MEYSAN, UPPER	MEYSAN CREEK	LONE PINE	12000		X				
MIDNIGHT	MF BISHOP CREEK	MT. GODDARD	11300		X				
MILLS	ROCK CREEK	MT. ABBOTT	11600				X		
MIRROR	MIRROR CREEK	MT. WHITNEY	10700		X				
MOONLIGHT	MF BISHOP CREEK	MT. GODDARD	11425		X				
MORGAN, LOWER	MORGAN CREEK	MT. TOM	10800	X					
MORGAN, MIDDLE	MORGAN CREEK	MT. TOM	10900	X	X				
MORGAN, UPPER	MORGAN CREEK	MT. TOM	· 10933	X					
MUIR	NF COTTONWOOD CREEK	OLANCHA	11010				X		
NORTH	NF BISHOP CREEK	MT. GODDARD	9255	X	X	X			
PARKER	SF OAK CREEK	MT. PINCHOT	10800		X				
PATRICIA	ROCK CREEK	MT. TOM	11000		X				
PEE-WEE	MF. BISHOP CREEK	MT. GODDARD	12000		X		X		
PETE'S POND	MF. BISHOP CREEK	MT. GODDARD	11700				X		
PHYLLIS	SF BISHOP CREEK	MT. GODDARD	11150	X	X				
PINE 1	PINE CREEK	MT. TOM	9700	X	X		X		
PINE 2	PINE CREEK	MT. TOM	10100	X	X		X		
PIUTE	NF BISHOP CREEK	MT. GODDARD	10400	X	X				
POT HOLE	INDEPENDENCE CREEK	MT. PINCHOT	11250		X				
RED MOUNTAIN	RED MOUNTAIN CREEK	BIG PINE	10480				X		
ROBINSON (GRACE)	INDEPENDENCE CREEK	MT. PINCHOT	10480	X	X				
ROCK CREEK	ROCK CREEK	MT. TOM	9682	X	X	X			
ROCKY BOTTOM	COYOTE CREEK	MT. GODDARD	10550	X					
RUBY	ROCK CREEK	MT. ABBOTT	11150	?	X				
RUWAU	SF BISHOP CREEK	MT. GODDARD	10950	X					
SABRINA	MF BISHOP CREEK	MT. GODDARD	9132	X	X				
SADDLEROCK	BISHOP CREEK	MT. GODDARD	11175	X	X				
SAILOR	MF BISHOP CREEK	MT. GODDARD	11040	X	X				
SAM MACK	BIG PINE CREEK	MT. GODDARD	12000		X				
SARDINE	SF OAK CREEK	MT. PINCHOT	11600		X				
SAWMILL	SAWMILL CREEK	MT. PINCHOT	9920	X		X			
SCHOEBER HOLE	MF BISHOP CREEK	MT. GODDARD	11700		X				
SCHOEBER HOLE 2	MF BISHOP CREEK	MT. GODDARD	11800		X				
SCHOEBER HOLE 3	MF BISHOP CREEK	MT. GODDARD	12000				X		
SECRET	MF ROCK CREEK	MT. TOM	10200	X	X				
SERENE	ROCK CREEK	MT. TOM	10200		X		X		
SLIM	INDEPENDENCE CREEK	MT. PINCHOT	10480	X	X				
SOUTH	MF BISHOP CREEK	MT. GODDARD	9755	X	X	X			
SOUTH FORK, LOWER	SF COTTONWOOD CREEK	OLANCHA	11040				X		
SPEARHEAD	SF BISHOP CREEK	MT. GODDARD	11000	X					
SPIRE	MORGAN CREEK	MT. TOM	11750		X		X		
SPLIT	MORGAN CREEK	MT. TOM	11300		X		X		
SUMMIT	NF BIG PINE CREEK	MT. GODDARD	10700		X				
SUNSET	MF BISHOP CREEK	MT. GODDARD	11550		X				
TABOOSE	TABOOSE CREEK	MT. PINCHOT	11440	X					
TAMARACK	ROCK CREEK	MT. TOM	11580		X		X		
THOMPSON	SF BISHOP CREEK	MT. GODDARD	12000		X		X		
THUMB	SF BISHOP CREEK	BIG PINE	11500				X		
THUMB, UPPER	SF BISHOP CREEK	BIG PINE	11700				X		
THUNDER AND LIGHTNING	BAKER CREEK	MT. GODDARD	11650	X	X				
TIMBERLINE TARN	SF BISHOP CREEK	MT. GODDARD	11050	X	X				
TIMBERLINE TARN	SF BISHOP CREEK	MT. GODDARD	11050	X	X				
TIMBERLINE TARN 2	SF BISHOP CREEK	MT. GODDARD	11150	X	X				
TINEMAHA	TINEMAHA CREEK	BIG PINE	11400				?		
TOPSY TURVY	MF BISHOP CREEK	MT. GODDARD	11000	X	X				
TREASURE 1	SF BISHOP CREEK	MT. GODDARD	10650				X		
TREASURE 1	SF BISHOP CREEK	MT. GODDARD	11150	X			X		
TREASURE 1	ROCK CREEK	MT. ABBOTT	11150		X		X		
TREASURE 2	SF BISHOP CREEK	MT. GODDARD	10650				X		
TREASURE 2	SF BISHOP CREEK	MT. GODDARD	11150	X			X		
TREASURE 2	ROCK CREEK	MT. ABBOTT	11200		X		X		
TREASURE 3	SF BISHOP CREEK	MT. GODDARD	11800				X		
TREASURE 3	SF BISHOP CREEK	MT. GODDARD	11150	X			X		
TREASURE 3	ROCK CREEK	MT. ABBOTT	11200		?		X		
TREASURE 4	SF BISHOP CREEK	MT. GODDARD	11850				X		
TREASURE 4	SF BISHOP CREEK	MT. GODDARD	11160	X			X		
TREASURE 5	SF BISHOP CREEK	MT. GODDARD	10950				X		
TREASURE 6	SF BISHOP CREEK	MT. GODDARD	10950				X		
TREASURE 7	SF BISHOP CREEK	MT. GODDARD	10975				X		
TYEE	SF BISHOP CREEK	MT. GODDARD	10300		X				
TYEE 2	SF BISHOP CREEK	MT. GODDARD	10400		X				
TYEE 3	SF BISHOP CREEK	MT. GODDARD	10800		X				
TYEE 4	SF BISHOP CREEK	MT. GODDARD	10900		X				
TYEE 5	SF BISHOP CREEK	MT. GODDARD	11000	X	X				
TYEE 6	SF BISHOP CREEK	MT. GODDARD	11000		X				
UNNAMED	EF ROCK CREEK	MT. TOM	9850		X				
WEIR	SF BISHOP CREEK	MT. GODDARD	9600	X	X	X			
WILLOW	BIG PINE CREEK	BIG PINE	9650		X				
WONDER 1	LAMARCK CREEK	MT. GODDARD	10800		X				
WONDER 2	LAMARCK CREEK	MT. GODDARD	11300		X				
WONDER 3	LAMARCK CREEK	MT. GODDARD	11600		X				

MADERA COUNTY LAKES

LAKE	TRIBUTARY TO	TOPO MAP	ELEV.	RB	BK	BN	GN	CT	LK
ADAIR	MERCED RVR	MERCED PEAK	9700				X		
AGNEW PASS	SAN JOAQUIN RVR	DEVIL'S POSTPILE	10000				?		
ALPINE	WF GRANITE CREEK	MERCED PEAK	10000				X		
ALTHA	SAN JOAQUIN RVR	DEVIL'S POSTPILE	9680	X					
ALTON	SLAB CREEK	MERCED PEAK	10200		X				
ANNE	WF GRANITE CREEK	MERCED PEAK	9500	X					
ANONA	KING CREEK	DEVIL'S POSTPILE	9080				X		
ASHLEY	KING CREEK	DEVIL'S POSTPILE	9550	X					
BADGER	SAN JOAQUIN RVR	DEVIL'S POSTPILE	9520	X					
BANNER	SAN JOAQUIN RVR	DEVIL'S POSTPILE	9840		X		X		
BARE ISLAND	IVAN CREEK	SHUTEYE PEAK	8500	X	X				
BECK, LOWER	KING CREEK	DEVIL'S POSTPILE	9760	X					
BECK, UPPER	KING CREEK	DEVIL'S POSTPILE	9800	?					
BENCH CANYON	BENCH CANYON CREEK	MERCED PEAK	10575				?		
BLUE	BENCH CANYON CREEK	MERCED PEAK	10500				X		
BREEZE	NO OUTLET	MERCED PEAK	9650	?	?	?			
BUENA VISTA	BUENA VISTA CREEK	YOSEMITE	9200	?	X				
BURRO	UPPER JACKASS LAKE	MERCED PEAK	9600		?				
CABIN	SHADOW CREEK	DEVIL'S POSTPILE	9520				X		
CASTLE	SAN JOAQUIN	DEVIL'S POSTPILE	9840	?					
CECIL	SHADOW CREEK	DEVIL'S POSTPILE	10300	?	X				
CHAIN, LOWER	MERCED RIVER	MERCED PEAK	9050	X	X				
CHAIN, UPPER	MERCED RIVER	MERCED PEAK	9250	X	X				
CHILNUALNA	NO OUTLET	YOSEMITE	8400		X				
CHIQUITO	CHIQUITO CREEK	MERCED PEAK	7923	X	X				
CHITTENDEN	SHIRLEY LAKE	MERCED PEAK	9500	X	X				
CLARIS	SAN JOAQUIN	DEVIL'S POSTPILE	9840	X	X				
CORA, LOWER	CORA CREEK	MERCED PEAK	8290		?				
CORA, MIDDLE	CORA CREEK	MERCED PEAK	8400	X					
CORA, UPPER	CORA CREEK	MERCED PEAK	8400		X				
CRATER	MF SAN JOAQUIN RVR	DEVIL'S POSTPILE	6500	X					
DEADHORSE	MINARET CREEK	DEVIL'S POSTPILE	10000		X				
DUTCHMAN	IRON CREEK	SHUTEYE PEAK	8900		X				
EDIZA	SHADOW CREEK	DEVIL'S POSTPILE	9300	X	X				
EDNA	MERCED RIVER	MERCED PEAK	10200	X	X	X			
EMERALD	SAN JOAQUIN RVR	DEVIL'S POSTPILE	9880	X	X				
EMILY	SAN JOAQUIN	DEVIL'S POSTPILE	9900	?					
FERN	KING CREEK	DEVIL'S POSTPILE	8760	X	X				
FERNANDEZ, LOWER	FERNANDEZ CREEK	MERCED PEAK	9400		X				
FERNANDEZ, MIDDLE	FERNANDEZ CREEK	MERCED PEAK	9500		X				
FERNANDEZ, UPPER	FERNANDEZ CREEK	MERCED PEAK	9600		X				
FLAT	MADERA CREEK	MERCED PEAK	9000	?	X				
FLORENCE, LOWER	FLORENCE CREEK	MERCED PEAK	10100	X					
FLORENCE, UPPER	FLORENCE CREEK	MERCED PEAK	10550	X					
GALE	SHIRLEY CREEK	MERCED PEAK	9700		X				
GARNET	SAN JOAQUIN RVR	MERCED PEAK	9840	X	X				
GIVENS	GIVENS CREEK	MERCED PEAK	10500	?	X				
GLADYS	SAN JOAQUIN RVR	DEVILS POSTPILE	9160	X					
GRAYLING	RED CREEK	MERCED PEAK	8850	X					
GRIZZLY	QUARTZ CREEK	SHUTEYE PEAK	8300	X	X				
HOGGEM	IRON CREEK	BASS LAKE	7580	X					
HOLCOMB	KING CREEK	DEVIL'S POSTPILE	9480	X					
HOOVER	HOOVER CREEK	MERCED PEAK	8700	?	X				
ICEBERG	SHADOW CREEK	DEVIL'S POSTPILE	9800		X		?		
IRON	IRON CREEK	DEVIL'S POSTPILE	10770				X		
IRON, LOWER	IRON CREEK	SHUTEYE PEAK	8100	X					
IRON, UPPER	IRON CREEK	SHUTEYE PEAK	8300	X					
ISEBERG, LOWER	SADLER LAKE	MERCED PEAK	9600		X		X		
ISEBERG, MIDDLE	EF GRANITE CREEK	MERCED PEAK	10100				X		
ISEBERG, NORTH	SADLER LAKE	MERCED PEAK	10000				X		
ISEBERG, UPPER	EF GRANITE CREEK	MERCED PEAK	10100				X		
JACKASS, LOWER	JACKASS CREEK	MERCED PEAK	8600	X					
JACKASS, MIDDLE	JACKASS CREEK	MERCED PEAK	9000	X					
JACKASS, UPPER	JACKASS CREEK	MERCED PEAK	9200		X				
JOE CRANE	GRANITE CREEK	MERCED PEAK	9700	X					
JOHNSON	JOHNSON CREEK	YOSEMITE	8300	X	X	?			
JOHNSON	SAN JOAQUIN RVR	DEVIL'S POSTPILE	8100		?				
JUNCTION	IRON CREEK	SHUTEYE PEAK	8270		X				
LADY	MADERA CREEK	MERCED PEAK	8700		X				
LAURA	SAN JOAQUIN RVR	DEVIL'S POSTPILE	9600	X					
LILLIAN	MADERA CREEK	MERCED PEAK	8880	X	X				
LOIS	SAN JOAQUIN RVR	DEVIL'S POSTPILE	10050	X	X				
LOST	LOST CREEK	SHUTEYE PEAK	8000		X				
LOST	NF SAN JOAQUIN RVR	DEVIL'S POSTPILE	9000		X				
MADERA	MADERA CREEK	MERCED PEAK	8800	X					
McCLURE	EF GRANITE CREEK	MERCED PEAK	9555	X					
McGEE	SADLER LAKE	MERCED PEAK	10050		X				
McGEE, LITTLE	SADLER LAKE	MERCED PEAK	10050	X					
MINARET	SAN JOAQUIN RVR	DEVIL'S POSTPILE	9800	X	X				
MINNOW	JOHNSON CREEK	YOSEMITE	8720		X				
MONUMENT	FLAT LAKE	MERCED PEAK	9000		X				
NORRIS	NORRIS CREEK	MERCED PEAK	8300		X				
NYDIVER, LOWER	SHADOW CREEK	DEVIL'S POSTPILE	10100		X				
NYDIVER, MIDDLE	SHADOW CREEK	DEVIL'S POSTPILE	10100		X				
NYDIVER, UPPER	SHADOW CREEK	DEVIL'S POSTPILE	10150		X				
OLAINE	SAN JOAQUIN RVR	DEVIL'S POSTPILE	8120	X					
OTTOWAY, LOWER	OTTOWAY CREEK	MERCED PEAK	9700	X					
POST, LOWER	POST CREEK	MERCED PEAK	10100		X				
POST, UPPER	POST CREEK	MERCED PEAK	10100		X				
RAINBOW	FLAT LAKE	MERCED PEAK	9200	X					
RATTLESNAKE	SF SAN JOAQUIN RVR	KAISER PEAK	5583	X					
RED DEVIL	MERCED RVR	MERCED PEAK	9800	?					
RED'S	RED'S CREEK	DEVIL'S POSTPILE	9320	X					
RITTER	SAN JOAQUIN RVR	DEVIL'S POSTPILE	9840		X		X		
ROCKBOUND	LONG CANYON CREEK	MERCED PEAK	10120				X		
ROSALIE	SAN JOAQUIN RVR	DEVIL'S POSTPILE	9320	X					
ROYAL ARCH	JOHNSON CREEK	YOSEMITE	8850	X	X	?			
RUBY	SAN JOAQUIN RVR	DEVIL'S POSTPILE	9880	X					
RUTH	RAINBOW LAKE	MERCED PEAK	9500	X					
RUTHERFORD	WF GRANITE CREEK	MERCED PEAK	9700	X	X				
SADLER	WF GRANITE CREEK	MERCED PEAK	9400	X	X	?			
SHADOW	SAN JOAQUIN RVR	DEVIL'S POSTPILE	8800	X	X				
SHIRLEY	SHIRLEY CREEK	MERCED PEAK	9500		X				
SLAB, LOWER	SLAB CREEK	MERCED PEAK	10000		X				
SLAB, MIDDLE	SLAB CREEK	MERCED PEAK	10000		X				
SLAB, UPPER	SLAB CREEK	MERCED PEAK	10000		X				
SOTCHER	SAN JOAQUIN RVR	DEVIL'S POSTPILE	7610	X	X	X			
STANFORD, LOWER	SHIRLEY CREEK	MERCED PEAK	8800	X	X				
STANFORD, UPPER	SHIRLEY CREEK	MERCED PEAK	8800		X				
STAR, LOWER	IRON CREEK	YOSEMITE	8000	X					
STAR, UPPER	IRON CREEK	YOSEMITE	8100	X					
STARKWEATHER	NO OUTLET	DEVIL'S POSTPILE	8000	X					
SUPERIOR	KING CREEK	DEVIL'S POSTPILE	9400	X					
THOUSAND ISLAND	SAN JOAQUIN	DEVIL'S POSTPILE	9850	X	X				
TWIN ISLAND, NORTH	NF SAN JOAQUIN RVR	DEVIL'S POSTPILE	9640				X		
TWIN ISLAND, SOUTH	NF SAN JOAQUIN RVR	DEVIL'S POSTPILE	9840		X				
VANDEBURG	MADERA CREEK	MERCED PEAK	8600		X				
VIVIAN	SAN JOAQUIN RVR	DEVIL'S POSTPILE	9400	X					
WARD, LOWER	McCLURE LAKE	MERCED PEAK	10000		X				

LAKE	TRIBUTARY TO	TOPO MAP	ELEV.	RB	BK	BN	GN	CT	LK
WARD, UPPER	LOWER WARD LAKE	MERCED PEAK	10000		X		X		
WASHBURN	MERCED RVR	MERCED PEAK	7600	X	X	?			
WINDY	BUENA VISTA CREEK	YOSEMITE	8400	?					

MARIPOSA COUNTY LAKES

LAKE	TRIBUTARY TO	TOPO MAP	ELEV.	RB	BK	BN	GN	CT	LK
BERNICE	LEWIS CREEK	TUOLUMNE MEADOWS	10217		X				
BOOTHE	EMERIG	TUOLUMNE MEADOWS	9920		X				
BUDD	BUDD CREEK	TUOLUMNE MEADOWS	10000		X				
CATHEDRAL, LOWER	TENAYA CREEK	TUOLUMNE MEADOWS	9350	?	X				
CATHEDRAL, UPPER	TENAYA CREEK	TUOLUMNE MEADOWS	9750	?	X				
EDSON	BUENA VISTA CREEK	YOSEMITE	8275	?	?				
FLETCHER	MERCED RVR	TUOLUMNE MEADOWS	10160		X				
GALLISON	MERCED RVR	TUOLUMNE MEADOWS	10400		X				
GRANT, LOWER	YOSEMITE CREEK	HETCH HETCHY	9250	X	?				
GRANT, UPPER	YOSEMITE CREEK	HETCH HETCHY	9500	X	?				
HANGING BASKET	TOWNSLEY LAKE	TUOLUMNE MEADOWS	10560					?	
HART	BUENA VISTA CREEK	YOSEMITE	8750	?	?				
HIDDEN	NO OUTLET	TUOLUMNE MEADOWS	8300	?	?				
MATTHES	ECHO CREEK	TUOLUMNE MEADOWS	9700		X				
MERCED	MERCED RVR	MERCED PEAK	7216	X	X	X			
MILDRED	TENAYA CREEK	TUOLUMNE MEADOWS	9600		X				
NELSON	ECHO CREEK	TUOLUMNE MEADOWS	9636		X				
OSTRANDER	BRIDAL VEIL CREEK	YOSEMITE	8600	X	X	?			
REYMANN	ECHO CREEK	TUOLUMNE MEADOWS	10000		X				
POLLY DOME	MURPHY CREEK	TUOLUMNE MEADOWS	8750	?	X				
SUNRISE, LOWER	TENAYA CREEK	TUOLUMNE MEADOWS	9450	?	?				
SUNRISE, MIDDLE	TENAYA CREEK	TUOLUMNE MEADOWS	9200	?	X	?			
SUNRISE, UPPER	TENAYA CREEK	TUOLUMNE MEADOWS	9200	?	?				
TENAYA	TENAYA CREEK	TUOLUMNE MEADOWS	8149	X	X	X		L	
TOWNSLEY	FLETCHER LAKE	TUOLUMNE MEADOWS	10350		X		?		
VOGELSANG	FLETCHER CREEK	TUOLUMNE MEADOWS	10341	X	?	?	?		

MONO COUNTY LAKES

LAKE	TRIBUTARY TO	TOPO MAP	ELEV.	RB	BK	BN	GN	CT	LK
AGNEW	RUSH CREEK	MONO CRATERS	8508	X	X				
ALGER 1	RUSH CREEK	MONO CRATERS	10700				X		
ALGER 2	RUSH CREEK	MONO CRATERS	10710				X		
ALGER 3	RUSH CREEK	MONO CRATERS	10880				X		
ALPINE	SLATE CREEK	TUOLUMNE MEADOWS	11350		?		X		
ANNA	LITTLE WALKER RVR	TOWER PEAK	10500				X		
ARROWHEAD	MAMMOTH CREEK	MT. MORRISON	9800	X	?				
AVALANCHE	ROBINSON CREEK	MATTERHORN PEAK	9800				?		
BALDWIN	McGEE CREEK	MT. MORRISON	10960				X		
BARNEY	ROBINSON CREEK	MATTERHORN PEAK	8300		X				
BARNEY	MAMMOTH CREEK	MT. MORRISON	10100	X	X				
BARRETT	MAMMOTH CREEK	DEVIL'S POSTPILE	9290		X				
BENCH	WEST WALKER RVR	TOWER PEAK	9520	X	X				
BERGONA	GREEN CREEK	MATTERHORN PEAK	10400		?				
BIGHORN	SF CONVICT CREEK	MT. MORRISON	10675		X		?		
BIGHORN	NO OUTLET	TUOLUMNE MEADOWS	10950		X				
BILLY	RUSH CREEK	MONO CRATERS	9200		X				
BLOODY	LAUREL CREEK	MT. MORRISON	10880		X				
BLUE	NO OUTLET	BODIE	9450	X	X				
BLUE	VIRGINIA CREEK	MATTERHORN PEAK	9740	X	X				
BONNIE	BENCH CREEK	TOWER PEAK	9400	X	X				
BRIDGEPORT RES.	EF WALKER RIVER	BRIDGEPORT	6455		X		X		
BRIGHT DOT	EF CONVICT CREEK	MT. MORRISON	10650		X				
BROWN	WF WALKER RVR	TOWER PEAK	9000	?					
BUNNY	WF CONVICT CREEK	MT. MORRISON	10960		X				
BURRO, LOWER	WF MILL CREEK	MATTERHORN PEAK	10480		X				
BURRO, MIDDLE	MONO LAKE	MATTERHORN PEAK	10500	X	X				
BURRO,UPPER	WF MILL CREEK	MATTERHORN PEAK	10550	X	X				
BUTTS	WF WALKER RVR	TOWER PEAK	8440	?					
CARMEN (KIRMAN)	MUD CREEK	SONORA PASS	7220		X			L	
CARSON	RUSH CREEK	MONO CRATERS	7223		X				
CASCADE	WF MILL CREEK	TUOLUMNE MEADOWS	10400		X		X		
CINKO	WF WALKER RVR	TOWER PEAK	9200	X	X				
CLARA	CINKO CREEK	TOWER PEAK	9500		X				
CLARK 1	RUSH CREEK	DEVIL'S POSTPILE	9760		X				
CLARK 2	RUSH CREEK	DEVIL'S POSTPILE	9780		X				
CLARK 3	RUSH CREEK	DEVIL'S POSTPILE	9840		X		X		
CLARK 4	RUSH CREEK	DEVIL'S POSTPILE	9840		X		X		
CLARK 5	RUSH CREEK	DEVIL'S POSTPILE	9850		X		X		
CLOVERLEAF	WF CONVICT CREEK	MT. MORRISON	10300				X		
CONNESS, LOWER	CONNESS CREEK	TUOLUMNE MEADOWS	10660				X		
CONNESS, MIDDLE	CONNESS CREEK	TUOLUMNE MEADOWS	10750				X		
CONNESS, UPPER	CONNESS CREEK	TUOLUMNE MEADOWS	10800				X		
CONSTANCE	SF CONVICT CREEK	MT. MORRISON	10950		X				
CONVICT	CONVICT CREEK	MT. MORRISON	7850	X	X	X			
COONEY	VIRGINIA CREEK	MATTERHORN PEAK	10100	X	X				
CORA	CASCADE CREEK	TOWER PEAK	9360	X	X				
CREST	CREST CREEK	MONO CRATERS	10480				X		
CROCKER	SF McGEE CREEK	MT. ABBOTT	10950		X				
CROWLEY	OWENS RVR	MT. MORRISON	6781	X	X	X		L	
CROWN	ROBINSON CREEK	MATTERHORN PEAK	9580		X				
CRYSTAL	WF MAMMOTH CREEK	DEVIL'S POSTPILE	9550	X	X	X			
DANA 1	LEE VINING CREEK	MONO CRATERS	10800		?				
DANA 2	LEE VINING CREEK	MONO CRATERS	10040		X				
DANA 3	LEE VINING CREEK	MONO CRATERS	10040				X		
DANA 4	LEE VINING CREEK	MONO CRATERS	11120				X		
DAVIS, LOWER	RUSH CREEK	DEVIL'S POSTPILE	10000		x				
DAVIS, UPPER	RUSH CREEK	DEVIL'S POSTPILE	10300		X				
DOROTHY	MF CONVICT CREEK	MT. MORRISON	10340	X	X				
EAST	MF GREEN CREEK	MATTERHORN PEAK	9464	X	X				
ED	CONVICT CREEK	MT. MORRISON	9840		X				
EDITH	WF CONVICT CREEK	MT. MORRISON	10100		X		X		
ELLERY	LEE VINING CREEK	MONO CRATERS	9489	X	X	X			
EMMA	POISON CREEK	FALES HOT SPRING	9300	X					
EXCELSIOR	WF MILLS CREEK	TUOLUMNE MEADOWS	10370		?		X		
FANTAIL	MINE CREEK	TUOLUMNE MEADOWS	10000	X	X				
FERN	FERN CREEK	DEVIL'S POSTPILE	8960		X				
FINGER	LEE VINING	TUOLUMNE MEADOWS	10750		X				
FRANCES	ROBINSON CREEK	MATTERHORN PEAK	10450		X				
FREMONT	WF WALKER RVR	SONORA PASS	8250	X	?				
FROG	NF LEE VINING CREEK	TUOLUMNE MEADOWS	10100		X				
FROG, LOWER	VIRGINIA CREEK	MATTERHORN PEAK	10350		X				
FROG, MIDDLE	VIRGINIA CREEK	MATTERHORN PEAK	10365		X				
FROG, UPPER	VIRGINIA CREEK	MATTERHORN PEAK	10375		X				
GARDISKY	GARDISKY CREEK	MONO CRATERS	10760		X				
GEM	RUSH CREEK	DEVIL'S POSTPILE	9052	X	X				
GENEVIEVE	WF CONVICT CREEK	MT. MORRISON	9910		X				
GEORGE	WF MAMMOTH CREEK	DEVIL'S POSTPILE	9060	X	X	X			
GIBBS	GIBBS CREEK	MONO CRATERS	9800				X		
GILMAN	EF GREEN CREEK	MATTERHORN PEAK	9500		X				
GLACIER	WF BLACKSMITH CREEK	MATTERHORN PEAK	10100		X				
GLENBERRY	CATTLE CANYON CREEK	MATTERHORN PEAK	10000		X				
GOLD	SF McGEE CREEK	MT. ABBOTT	10350				X		
GRANT	OWENS RIVER	MONO CRATERS	7135	X		X			
GRASS	EF McGEE CREEK	MT. MORRISON	9650	X	X				
GREEN	WF GREEN CREEK	MATTERHORN PEAK	9000	X	X	?			
GREEN	SLATE CREEK	TUOLUMNE MEADOWS	10300		X				
GREENSTONE	NF LEE VINING CREEK	TUOLUMNE MEADOWS	10120	X	X			L	
GRIZZLY	WF WALKER RIVER	TOWER PEAK	9840				?		
GULL	REVERSE CREEK	MONO CRATERS	7598	X	X	X			
HAMMIL	MAMMOTH CREEK	MT. MORRISON	10000		X				
HARDING	WF WALKER RIVER	TOWER PEAK	8600	X					
HARRIET	BENDER CREEK	TOWER PEAK	9200	X	X				
HEART	MAMMOTH CREEK	MT. MORRISON	9600	X	X				
HELEN	WF MILL CREEK	MATTERHORN PEAK	10100		X		X		
HELEN	CASCADE CREEK	TOWER PEAK	9680	X					
HERMIT	LEE VINING CREEK	TUOLUMNE MEADOWS	9700		?				
HIDDEN	LEE VINING CREEK	TUOLUMNE MEADOWS	9920				X		
HIDDEN	WF WALKER RVR	SONORA PASS	7740	X					
HILTON 1	HILTON CREEK	MT. ABBOTT	9800	X	X				
HILTON 10	HILTON CREEK	MT. ABBOTT	11360		X		X		
HILTON 10	HILTON CREEK	MT. ABBOTT	11360		X		X		
HILTON 2	HILTON CREEK	MT. ABBOTT	9900	X					
HILTON 3	HILTON CREEK	MT. ABBOTT	10300	X					
HILTON 4	HILTON CREEK	MT. ABBOTT	10350	?	X				
HILTON 5	HILTON CREEK	MT. ABBOTT	10620	X	X		X		
HILTON 6	HILTON CREEK	MT. ABBOTT	10720		X				
HILTON 7	HILTON CREEK	MT. ABBOTT	10725		X				
HILTON 8	HILTON CREEK	MT. ABBOTT	10750	?	X				
HILTON 9	HILTON CREEK	MT. ABBOTT	11200		X		X		
HOOVER, LOWER	EF GREEN CREEK	MATTERHORN PEAK	9760		X				
HOOVER, UPPER	EF GREEN CREEK	MATTERHORN PEAK	9840		X				
HORSE CANYON	HORSE CANYON CREEK	MATTERHORN PEAK	8250	?					
HORSESHOE	MAMMOTH CREEK	DEVIL'S POSTPILE	8880	?					
HUMMINGBIRD	NF LEE VINING CREEK	TUOLUMNE MEADOWS	10280		X				
HUNEWILL	TAMARACK CREEK	MATTERHORN PEAK	10120		X		?		
ICE	LITTLE SLIDE CANYON CREEK	MATTERHORN PEAK	9950	X	X				
IDA	EF MILL CREEK	MONO CRATERS	10000		X				
ISLAND PASS	RUSH CREEK	DEVIL'S POSTPILE	10000				X		
JUNCTION RES.	WF WALKER RVR	FALES HOT SPRING	7040	X	X				
JUNE	REVERSED CREEK	MONO CRATERS	7616	X	X	X			
KIDNEY	GIBBS CREEK	MONO CRATERS	10500				?		
KIRKWOOD	KIRKWOOD CREEK	TOWER PEAK	10280		X				
KOENIG	LEAVITT CREEK	SONORA PASS	9600				X		
LANE	WF WALKER RVR	SONORA PASS	7300		X			L	
LATOPIE	LEAVITT CREEK	SONORA PASS	10400	?			X		
LAUREL 1	LAUREL CREEK	MT. MORRISON	10000				X		
LAUREL 2	LAUREL CREEK	MT. MORRISON	10050				X		
LEAVITT	LEAVITT CREEK	SONORA PASS	9556	X	X			L	
LOBDELL	DESERT CREEK	FALES HOT SPRING	9200	X	X				
LONG, LOWER	WF WALKER RIVER	TOWER PEAK	8600	X					
LONG, UPPER	WF WALKER RVR	TOWER PEAK	8600	X					
LOST	SHERWIN CREEK	MT. MORRISON	9050		X				
LOST 1	LOST CREEK	MONO CRATERS	10400	?			X		
LOST 2	LOST CREEK	MONO CRATERS	10400				X		
LOST 3	LOST CREEK	MONO CRATERS	9600				X		
LUNDY	MILL CREEK	BODIE	7750	X	X	X			
MALTBY	LITTLE SLIDE CANYON CREEK	MATTERHORN PEAK	9750	X	X				
MAMIE	MAMMOTH CREEK	DEVIL'S POSTPILE	8800	X	X	X			
MARIE, LOWER	RUSH CREEK	DEVIL'S POSTPILE	10850	X	X				
MARIE, UPPER	RUSH CREEK	DEVIL'S POSTPILE	11240	X					
MARY	MAMMOTH CREEK	DEVIL'S POSTPILE	8931	X	X	X			
MAUL	SLATE CREEK	TUOLUMNE MEADOWS	10303		X				
McCLOUD	MAMMOTH CREEK	DEVIL'S POSTPILE	9250		X			L	
McGEE, LOWER	McGEE CREEK	MT. ABBOTT	10557		X				
McGEE, UPPER	McGEE CREEK	MT. ABBOTT	11050		X				
McMILLAN	MOLYBDENITE CREEK	MATTERHORN PEAK	9120		X				
MEADOW	McGEE CREEK	MT. MORRISON	10150		X				
MIDDLE	LEE VINING CREEK	TUOLUMNE MEADOWS	9690		X				
MIDDLE	MINE CREEK	TUOLUMNE MEADOWS	9850	?					
MILDRED	CONVICT CREEK	MT. MORRISON	9850	?					
MILLIE	POORE CREEK	SONORA PASS	6980	X					
MOAT	VIRGINIA CREEK	MATTERHORN PEAK	10450		?		X		
NUTTER	GREEN CREEK	MATTERHORN PEAK	9600	X					
OAK CREEK	OAK CREEK	MT. PINCHOT	11100		X				
ODELL	MILL CREEK	TUOLUMNE MEADOWS	10240				X		
ONEIDA	MILL CREEK	MONO CRATERS	9656	X					
PAGE	GREEN CREEK	MATTERHORN PEAK	10120	?					
PAR VALUE, LOWER	GREEN CREEK	MATTERHORN PEAK	10240		X		?		
PAR VALUE, UPPER	GREEN CREEK	MATTERHORN PEAK	10320		?		?		
PARKER	MONO LAKE	MONO CRATERS	8350		X				
PASS	ROBINSON CREEK	MATTERHORN PEAK	9720		X				
PEELER	ROBINSON CREEK	MATTERHORN PEAK	9440	X					
POORE	POORE CREEK	SONORA PASS	7214	X	X				
POTTER	MILL CREEK	TUOLUMNE MEADOWS	10400		?		X		
RED	VIRGINIA CREEK	MATTERHORN PEAK	9400	X	X				
RED LAKE	MAMMOTH CREEK	MT. MORRISON	10100	X	X				
RICHARDSON TARN	SF LEE VINING CREEK	MONO CRATERS	9500		X		X		
ROBINSON, LOWER	ROBINSON CREEK	MATTERHORN PEAK	9150	X	X				

LAKE	TRIBUTARY TO	TOPO MAP	ELEV.	RB	BK	BN	GN	CT	LK
ROBINSON, UPPER	ROBINSON CREEK	MATTERHORN PEAK	9200	X	X				
RODGERS, LOWER	RUSH CREEK	DEVIL'S POSTPILE	10080		?				
RODGERS, UPPER	RUSH CREEK	DEVIL'S POSTPILE	10840		X				
ROOSEVELT	WF WALKER RVR	SONORA PASS	7300		X			L	
ROUND	McGEE CREEK	MT. MORRISON	9950	X					
RUTH	WF WALKER RVR	TOWER PEAK	9680		X				
SADDLEBAG	LEE VINNING CREEK	TUOLUMNE MEADOWS	10081	X	X				
SARDINE, LOWER	WALKER CREEK	MONO CRATERS	9850	X					
SARDINE, UPPER	WALKER CREEK	MONO CRATERS	10450		X				
SECRET	POORE CREEK	SONORA PASS	7500		?		?		
SHAMROCK	MILL CREEK	TUOLUMNE MEADOWS	10250		X				
SHELL	MINE CREEK	TUOLUMNE MEADOWS	9680	?					
SHERWINS 1-4	SHERWIN CREEK	MT. MORRISON	8600	X	X				
SILVER	RUSH CREEK	MONO CRATERS	7212	X		X			
SKELTON	MAMMOTH CREEK	MT. MORRISON	9900	X	X				
SKI	LEAVITT CREEK	SONORA PASS	9800				X		
SNOW	ROBINSON CREEK	MATTERHORN PEAK	10200				?		
SPULLER	MINE CREEK	TUOLUMNE MEADOWS	10250		?				
STANFORD	HILTON CREEK	MT. ABBOTT	11440				X		
STEELHEAD	McGEE CREEK	MT. MORRISON	10480	X	X				
STEELHEAD	MILL CREEK	TUOLUMNE MEADOWS	10440	X	X			L	
STEELHEAD, LITTLE	MILL CREEK	TUOLUMNE MEADOWS	10450		X		X		
STELLA	WF WALKER RVR	TOWER PEAK	9480	X	X				
SULLIVAN	RUSH CREEK	DEVIL'S POSTPILE	9400		X				
SUMMIT	GREEN CREEK	MATTERHORN PEAK	10240		X				
TAMARACK	TAMARACK CREEK	MATTERHORN PEAK	9700				X		
TEE JAY	TEE JAY CREEK	DEVIL'S POSTPILE	9250	X					
THIMBLE, LOWER	LEE VINING CREEK	TUOLUMNE MEADOWS	9800		X				
THIMBLE, UPPER	LEE VINING CREEK	TUOLUMNE MEADOWS	9800		X				
TIOGA	LEE VINING CREEK	TUOLUMNE MEADOWS	9651	X	X				
TOPAZ	WF WALKER RVR	TOPAZ LAKE	4990	X		X			
TOWER	TOWER CANYON CREEK	TOWER PEAK	9600				X		
TOWSER	MILL CREEK	TUOLUMNE MEADOWS	10400				X		
TREBLE	SLATE CREEK	TUOLUMNE MEADOWS	10300		X				
TRUMBULL	VIRGINIA CREEK	MATTERHORN PEAK	9200	X	X				
TURQOISE	CATTLE CANYON CREEK	MATTERHORN PEAK	10450		X				
TWIN	LEE VINING CREEK	TUOLUMNE MEADOWS	10400		X				
TWIN LAKE, LOWER	ROBINSON CREEK	MATTERHORN PEAK	7081	X		X			
TWIN LAKE, UPPER	ROBINSON CREEK	MATTERHORN PEAK	7092	X		X			
TWIN LAKES	MAMMOTH CREEK	DEVIL'S POSTPILE	8480	X	X	X			
VALENTINE	SHERWIN CREEK	MT. MORRISON	9900		X				
VIRGINIA, LOWER	VIRGINA CREEK	MATTERHORN PEAK	9250	X		X			
VIRGINIA, UPPER	VIRGINIA CREEK	MATTERHORN PEAK	9300	X		X			
WALKER, LITTLE	WALKER CREEK	MONO CRATERS	7962	X		X			
WASCO	LEE VINING CREEK	TUOLUMNE MEADOWS	10100		X				
WAUGH	RUSH CREEK	MONO CRATERS	9424		X				
WEBER	RUSH CREEK	DEVIL'S POSTPILE	9900		X				
WEST	GREEN CREEK	MATTERHORN PEAK	9875	X	X	X			
WITSANAPAH	CONVICT CREEK	MT. MORRISON	10760		X				
WOODS, LOWER	MAMMOTH CREEK	MT. MORRISON	10000	X	X				
WOODS, UPPER	MAMMOTH CREEK	MT. MORRISON	10100	X					
YOST	MAHOGAN CREEK	DEVIL'S POSTPILE	9200		?				
Z	LEE VINING CREEK	TUOLUMNE MEADOWS	10480		X				

NEVADA COUNTY LAKES

LAKE	TRIBUTARY TO	TOPO MAP	ELEV.	RB	BK	BN	GN	CT	LK
ANGELA	LAKE VAN NORDEN	DONNER PASS	7193		X				
AZALEA	NO OUTLET	DONNER PASS	7400		X				
BALTIMORE	FRENCH LAKE	EMIGRANT GAP	6975		X				
BARBARA	GRANITE CREEK	EMIGRANT GAP	7500					L	
BEYERS, LOWER	FORDYCE CREEK	EMIGRANT GAP	6800		X			L	
BEYERS, UPPER	FORDYCE CREEK	EMIGRANT GAP	6800		X				
BIGLEY	NEXT LAKE	DONNER PASS	7000	?	?				
BLUE	RUCKER LAKE	EMIGRANT GAP	5964	X					
BOCA	LITTLE TRUCKEE RVR	TRUCKEE	5590	X		X			
BOWMAN	CANYON CREEK	EMIGRANT GAP	5565	X		X			
BUCKHORN	FORDYCE CREEK	EMIGRANT GAP	7100	X					
BULLPEN	TEXAS CREEK	EMIGRANT GAP	6700	X					
BUZZARD'S ROOST	NORTH CREEK	DONNER PASS	7560		X				
CALIFORNIA	MEADOW LAKE	DONNER PASS	6200	X	X				
CARR	LAKE CREEK	EMIGRANT GAP	6935		X				
CATFISH	MF YUBA RVR	EMIGRANT GAP	6430	?					
CAVE	LINDSEY CREEK	EMIGRANT GAP	6800		X			L	
CHUBB	LAKE SPAULDING	EMIGRANT GAP	5200	?					
CHUCK	FEELY LAKE	EMIGRANT GAP	6850		X				
CROOKED, LOWER	SAWMILL	EMIGRANT GAP	6750		X				
CROOKED, MIDDLE	LOWER CROOKED LAKE	EMIGRANT GAP	6750		X				
CROOKED, UPPER	MIDDLE CROOKED LAKE	EMIGRANT GAP	6756		X				
CULBERTSON	TEXAS CREEK	EMIGRANT GAP	6480	X					
DEVILS OVEN	WARREN LAKE	DONNER PASS	7840				?		
DONNER	DONNER CREEK	DONNER PASS	5935	X		X			X
DONNER EUER VALLEY	NO OUTLET	DONNER PASS	6600		X				
DOWNEY	LITTLE DOWNEY LAKE	EMIGRANT GAP	6600		X				
EASTERN BROOK, LOWER	FORDYCE CREEK	DONNER PASS	7000		X				
EASTERN BROOK, UPPER	FORDYCE CREEK	DONNER PASS	7000		X				
ECHO	FRENCH CREEK	EMIGRANT GAP	7700				X		
EILEEN	SAWMILL LAKE	EMIGRANT GAP	6600		X			L	
ELAINE	FAUCHERIE LAKE	EMIGRANT GAP	6940	X	X				
EMERALD	GRANITE CREEK	EMIGRANT GAP	5700		X				
EMERALD, LITTLE	GRANITE CREEK	EMIGRANT GAP	5700		X				
EVELYN	QUEEN LAKE	DONNER PASS	7000	X	X				
FAUCHERIE	CANYON CREEK	EMIGRANT GAP	6160	X		X			
FEELY	CARR	EMIGRANT GAP	6721	X	X				
FLORENCE	FORDYCE LAKE	DONNER PASS	7000		X				
FORDYCE	FORDYCE CREEK	DONNER PASS	6400	X		X			
FREEMAN	FORDYCE LAKE	DONNER PASS	7000		X				
FRENCH	CANYON CREEK	EMIGRANT GAP	6700	X		X			
FROG	SF PROSSER CREEK	DONNER PASS	7900		X				
FULLER	JORDAN CREEK	EMIGRANT GAP	5339	X	X	X			
GLACIER	FAUCHERIE LAKE	EMIGRANT GAP	7500				?		
HELEN	MEYERS LAKE	EMIGRANT GAP	7100		X				
INDEPENDENCE	INDEPENDENCE CREEK	DONNER PASS	6950		X			L	
ISLAND, BIG	LILYPUT POND	EMIGRANT GAP	6800	X					
ISLAND, LITTLE	BIG ISLAND LAKE	EMIGRANT GAP	6800	X					
JACKSON	JACKSON CREEK	EMIGRANT GAP	6600	X	X				
JACKSON MEADOW	MF YUBA RVR	EMIGRANT GAP	6035	X	X	X		L	
JAKES	SF YUBA RVR	EMIGRANT GAP	5700	?					
JAY	BIG ISLAND LAKE	EMIGRANT GAP	6850		X				
JOHANNA	NO OUTLET	EMIGRANT GAP	6200					L	
JOHANNA, LITTLE	NO OUTLET	EMIGRANT GAP	6200					L	
KANEEN	FORDYCE CREEK	EMIGRANT GAP	7400				?		?
KILBORN	DEER LAKE	DONNER PASS	6680		X				
LILYPUT POND	SHOTGUN LAKE	EMIGRANT GAP	6800	?	?				
LINDSEY, LOWER	LINDSEY CREEK	EMIGRANT GAP	6508	X	X				
LINDSEY, UPPER	LOWER LINDSEY LAKE	EMIGRANT GAP	6705	X	X			L	
LOLA MONTEZ, LOWER	LOLA MONTEZ CREEK	DONNER PASS	7100	X	X				
LOLA MONTEZ, UPPER	LOLA MONTEZ CREEK	DONNER PASS	7500	X	X				
LONG	UPPER CROOKED CREEK	EMIGRANT GAP	6800	X	X				
LONG	FORDYCE CREEK	EMIGRANT GAP	7100	?	?			?	
MARIA	CASTLE CREEK	DONNER PASS	7200		X				
MARTIS CREEK RES.	MARTIS CREEK	TRUCKEE	5858	X		X		L	
MAX	FORDYCE CREEK	EMIGRANT GAP	6750		X				
McMURRAY	WEAVER CREEK	EMIGRANT GAP	6000	X		X			
MEADOW	FORDYCE LAKE	DONNER PASS	7250	X					
MEYERS	BOWMAN LAKE	EMIGRANT GAP	7100		X				
MIDDLE	SF CANYON CREEK	EMIGRANT GAP	6700		X				
MILK	UPPER CROOKED CREEK	EMIGRANT GAP	6800	X					
MILTON RES.	MF YUBA RVR	SIERRA CITY	5690	X	X	X		L	
MOSSY POND	FORDYCE CREEK	DONNER PASS	6875		?				
PARADISE	NORTH CREEK	DONNER PASS	7700	X					
PENNER	DRY LAKE	EMIGRANT GAP	6850	X					
PROSSER	PROSSER CREEK	TRUCKEE	5740	X	X	X			
QUEEN	FORDYCE CREEK	EMIGRANT GAP	6900		X				
ROCK, LOWER	TEXAS CREEK	EMIGRANT GAP	6900		X				
ROCK, UPPER	LOWER ROCK LAKE	EMIGRANT GAP	6985		X				
ROUND	UPPER CROOKED LAKE	EMIGRANT GAP	6800	X	X				
RUCKER	RUCKER CREEK	EMIGRANT GAP	5462	X					
SAMS	EMERALD LAKE	EMIGRANT GAP	6700		X				
SANDRIDGE	NORTH CREEK	DONNER PASS	7750	X	X				
SANFORD	LONEY LAKE	EMIGRANT GAP	7100	X					
SAWMILL	BOWMAN LAKE	EMIGRANT GAP	5863	X					
SECRET	MF YUBA RVR	EMIGRANT GAP	6450	X					
SECTIONAL LINE	FORDYCE LAKE	DONNER PASS	7000		X				
SHOTGUN	UPPER CROOKED LAKE	EMIGRANT GAP	6800	X					
SPAULDING	YUBA RVR	EMIGRANT GAP	5011	X		X			
STERLING	FORDYCE LAKE	DONNER PASS	6987	X					
SUMMIT	BILLY MACK CANYON	DONNER PASS	7460		X				
TALBOT	FORDYCE LAKE	DONNER PASS	7000		X				
TOLLHOUSE	NF YUBA RVR	EMIGRANT GAP	7100	X					
TUTTLE	NO OUTLET	EMIGRANT GAP	6700	X	X				
UNNAMED 1	JOHANNA CREEK	EMIGRANT GAP	6000		X				
UNNAMED 2	JOHANNA CREEK	EMIGRANT GAP	6200		X				
VIEW	UPPER LINDSEY LAKE	EMIGRANT GAP	6749	X					
VIRGINIA	FORDYCE LAKE	DONNER PASS	7000		X				
WAGON WHEEL	FORDYCE LAKE	DONNER PASS	7100		X			L	
WARREN	NF PROSSER CREEK	DONNER PASS	7400					L	
WEAVER	EF YUBA RVR	EMIGRANT GAP	5690	X		X			X
WEIL	CANYON CREEK	EMIGRANT GAP	6400	X	X				
WEST, LOWER	BILLY MACK CANYON	DONNER PASS	7760		X				
WEST, UPPER	LOWER WEST LAKE	DONNER PASS	7820		X				
WHITE ROCK	WHITE ROCK CREEK	DONNER PASS	7940	X					

PLACER COUNTY LAKES

LAKE	TRIBUTARY TO	TOPO MAP	ELEV.	RB	BK	BN	GN	CT	LK
BEAR	BARKER CREEK	TAHOE	7550		X				
BUCK	McKINNEY CREEK	TAHOE	7450	X	X				
BUNKER	RUBICON RVR	GRANITE CHIEF	6530		X				
CASCADE, LOWER	SF YUBA RVR	DONNER PASS	6722	X					
CASCADE, UPPER	LOWER CASCADE LAKE	DONNER PASS	6750	X	X				
DAN	LONG LAKE	DONNER PASS	6800		X				
DEVIL'S PEAK	DAN LAKE	DONNER PASS	6800		X				
DRUM FOREBAY	BEAR RVR	EMIGRANT GAP	4766	X					
ELLIS	BLACKWOOD CREEK	TAHOE	8200		X				
FERN	RUBICON RIVER	GRANITE CHIEF	6260	X					
FISHER	GRANITE CREEK	DONNER PASS	7030		X				
FIVE 1	BEAR CREEK	TAHOE	7510	X	X				
FIVE 2	FIVE LAKES CREEK	TAHOE	7510	X	X				
FIVE 3	FIVE LAKES CREEK	TAHOE	7550	X					
FRENCH MEADOW	MF AMERICAN RVR	GRANITE CHIEF	5260	X					
HELL HOLE	RUBICON RVR	GRANITE CHIEF	4630	X		X			X
HIDDEN	PALISADE CREEK	DONNER PASS	6600		X				
HUNTLEY MILL	GRANITE CREEK	DONNER PASS	6600		X				
HUYSINK	BIG VALLEY CREEK	EMIGRANT GAP	6846		X				
JIM	BIG GRANITE CREEK	DONNER PASS	7000		X				
KELLY	NF AMERICAN RVR	EMIGRANT GAP	5910	X					
KIDD	SF YUBA RVR	DONNER PASS	6628		X				
LAKE VALLEY RES.	NF AMERICAN RVR	EMIGRANT GAP	5786	X					
LOCH LEVEN, HIGH	MIDDLE LOCH LEVEN LAKE	DONNER PASS	6860	X	X				
LOCH LEVEN, LOWER	LITTLE GRANITE CREEK	EMIGRANT GAP	6780	X					
LOCH LEVEN, MIDDLE	LOWER LOCH LEVEN LAKE	EMIGRANT GAP	6780		X				
LOCH LEVEN, UPPER	LOWER LOCH LEVEN LAKE	EMIGRANT GAP	6790	X					
LONG	UPPER CASCADE CREEK	DONNER PASS	6260	X					
LONG	RUBICON RVR	GRANITE CHIEF	6620		X				
MARY	NO OUTLET	DONNER PASS	7026		X				
McKINSTRY	JERRET CREEK	GRANITE CHIEF	6900		X				
MILDRED	NF AMERICAN RVR	EMIGRANT GAP	7970		?		?		
MILLER	MILLER CREEK	TAHOE	7115		X				
NATALIE	GRANITE CREEK	DONNER PASS	6390					L	
NEEDLE	NF AMERICAN RVR	GRANITE CHIEF	8490				X		
NEEDLE, LITTLE	NF AMERICAN RVR	GRANITE CHIEF	8050		?		?		
PALISADE	PALISADE CREEK	DONNER PASS	6520	X		X			
QUAIL	LAKE TAHOE	TAHOE	6707		X				
RANI	NF AMERICAN	GRANITE CHIEF	4000	X					
SALMON, SOUTH	LITTLE GRANITE CREEK	EMIGRANT GAP	7750		X				
SERENE	SERENE CREEK	DONNER PASS	6872	X	X				

LAKE	TRIBUTARY TO	TOPO MAP	ELEV.	RB	BK	BN	GN	CT	LK
TAHOE	TRUCKEE RVR	TAHOE	6224	X	?	X			X
WATSON	WATSON CREEK	TAHOE	7780		X				

PLUMAS COUNTY LAKES

LAKE	TRIBUTARY TO	TOPO MAP	ELEV.	RB	BK	BN	GN	CT	LK
BALD EAGLE, NORTH	MILK RANCH CREEK	BUCKS LAKE	5900		X				
BALD EAGLE, SOUTH	MILK RANCH CREEK	BUCKS LAKE	6205	X	X				
BEAR, BIG	GRAYEAGLE CREEK	SIERRA CITY	6475	X	X	X			
BEAR, LITTLE	BIG BEAR LAKE	SIERRA CITY	6500	X	X				
BUCKS	BUCKS CREEK	BUCKS LAKE	5155	X		X			
BUCKS, LOWER	BUCKS CREEK	BUCKS LAKE	5008	X					
CUB	BEAR LAKE	SIERRA CITY	6590		X				
ELWELL	GRAYEAGLE CREEK	SIERRA CITY	6487		X				
EUREKA	EUREKA CREEK	BLAIRSDEN	4360	X	X				
FRENCHMAN	LITTLE LAST CHANCE	PORTOLA	5590	X	X				
GOLD	SILVER CREEK	BUCKS LAKE	5720		X	X			
GRAYEAGLE POND	GRAYEAGLE CREEK	BLAIRSDEN	4360	X					
GRASS	JAMISON CREEK	SIERRA CITY	6200	X	X	X		?	
GRASSY	GRAYEAGLE CREEK	SIERRA CITY	5842	X	X				
GRIZZLY	GRIZZLY CREEK	QUINCY	5150	X	X	X			
JAMISON	ROCK CREEK	SIERRA CITY	6260	X	X				
LILY	GRAYEAGLE	SIERRA CITY	5900	X	X				
LITTLE GRASS VALLEY	SF FEATHER RVR	DOWNIEVILLE	5045	X				L	
LONG	GRAYEAGLE CREEK	SIERRA CITY	6456	X					
LOST	MILL CREEK	BUCKS LAKE	6420		X				
ROCK	GRASS LAKE	SIERRA CITY	4500		X				
ROUND	BIG BEAR LAKE	SIERRA CITY	6714		X				
SILVER	CUB LAKE	SIERRA CITY	6654		X		?		
SILVER	SILVER CREEK	BUCKS LAKE	5824	X	X				
SMITH	SMITH CREEK	SIERRA CITY	6094	X	X				
THREE, LOWER	MILL RANCH CREEK	BUCKS LAKE	6080		X				
THREE, MIDDLE	LOWER THREE LAKES	BUCKS LAKE	5820		X				
THREE, UPPER	MIDDLE THREE LAKES	BUCKS LAKE	5900		X				
WADES	JAMISON CREEK	SIERRA CITY	6540		X				

SIERRA COUNTY LAKES

LAKE	TRIBUTARY TO	TOPO MAP	ELEV.	RB	BK	BN	GN	CT	LK
CALPINE	CALPINE CHANNEL	SIERRAVILLE	5100	X					
COBURN	BERRY CREEK	SIERRAVILLE	7380	X					
COLDSTREAM	COLD STREAM	SIERRAVILLE	5600	X		X			
DEADMAN	YUBA	SIERRA CITY	6638	X		X		L	
DEER, BIG	SAWMILL	SIERRA CITY	7110	X	X				
DEER, LITTLE	PAULEY CREEK	SIERRA CITY	6957	X	X				
DELHANTY	SACKETT CREEK	DOWNIEVILLE	5750	X					
DUGAN POND	PACKER CREEK	SIERRA CITY	6400		X				
GOLD	FRAZIER CREEK	SIERRA CITY	6409	X	X	X			
GOLD, LITTLE	GOLD LAKE	SIERRA CITY	6430		X				
GOOSE	FRAZIER CREEK	SIERRA CITY	6750	X	X				
GRASSY	GRASSY LAKE CREEK	SIERRA CITY	6500	X	X				
HAVEN	FRAZIER CREEK	SIERRA CITY	6750	X	X				
HAWLEY	PAULEY CREEK	SIERRA CITY	6200	X	X				
INDEPENDENCE	INDEPENDENCE CREEK	DONNER PASS	6949	X	X			L	
LAKE OF THE WOOD	WEBBER LAKE	SIERRAVILLE	7420	X	X	X			
PACKER	NF YUBA RVR	SIERRA CITY	6550	X					
SALMON, LOWER	SALMON CREEK	SIERRA CITY	6390	X	X	?			
SALMON, MIDDLE	LOWER SALMON LAKE	SIERRA CITY	6460	X					
SALMON, UPPER	LOWER SALMON LAKE	SIERRA CITY	6495	X	X	?			
SAND	SALMON CREEK	SIERRA CITY	5850	X		X			
SARDINE, LOWER	SARDINE CREEK	SIERRA CITY	5759	X	X	?			
SARDINE, UPPER	LOWER SARDINE LAKE	SIERRA CITY	6580		X				
SAXONIA	SALMON CREEK	SIERRA CITY	6430	X	X				
SMITH	SMITH CREEK	SIERRA CITY	6030	X					
SNAG	SALMON CREEK	SIERRA CITY	6600	X	X				
SNAKE	PAULEY CREEK	SIERRA CITY	6970	X					
SPENCER, LOWER	SPENCER CREEK	SIERRA CITY	6380	X	X				
SPENCER, UPPER	LOWER SPENCER LAKE	SIERRA CITY	6580		X				

LAKE	TRIBUTARY TO	TOPO MAP	ELEV.	RB	BK	BN	GN	CT	LK
SQUAW	GOLD LAKE	SIERRA CITY	6530	X	X	X			
STAMPEDE	BOCA RESERVOIR	TRUCKEE	5768	X		X			
TAMARACK, LOWER	DUGAN POND	SIERRA CITY	6690		X				
TAMARACK, UPPER	LOWER TAMARACK LAKE	SIERRA CITY	6732		X				
VOLCANO	SALMON CREEK	SIERRA CITY	5980		X				
WEBBER	LITTLE TRUCKEE RIVER	DONNER PASS	6770	X	X	X			
YOUNG AMERICA	UPPER SARDINE LAKE	SIERRA CITY	7200		X	X	?		

TULARE COUNTY LAKES

LAKE	TRIBUTARY TO	TOPO MAP	ELEV.	RB	BK	BN	GN	CT	LK
ANSEL	EF KAWEAH	MT. GODDARD	10500	X					
ASTER	MARBLE FORK KAWEAH	TRIPLE DIVIDE	9000	X					
BALCH, BIG	TULE RVR	CAMP NELSON	6400	X					
BALCH, LITTLE	TULE RIVER	CAMP NELSON	6350	X					
BIG BIRD	ROARING RVR	TRIPLE DIVIDE	9775	?	X				
BIG BASIN	SUGARLOAF	TRIPLE DIVIDE	10880	X					
BEVILLE	SF SUGARLOAF	TRIPLE DIVIDE	9450		X				
BLOSSOM 1	SF KAWEAH	MINERAL KING	10300		X				
BLOSSOM 4	SF KAWEAH	MINERAL KING	10400		X				
BREWER	SUGARLOAF	TRIPLE DIVIDE	10880	X					
BULLFROG, LOWER	LITTLE KERN RVR	MINERAL KING	10700				X		
BULLFROG, UPPER	LITTLE KERN RVR	MINERAL KING	10900				X		
CENTER BASIN	BUBBS CREEK	MT. WHITNEY	11776	X					
CHICKEN SPRINGS	GOLDEN TROUT CREEK	OLANCHA	11250				X		
COBALT, LOWER	EF KAWEAH RVR	MINERAL KING	9975		X				
COBALT, UPPER	EF KAWEAH RVR	MINERAL KING	10200		?				
CRYSTAL, LOWER	EF KAWEAH RVR	MINERAL KING	10880		X				
EAGLE	EF KAWEAH RVR	MINERAL KING	10000		X				
EMERALD	MARBLE FORK KAWEAH	TRIPLE DIVIDE	9200		X				
FERGUSON 1	WF FERGUSON	TRIPLE DIVIDE	10080	X					
FERGUSON 2	WF FERGUSON	TRIPLE DIVIDE	10320	X					
FRANKLIN, LOWER	EF KAWEAH RVR	MINERAL KING	10300		X				
FRANKLIN, UPPER	EF KAWEAH RVR	MINERAL KING	10525		X				
FUNSTON	FUNSTON CREEK	KERN PEAK	10840				?		
GALENA	MINERAL CREEK	MINERAL KING	9759	X					
GOLD	MINERAL CREEK	MINERAL KING	9500	X					
GOLDEN BEAR	BUBBS CREEK	MT. WHITNEY	11175	X			X		
HIDDEN	LITTLE KERN	MINERAL KING	9200				X		
HITCHCOCK 1	WHITNEY CREEK	MT. WHITNEY	11600	X			X		
HITCHCOCK 2	WHITNEY CREEK	MT. WHITNEY	11600				X		
JENNIE	BOULDER CREEK	GIANT FOREST	8500	X					
JOSEPHINE	SUGARLOAF	TRIPLE DIVIDE	10430	X					
KERN	KERN RVR	KERN PEAK	6233	X					
KERN, LITTLE	KERN RVR	KERN PEAK	6150	X					
LITTLE 1	MARBLE FORK KAWEAH RVR	TRIPLE DIVIDE	10200		X				
LITTLE CLAIRE	SODA CREEK	MINERAL KING	10400		X				
LITTLE FIVE LAKES	BIG ARROYO	TRIPLE DIVIDE	10410		X				
LITTLE MOUSE	MF KAWEAH RVR	TRIPLE DIVIDE	9500		X				
LOST	SUGARLOAF	TRIPLE DIVIDE	9140	?	X				
MAGGIE, LOWER	PECKS CANYON CREEK	MINERAL KING	9000		X		?		
MAGGIE, UPPER	PECKS CANYON CREEK	MINERAL KING	9100		X		?		
MICA	MINERAL CREEK	MINERAL KING	9625				?		
MONARCH, LOWER	KAWEAH RVR	MINERAL KING	10350		X	X			
MONARCH, UPPER	KAWEAH RVR	MINERAL KING	10375		X				
MOOSE	BUCK	TRIPLE DIVIDE	10530		X				
MOSQUITO 1	EF KAWEAH	MINERAL KING	9000		X				
MOSQUITO 2	MOSQUITO 1	MINERAL KING	9500	X	X				
MOSQUITO 3	MOSQUITO 2	MINERAL KING	9800		X				
MOSQUITO 5	MOSQUITO 4	MINERAL KING	9950		X				
MT. WHITNEY 3	TYNDALL CREEK	MT. WHITNEY	12000				?		
MT. WHITNEY 4	KERN HEADWATERS	MT. WHITNEY	12460	X			X		
NINE	BOG ARROYO	TRIPLE DIVIDE	10400		X				
PEAR	MARBLE FORK KAWEAH RVR	TRIPLE DIVIDE	9510		X				
RANGER 1	SUGARLOAF	TRIPLE DIVIDE	9200	?	?				
RANGER 2	SUGARLOAF	TRIPLE DIVIDE	9200	?	?				
REDWOOD	BEAR CREEK	CAMP NELSON	6200	X					
ROCKY BASIN 1	GOLDEN TROUT CREEK	KERN PEAK	10745				X		
ROCKY BASIN 2	GOLDEN TROUT CREEK	KERN PEAK	10800				X		

LAKE	TRIBUTARY TO	TOPO MAP	ELEV.	RB	BK	BN	GN	CT	LK
ROCKY BASIN 3	GOLDEN TROUT CREEK	KERN PEAK	10750				X		
ROCKY BASIN 4	GOLDEN TROUT CREEK	KERN PEAK	10760				X		
SEVILLE	SUGARLOAF	TRIPLE DIVIDE	8500	X	X				
SKY BLUE	ROCK CREEK	MT. WHITNEY	11600				X		
SOUTH AMERICA	KERN RIVER	MT. WHITNEY	11941				X		
SOLDIER	KERN RVR	MT. WHITNEY	11180				X		
SPHINX	SF KINGS RVR	TRIPLE DIVIDE	9610	?					
SPHINX 3	SF KINGS RVR	TRIPLE DIVIDE	10520	X					
SPHINX 4	SF KINGS RVR	TRIPLE DIVIDE	10540	?					
SPHINX 6	SF KINGS RVR	TRIPLE DIVIDE	11140	X					
SPHINX 8	SF KINGS RVR	TRIPLE DIVIDE	11140	X					
SPHINX 9	SF KINGS RVR	TRIPLE DIVIDE	10880	X					
SUMMIT	MF TULE	MINERAL KING	9300		X				
TAMARACK	MF KAWEAH RVR	TRIPLE DIVIDE	9300		X				
TWIN	PECK CANYON CREEK	MINERAL KING	9200		X				
TWIN 1	MARBLE FORK KAWEAH RVR	TRIPLE DIVIDE	9759		X				
TWIN 2	MARBLE FORK KAWEAH RVR	TRIPLE DIVIDE	9759		X				
VERSTEEG	WRIGHT CREEK	MT. WHITNEY	11952	X			X		
WEAVER	BIG MEADOW CREEK	GIANT FOREST	8600		X				
WHITE CHIEF	EF KAWEAH RVR	MINERAL KING	10400	X	X				
WOODS	SF KINGS RVR	MT. PINCHOT	10720		X				
WRIGHT	WRIGHT CREEK	MT. WHITNEY	11122	X			X		

TUOLUMNE COUNTY LAKES

LAKE	TRIBUTARY TO	TOPO MAP	ELEV.	RB	BK	BN	GN	CT	LK
"W"	NO OUTLET	TOWER PEAK	9160		X				
ANDREWS	NO OUTLET	TOWER PEAK	7650	X					
ARDETH	NO OUTLET	TOWER PEAK	8350	X					
AVONELLE	NO OUTLET	TOWER PEAK	8400	X					
BABCOCK	FLETCHER CREEK	TUOLUMNE MEADOWS	8983		X				
BANANA	WF CHERRY CREEK	PINECREST	9000	?	X				
BEAR	LILY CREEK	PINECREST	8400	X	X				
BEAR	BREEZE CREEK	TOWER PEAK	8975	X					
BEARUP	TUOLUMNE RVR	TOWER PEAK	7600	X					
BENSON	TUOLUMNE RVR	TOWER PEAK	7600		X				
BIG	CHERRY CREEK	PINECREST	6700	X					
BIGELOW	EF CHERRY CREEK	TOWER PEAK	9700	X	X				
BINGAMAN	PARKER PASS CREEK	MONO CRATERS	11350		X		X		
BLACK BEAR	EF CHERRY CREEK	TOWER PEAK	9200	X					
BLACK HAWK	SUMMIT CREEK	TOWER PEAK	9600				X		
BLUE CANYON	BLUE CANYON CREEK	SONORA PASS	10080	X			X		
BOUNDARY	LITTLE BEAR LAKE	PINECREST	7600	X					
BRANIGAN	LAKE VERNON	TOWER PEAK	7350	X					
BUCK, LOWER	WF CHERRY CREEK	TOWER PEAK	7700	X					
BUCK, UPPER	LOWER BUCK LAKE	TOWER PEAK	7750	X					
BURGSON	WHEATS MEADOW CREEK	DARDANELLES CONE	6800		X				
CAMP	BELL MEADOW CREEK	PINE CREST	8000	X					
CATFISH	HERRING CREEK	PINE CREST	5900		X				
CHAIN, LOWER	GROUSE LAKE	PINE CREST	7700		X				
CHERRY	CHERRY CREEK	PINE CREST	4700	X		X			
CHEWING GUM	LILY CREEK	PINE CREST	9000		X				
CLEAR	ROCK CREEK	PINE CREST	6600	X					
COW MEADOW	NF CHERRY CREEK	TOWER PEAK	7400	X					
COYOTE	BIG LAKE	PINE CREST	7500	X					
DEADMAN	DEADMAN CREEK	SONORA PASS	10300				?		
DEER	BUCK MEADOW CREEK	PINE CREST	7500	X					
DOE	PIUTE CREEK	MATTERHORN PEAK	9200	X					
DOG	TUOLUMNE RVR	TUOLUMNE MEADOWS	9240	?	X				
DONNELL'S RES.	MF STANISLAUS RVR	DARDANELLES CONE	4900	X		X			
DOROTHY, BIG	TUOLUMNE RVR	TOWER PEAK	9440	X					
DOROTHY, LITTLE	TUOLUMNE RVR	TOWER PEAK	9440	X					
DOUGLAS	HUCKLEBERRY CREEK	TOWER PEAK	8300	X					
DUTCH	BOURLAND CREEK	PINECREST	7700	X					
EDYTH	KENDRICK CREEK	PINECREST	6300	X					
ELEANOR RES.	ELEANOR CREEK	LAKE ELEANOR	4657	X					
ELIZABETH	UNICORN CREEK	TUOLUMNE MEADOWS	9508	?	X				
EMERIC	FLETCHER CREEK	TUOLUMNE MEADOWS	9350	?	X				

LAKE	TRIBUTARY TO	TOPO MAP	ELEV.	RB	BK	BN	GN	CT	LK
EMIGRANT MEADOW	NF CHERRY CREEK	TOWER PEAK	9500	X					
EMIGRANT, LOWER	NF CHERRY CREEK	TOWER PEAK	8800	X					
EMIGRANT, MIDDLE	NF CHERRY CREEK	TOWER PEAK	9000	X	X				
EMIGRANT, UPPER	NF CHERRY CREEK	TOWER PEAK	9700	X					
EVELYN	RAFFERTY CREEK	TUOLUMNE MEADOWS	10328	X	?				
FLORA	BARTLETT CREEK	PINECREST	7050	?					
FRASER	NO OUTLET	TOWER PEAK	9300		X				
FROG	LERTORA LAKE	TOWER PEAK	8350	X	?				
GAYLOR, LOWER	TUOLUMNE RVR	TUOLUMNE MEADOWS	10100	?	X			?	
GAYLOR, MIDDLE	TUOLUMNE RVR	TUOLUMNE MEADOWS	10350	?	X			?	
GAYLOR, UPPER	TUOLUMNE RVR	TUOLUMNE MEADOWS	10550	?	X			?	
GEM	BUCK MEADOW LAKE	PINECREST	8200	X					
GERTRUDE	SF STANISLAUS RVR	PINECREST	7300	X					
GRANITE	CLAVEY RVR	PINECREST	8000		X				
GRANITE, LOWER	GAYLOR CREEK	TUOLUMNE MEADOWS	9500	X	?				
GRANITE, UPPER	GAYLOR LAKE	TUOLUMNE MEADOWS	10400	?	?				
GRAVEL PIT	MIGUEL CREEK	LAKE ELEANOR	5300	?	?				
GRIZZLY PEAK, EAST	EF CHERRY CREEK	TOWER PEAK	9600	X					
GRIZZLY PEAK, WEST	EF CHERRY CREEK	TOWER PEAK	9600	X					
GROUSE	LILY CREEK	PINECREST	7100		X				
GROUSE CREEK	GROUSE CREEK	TOWER PEAK	7100		X				
HARDEN	NO OUTLET	HETCH HETCHY	7575	?	?				
HELEN	PARKER PASS CREEK	MONO CRATERS	10880		X				
HERRING CREEK RES.	HERRING CREEK	DARDANELLES CONE	7360	X					
HETCH HETCHY	TUOLUMNE RVR	HETCH HETCHY	3796	X		X			
HUCKLEBERRY	EF CHERRY CREEK	TOWER PEAK	7700	X	X				
HYATT	CHERRY CREEK	PINECREST	7300	X					
ICELAND	SUMMIT CREEK	TOWER PEAK	9100				X		
INFERNO, LOWER	SPOTTED FAWN LAKE	PINECREST	7900	?					
INFERNO, UPPER	SPOTTED FAWN LAKE	PINECREST	7950	?					
JEWELRY	BUCK MEADOW CREEK	PINECREST	8300	X					
JOHNSON PEAK	SF MERCED	TUOLUMNE MEADOWS	10350		X				
KARL'S	LEIGHTON LAKE	PINECREST	8400	X					
KENNEDY	EF STANISLAUS RVR	SONORA PASS	8000	X		X			
KIBBIE	KIBBIE CREEK	PINECREST	6450	X					
KOLE	YELLOWHAMMER LAKE	PINE CREST	7500	X					
KUNA	PARKER PASS CREEK	TUOLUMNE MEADOWS	10850	?	X				
LAUREL	FROG CREEK	LAKE ELEANOR	6675	X					
LEIGHTON	LOWER YELLOWHAMMER LAKE	PINECREST	8400	X					
LEOPOLD	WF CHERRY CREEK	PINECREST	8600	X					
LERTORA	NF CHERRY CREEK	TOWER PEAK	8500	X					
LEWIS	SUMMIT CREEK	TOWER PEAK	9100		X				
LEWIS, LOWER	SUMMIT CREEK	TOWER PEAK	8800		X				
LEWIS, UPPER	SUMMIT CREEK	TOWER PEAK	9770		X				
LITTLE BEAR	BARTLETT CREEK	PINECREST	7800	?					
LONG	DEER LAKE	PINECREST	8600	X					
LOST	KENNEDY LAKE	TOWER PEAK	8100		X				
LUKENS	TUOLUMNE RVR	HETCH HETCHY	8250	?	?	?			
LYON'S RES.	SF STANISLAUS RVR	LONG BARN	4226	X		X			
MARY	TILDEN CREEK	TOWER PEAK	9600	X		X			
MATTE, BIG	MATTE CREEK	TUOLUMNE MEADOWS	9448		X				
MATTE, LITTLE	MATTE CREEK	TUOLUMNE MEADOWS	9650		X				
MAXWELL	EF CHERRY CREEK	TOWER PEAK	8800	X	X				
MAY	SNOW CREEK	TUOLUMNE MEADOWS	9350	X	?				
McCABE, LOWER	McCABE CREEK	TUOLUMNE MEADOWS	9950	X					
McCABE, MIDDLE	McCABE CREEK	TUOLUMNE MEADOWS	10250	X					
McCABE, UPPER	McCABE CREEK	TUOLUMNE MEADOWS	10480	X		X			
MERCUR, LOWER	CHERRY CREEK	PINECREST	7200		X				
MERCUR, UPPER	CHERRY CREEK	PINECREST	7400		X				
MILLER	RETURN CREEK	TUOLUMNE MEADOWS	9500	?					
MIWOK	FROG CREEK	TOWER PEAK	8200	?					
MOSQUITO	NF CHERRY CREEK	TOWER PEAK	9700	?					
MUD	NO OUTLET	PINECREST	7000	?					
NEALL	TUOLUMNE RVR	HETCH HETCHY	9250	X					
OLIVER	EF CHERRY CREEK	TOWER PEAK	7900		X				
OTTER, BIG	FROG CREEK	TOWER PEAK	8850					?	
OTTER, LITTLE	FROG CREEK	TOWER PEAK	8850	?					
PENINSULA	FROG LAKE	TOWER PEAK	8875	X					
PINECREST	SF STANISLAUS RVR	PINECREST	5800	?					

LAKE	TRIBUTARY TO	TOPO MAP	ELEV.	RB	BK	BN	GN	CT	LK
PINGREE	NF CHERRY CREEK	PINECREST	8200	X					
PINTO	WF CHERRY CREEK	PINECREST	9440	X					
PIUTE	NO OUTLET	PINECREST	7928	X					
POWELL	SF STANISLAUS	PINECREST	8900		X				
PRUITT	EF CHERRY CREEK	PINECREST	8000	X					
RED CAN	FIVE ACRE LAKE	PINECREST	8300	X					
RELIEF RES.	SUMMIT MCREEK	SONORA PASS	7200	X	X				
RELIEF, NORTH	RELIEF CREEK	PINECREST	8000	?	X				
RELIEF, SOUTH	RELIEF CREEK	PINECREST	7950	?	X				
RETURN	RETURN CREEK	MATTERHORN PEAK	10250	?	X				
RIDGE	NO OUTLET	TOWER PEAK	9450				X		
RODGERS	RODGERS CREEK	TUOLUMNE MEADOWS	9460	X	?				
ROOSEVELT	CONNESS	TUOLUMNE MEADOWS	10184						
ROSASCO	CHERRY CREEK	PINECREST	7800	X	?				
SADDLEHORSE	PIUTE CREEK	HETCH HETCHY	7500	?					
SARDELLA	NO OUTLET	TOWER PEAK	9700				X		
SHALLOW	NF CHERRY CREEK	TOWER PEAK	9200		X				
SHEPARD	RETURN CREEK	MATTERHORN PEAK	8320	X					
SISTER	PIUTE CREEK	MATTERHORN PEAK	9550	X					
SKELTON	DELANEY CREEK	TUOLUMNE MEADOWS	10560		X				
SMEDBERG	PIUTE CREEK	MATTERHORN PEAK	9223	X					
SNOW	EF CHERRY CREEK	TOWER PEAK	9500	X					
SPILLWAY	PARKER PASS CREEK	MONO CRATERS	10450	X	X	X			L
SPOTTED FAWN	BARTLETT CREEK	PINECREST	7350	?					
STARVATION	NO OUTLET	PINECREST	8800		X				
STRAWBERRY	SF STANISLAUS RVR	LONGBARN	5600	X		X			
SURPRISE	PIUTE CREEK	MATTERHORN PEAK	9400	?					
SWAMP	LAKE ELEANOR	LAKE ELEANOR	5100	X					
TABLE	PIUTE CREEK	HETCH HETCHY	7100	X					
TALLULAH	PIUTE CREEK	MATTERHORN PEAK	9850	x					
TEN 1	TUOLUMNE RVR	HETCH HETCHY	9100	?	?	?			
TEN 2	TUOLUMNE RVR	HETCH HETCHY	9050	x	x	?			
TEN 3	TUOLUMNE RVR	HETCH HETCHY	9100	X	X	?			
TEN 4	TUOLUMNE RVR	HETCH HETCHY	9250	X	X				
TEN 5	TUOLUMNE RVR	HETCH HETCHY	9400	X	?				
TEN 6	TUOLUMNE RVR	HETCH HETCHY	9400	X	?				
TEN 7	TUOLUMNE RVR	HETCH HETCHY	8950	?	?	?			
TILDEN	TILDEN CREEK	TOWER PEAK	8850	X					
TOE JAM	PIUTE CREEK	PINECREST	8800	X					
TWIN MEADOW	WHEATS MEADOW CREEK	DARDANELLES CONE	6900		X				
UNNAMED CHAIN	KENDRICK CREEK	PINECREST	6100	X					
VERNON	FALLS CREEK	TOWER PEAK	6600	X					
VIRGINIA	NO OUTLET	TUOLUMNE MEADOWS	9230	?	X	?			
WATERHOUSE	SF STANISLAUS RVR	PINECREST	7450	X					
WEGNER	NO OUTLET	HETCH HETCHY	9250	?		?			
WILLOW	TUOLUMNE RVR	LAKE ELEANOR	4600	X					
WILSON MEADOW	SPRING CREEK	TOWER PEAK	9600				X		
WIRE, NORTH	WF CHERRY CREEK	PINECREST	9000		X				
WIRE, SOUTH	WF CHERRY CREEK	PINECREST	9000		X				
WOOD	WF CHERRY CREEK	PINECREST	8900	X					
YELLOWHAMMER	CHERRY VALLEY CREEK	PINECREST	7720	X					
YOUNG	CONNESS CREEK	TUOLUMNE MEADOWS	10000		X				

DOUGLAS COUNTY, NEVADA LAKES

LAKE	TRIBUTARY TO	TOPO MAP	ELEV.	RB	BK	BN	GN	CT	LK
BLISS	BLISS CREEK	CARSON CITY	6885	X					
SPOONER	NO OUTLET	CARSON CITY	7120	X	X	X		?	
ZEPHYR PT (McFAUL)	LAKE TAHOE	FREEL PEAK	6800	X		X			

WASHOE COUNTY, NEVADA LAKES

LAKE	TRIBUTARY TO	TOPO MAP	ELEV.	RB	BK	BN	GN	CT	LK
FULLER, UPPER	TRUCKEE RVR	MT. ROSE	6080		X				
FULLER, LOWER	TRUCKEE RVR	MT. ROSE	6000	X					
GINNEY	THIRD CREEK	MT. ROSE	8200	X	X				
HOBART CREEK RES.	FRANKTOWN CREEK	CARSON CITY	9060	X		X			
HUNTER CREEK RES.	HUNTER CREEK	MT. ROSE	4800	X					

LAKE	TRIBUTARY TO	TOPO MAP	ELEV.	RB	BK	BN	GN	CT	LK
HUNTER	HUNTER CREEK	MT. ROSE	8200		X				
INCLINE	THIRD CREEK	MT. ROSE	8500		X	X			
JOY	NO OUTLET	MT. ROSE	5840	X					
MARLETTE	MARLETTE CREEK	CARSON CITY	7823						L
MARLETTE RES.	MARLETTE CREEK	CARSON CITY	6400						L
ROCK	OPHIR CREEK	MT. ROSE	6700					?	
TAMARACK	OUTLET UNNAMED	MT. ROSE	8800		X				

GLOSSARY

Alluvial: A deposit of rock, sand, or mud formed by flowing water. An **Alluvial Fan** is the fan shaped alluvial deposit at the mouth of a canyon. This is a very typical landform on the east flank of the Sierra. Alluvial fans often contain a wide spectrum of minerals which can result in highly productive water if a stream flows through the fan.

Anadromous: The act of migrating from salt water to fresh water to spawn.

Anchor ice: Ice that forms on river beds. When enough ice develops, it floats to the surface and rips out the stream bed it was frozen to. This grit encrusted anchor iceberg drifts with the current and grinds the streambed.

Basibranchial teeth: Three median bones on the floor of the gill chamber.

Behavioral drift: A synchronous event where common organisms voluntarily become transported with the current.

Biomass: The amount of living matter in a given habitat. A water that can support a biomass of 10 pounds of trout can hold ten one pound fish or one ten pounder.

California Wild Trout Program: A program of the California Department of Fish and Game where selected waters are managed for wild trout. This management includes habitat protection, cessation of hatchery trout plants, and fishing regulations that minimizes harvest of trout before they can reproduce.

Electrophoresis: Method of sorting proteins according to their response to an electrical charge. A highly accurate method for "fingerprinting" the genetics of an organism.

Electroshock: A method of electrically stunning fish so that they may be studied.

Evaporative lakes: Lakes with a high ion count due to concentration of its waters by evaporation. These lakes are highly productive.

Exotic trout: Trout other than those which naturally occurred in a given habitat. The vast majority of high elevation lakes where barren and their fish populations were introduced by humans; thus, most high elevation waters contain exotic trout.

Hybrid: Bred from two distinct races or species.

Hybrid vigor: (Heterosis) The increased growth, strength, fecundity and other traits displayed by hybrids over their parents.

Hyoid teeth: See basibranchial.

Lie: A specific geographical position taken by a trout. A feeding lie is a position taken by a trout to feed; A resting lie is a place where a trout can remain protected from current; A protective lie is a place a trout can remain protected from enemies; A prime lie is a place where a trout can find food and protection from enemies and current.

Limnology: The study of bodies of fresh water.

Native trout: A trout that naturally evolved in a given system. Not all wild trout are native trout.

Ocelli: A primitive eye found on many insects. It can detect light and dark as well as ultra violet light.

Onchorynchus: Latin for "hooked jaw." Onchorynchus is the family of fish that include the Pacific salmon, cutthroat, rainbow, gilbert, and golden trout.

Photosynthesis: The process where sunlight energy is combined with inorganic carbon to produce organic material. Oxygen is a byproduct.

Phytoplankton: The portion of the plankton community comprised of algae and Cyanobacteria.

Plankton: Tiny plants and animals that drift, float, or swim feebly in the water. Planktonic individuals are called Plankters; the animals are called Zooplankton and the plant plankters are called Phytoplankton.

Productivity: Is the growth of photosynthetic plants that provide the source of food and energy for the aquatic food chain. Productivity can be measured as the rate in which inorganic carbon is transformed into organic carbon through photosynthesis.

Salmo: The family of "true" trout which contains the brown trout and the Atlantic salmon.

Salvelinus: The family of char which includes the brook trout, lake trout, arctic char, Dolly Varden and bull trout.

Seston: The living and nonliving organic particulate debris drifting in water.

Total dissolved solids: (TDS) The residue left after water is evaporated. TDS is an accurate barometer of the potential biomass of a body of water.

Teneral: The newly hatched adult damselfly or dragonfly. Tenerals lack adult pigmentation or maximal structural integrity.

Tippet: The skinniest portion of a leader. This usually where the fly get tied on. Tippet material is sold in spools to replace the end of the leader as it is removed.

Topographic map: A map that shows geographic topography with contour lines. Topo maps are the basic reference for Sierra geography.

Up-slope-blow-in: A phenomena where air warmed in the lowlands rises and carries with it lowland insects. As the air rises it cools and drops its load of insects. Many Sierra fauna feed heavily on this windfall.

Wild trout: Wild trout are trout that were conceived, hatched, and reared in the wilds. Wild trout are not necessarily native trout.

Winter kill: Winter kill can be the outright freezing of trout or it can be the suffocation of trout caused by a heavy blanket of snow preventing oxygen producing photosynthesis from occurring in a water.

Appendix I
SIERRA OUTFITTERS

High Sierra Packers Association. 690 N. Main St., Bishop, CA 93514. (619) 873-8405.

HIGH SIERRA PACKERS

Little Antelope Valley Pack Station. P.O. Box 179, Coleville, CA 96107. (702) 782-4960.

Leavitt Meadows Pack Station. P.O. Box 1224A. Bridgeport, CA 93517. (916) 495-2257.

Virginia Lakes Pack Outfit. HC Route 1, Box 1076, Bridgeport, CA 93517. (702) 867-2591.

Frontier Pack Train. Box 18, Star Rt. 33, June Lake, CA 93529. (619)648-7701

Agnew Meadows Pack Train. Box 395, Mammoth Lakes, CA 93546. (619) 873-3928 (winter). (619) 873-3928 (summer).

McGee Creek Pack Station. Star Rt. 1, Box 100A, Independence, CA 93526 (619) 878-2207 (winter). Rt. 1, Box 162, Mammoth Lakes, CA 93546. (619) 935-4324 (summer).

Rock Creek Pack Station. Box 248, Bishop, CA 93514 (winter). (619) 935-4493 (summer).

Pine Creek Pack Station. P.O. Box 968, Bishop, CA 93515. (619) 387-2797.

Schober Pack Station. Rt. 1, Box AA-4, Bishop, CA 93524. (619) 387-2343 (winter). (619) 935-4493 (summer).

Sequoia Kings Pack Trains. Onion Valley hdqtrs. P.O. Box 209. Independence, CA 93526. (619) 387-2797.

Mt. Whitney Pack Trains. P.O. Box 1514, Bishop, CA 93514. (619) 872-8331 (winter). (619) 935-4493 (summer).

Cottonwood Pack Station. Star Rt 1, Box 81A, Independence, CA 93526. (619) 878-2015.

Kennedy Meadows Pack Trains. P.O. Box 1300 Weldon, CA 93283. (818) 896-4809 (winter). (619) 378-2232 (summer).

Appendix II
BACKPACK CHECKLIST

Fishing license
4 to 6 weight fly rod
Reel
Spool with floating line
Spool with sinking shooting head
Metal rod tube
Polaroid glasses
Leaders 7 to 13 feet
Tippet 4X to 7X
Split shot
Hemostats
Snips
Fly floatant, paste and powder
Vest or Fanny pack
Waders
Wading shoes (Aqua socks)
Float tube
Pump
Fins
Sherpa (to carry all this stuff)

FLIES

FOUNDATION:
Adams: size 12-18
Elk Hair Caddis: size 12-18
Ant: size 12-18
Gold Rib Hare's Ear: size 12-18
Royal Trude: size 14-18
Woolly Bugger (brown): size 6

VERSATILE:
More Elk Hair Caddis
Bird's Nest: size 10-20
Soft Hackle: size 10-20

PT Nymph: size 12-18
Zug Bug: size 12-18
Green Rockworm: size 12
Chironomid Pupa: size 18-24
EC Caddis: size 14
Bivisible Dun: size 12-16
Parachute (Hare's Ear): size 12-22
Stimulator: size 8-12
Woolly Bugger (brown): size 4-10

KITCHEN SINK
More Bird's Nests
Bucktail Caddis: size 6-8
Goddard Caddis: size 6-10
Perfect Little Yellow Stone: size 12-16
Stimulator: size 6-14
Sofa Pillow: size 4
Parachute (tan, olive, red): size 12-20
Light Cahill: size 14-18
Red Quill: size 14-28
Polywing Spinner: size 14-18
Trico Spinner: size 18-22
Griffith Gnat: size 18-22
Quiggly Cripple (gray): size 12-18
Mini-Egg: size 18
Tangerine Dream: size 6
Simulator (brown): size 6-10
LaFontaine Sparkle Pupa (green, gray, and gold): size 10-18
Damsel Nymph: size 10-14
Woolly Bugger (black, olive): size 4-10
Marabou Leech (black): size 4-10

Appendix III
FISHING GEAR CHECKLIST

BASICS
Backpack
Tent
Sleeping bag
Sleeping pad
Groundcloth

CLOTHING
Hat
Rain coat
Rain Pants
Warm coat
Long sleeve shirt
Tee shirt
Shorts
Long pants
Socks
Bandanna
Underwear
Boots
Camp shoes

COOKING
Stove
Fuel
Matches or lighter
Pot
Cup
Spoon
Small Swiss Army knife
Water bottle
Water filter
Food

TOILETRIES
Toothbrush
Toothpaste
Brush/comb
Mirror
Towel
Solar shower
Castile soap
Lotion
Toilet paper
Tampon
Medication

FIRST AID
White tape
4X4 bandage
Triangular bandage
Second Skin TM
Moleskin
Snake bite kit
Chapstick
Sun screen
Needle
Acetaminophen
Percocet
Diamox
Imodium

ODDS N' ENDS
This book
Topo maps
Wilderness permit
Insect repellent
Sun glasses
1/4 nylon rope
Flashlight
Camera/lenses/film
Ice axe
Crampons

Appendix IV
MAPS, INFORMATION, AND PERMITS

Topographic Maps

FREE topographical *map indexes* can be ordered from: U.S. Geological Survey, Box 25286, Federal Center, Bldg. 41, Denver, CO 80225. The indexes are cataloged by state.

U.S.G.S. topo maps are often horribly outdated. Wilderness Press prints up to date, water resistance topos, that have convenient notes and indexes along the margins. To make a good map even better, the Wilderness Press topos are cheaper than the government issue. Wilderness Press also publishes an *excellent* series of trail guides for the Sierra...ask for a catalog. Contact: The Map Center, 2440 Bancroft Way, Berkeley, CA 94704. (415) 841-MAPS.

The best deal going on maps are the California Atlas and Gazetter books by DeLorme Publishing. There are two books, one for each half of the state. Each map shows paved and dirt roads, 100 meter topo lines, campgrounds, and even very small lakes and creeks. The topographic detail is too gross for backpacking, but for car camping and overview purposes, the maps are unexcelled.

Write to: DeLorme Publishing Co., P.O. Box 298NC, Freeport, Maine 04032. Order either the Northern California or Southern California Atlas & Gazetter for $12.95 each or get the set for $25.00.

Mineral and Geology Maps

Mineral maps are very expensive when bought from private mapping agencies; however, California sells an inexpensive series of gravity maps superimposed on highly accurate mineral and geology maps.

Bureau of Mines and Geology, Box 2980, Sacramento, CA 95812-2980. (916) 445-5716. Ask for the free "List of Available Publications."

U.S. Forest Service Maps

U.S. Forest Service maps have good, up to date references of logging roads and campgrounds, but are next to worthless for hiking. USFS base maps are free for the asking at: U.S. Forest Service, 630 Sansome St., San Francisco, CA 94111.

Wilderness Permits, Grazing and Trail Information

El Dorado National Forest, 100 Forni Rd., Placerville, CA 95667 (916) 644-6048.

Inyo National Forest, 2957 Birch St., Bishop, CA 93514 (619) 876-5542.

Kings Canyon/Sequoia National Park, Three Rivers, CA 93271 (209) 565-03351.

Plumas National Forest, 159 Lawrence St., Quincy, CA 95971 (916) 283-2050.

Sequoia National Forest, P.O. Box 391. Porterville, CA 93528 (209) 784-1500.

Sierra National Forest, 1130 'O' St., Fresno, CA 93721 (916) 246-5222.

Stanislaus National Forest, 175 S. Fairview Ln., Sonora, CA 95370 (209) 532-3671.

Tahoe National Forest, Hwy. 49 and Coyote. Nevada City, CA 95959 (916) 265-4531.

Toiyabe National Forest, 1200 N. Franklin Wy., Sparks, NV (702) 355-5302.

Yosemite National Park, Box 577, Yosemite, CA 95389 (209) 372-4461.

For information regarding *Wilderness Areas*, contact the managing Forest Service office.

Ansel Adams Wilderness—Inyo and Sierra National Forests.

Desolation Wilderness—El Dorado National Forest.

Emigrant Wilderness—Stanislaus National Forest.

Golden Trout Wilderness—Inyo and Sequoia National Forests.

Granite Chief Wilderness—Tahoe National Forest.

Hoover Wilderness—Toiyabe and Inyo National Forests.

John Muir Wilderness—Sierra and Inyo National Forests.

Mokelumne Wilderness—El Dorado National Forest.

South Sierra Wilderness—Sequoia and Inyo National Forests.

Appendix V
ENVIRONMENTAL ORGANIZATIONS

Fishing groups

Trout groups don't necessarily represent trout, they represent their constituency: trout fisherman. Usually these groups are environmentally oriented; however, when ecological values and good trout fishing diverge, these groups support fishing. As an example, waters are poisoned to rid them of native "trash" fish such as chubs and suckers so that introduced trout can grow without interference.

California Sportfishing Protection Alliance, 5720 Roseville Rd., Suite 'C', Sacramento, CA 95842

California Trout Inc., P.O. Box 2046, San Francisco, CA 94126

Federation of Fly Fishers, Box 1088, West Yellowstone, MT 59758

Trout Unlimited, 501 Church St. N.E., Vienna, VA 22180

Environmental Groups that Work with the Sierra

American Rivers, 801 Pennsylvania Ave. S.E., No. 301 Washington, DC 20003

Earth First!, Box 5871, Tucson, AZ 85703

Friends of the River, Fort Mason Center, Building 'C', San Francisco, CA 94123

National Audubon Society, 950 Third Ave, New York, NY 10022

Natural Resources Defense Council, 40 W. 20th St., New York, NY 10011

Planning and Conservation League, 909 12th. St., No. 203. Sacramento, CA 95814

Sierra Club, 730 Polk St, San Francisco, CA 94109

INDEX